FACING MARIANO RIVERA

PLAYERS RECALL THE GREATEST RELIEF PITCHER WHO EVER LIVED

EDITED BY DAVID FISCHER

FOREWORD BY DAVE ANDERSON

SPORTS
PUBLISHING

Sports Publishing books may be purchased in bulk at special discounts for sales promotion, corporate gifts, fund-raising, or educational purposes. Special editions can also be created to specifications. For details, contact the Special Sales Department, Sports Publishing, 307 West 36th Street, 11th Floor, New York, NY 10018 or sportspubbooks@skyhorsepublishing.com.

Sports Publishing® is a registered trademark of Skyhorse Publishing, Inc.®, a Delaware corporation.

Visit our website at www.sportspubbooks.com.

10 9 8 7 6 5 4 3 2 1

Library of Congress Cataloging-in-Publication Data is available on file.

ISBN: 978-1-61321-639-2

Printed in the United States of America

For my grandpa Jack Baron, a Brooklyn Dodgers fanatic, who told me stories about another legendary No. 42, Jackie Robinson.

CONTENTS

Foreword   *xi*

Introduction   *1*

Section One: Infielders   **5**

  Roberto Alomar   7

  David Adams   8

  Mike Blowers   8

  Aaron Boone   10

  Mike Bordick   10

  Robinson Cano   12

  Eric Chavez   13

  Jeff Conine   14

  Carlos Delgado   15

  Mark DeRosa   16

  Robert Eenhoorn   18

  Matt Franco   19

  Nomar Garciaparra   21

  Jason Giambi   22

  Ozzie Guillen   25

  Scott Hatteberg   26

  Todd Helton   28

  Derek Jeter   29

  Chipper Jones   31

  Eric Karros   31

  Ryan Klesko   33

  Corey Koskie   33

  Kevin Kouzmanoff   36

  Tino Martinez   37

  Lou Merloni   39

CONTENTS

Doug Mientkiewicz   41

Kevin Millar   42

Bill Mueller   46

Lyle Overbay   48

Dustin Pedroia   50

Mark Reynolds   51

Kevin Seitzer   52

Bill Selby   54

Ed Sprague   58

Jason Smith   60

Mark Teixeira   61

Jim Thome   63

Robin Ventura   64

Ty Wigginton   65

Tony Womack   66

David Wright   68

Kevin Youkilis   70

Section Two: Outfielders   **73**

Brady Anderson   75

Garret Anderson   79

Frank Catalanotto   81

Bubba Carpenter   83

Johnny Damon   85

Jim Edmonds   87

Darin Erstad   88

Lew Ford   91

Brett Gardner   92

Luis Gonzalez   93

Curtis Granderson   98

Gabe Gross   100

David Hulse   103

Mike Humphreys   105

Torii Hunter   106

Raul Ibanez   109

Reed Johnson   111
Adam Jones   113
Mark Kotsay   116
Paul O'Neill   118
Jay Payton   120
Alex Rios   123
Dave Roberts   124
Tim Salmon   126
Mike Simms   128
Matt Stairs   131
Ichiro Suzuki   133
Nick Swisher   135
B.J. Upton   136
Shane Victorino   138
Vernon Wells   139

Section Three: Catchers   **143**

Sal Fasano   145
Francisco Cervelli   146
John Flaherty   146
Darrin Fletcher   148
Todd Greene   149
Jesse Levis   152
Russell Martin   155
Chad Moeller   157
Gustavo Molina   159
Salvador Perez   160
Wil Nieves   160
A.J. Pierzynski   161
Jorge Posada   163
Austin Romine   166
Terry Steinbach   167
Chris Stewart   169
Kelly Stinnett   170
Tom Wilson   172

CONTENTS

Gregg Zaun   172

Section Four: Designated Hitters   **179**

Jack Cust   181
Eric Hinske   184
Kevin Maas   184
Edgar Martinez   186
David Ortiz   189
Luke Scott   191
Mike Sweeney   193

Section Five: Pitchers   **197**

Jonathan Albaladejo   199
Bronson Arroyo   200
Dellin Betances   201
Joba Chamberlain   202
David Cone   203
Dennis Eckersley   205
Tom Gordon   207
Rich Goose Gossage   208
Jason Grimsley   209
David Huff   210
Phil Hughes   211
Jason Isringhausen   212
Shawn Kelley   212
Pedro Martinez   214
Al Leiter   214
Joe Nathan   215
Denny Neagle   218
Jeff Nelson   221
Andy Pettitte   223
J.J. Putz   224
David Robertson   226
CC Sabathia   227
Curt Schilling   228

CONTENTS

John Smoltz ... 229
Mike Stanton ... 231
Tanyon Sturtze ... 233
Rick Sutcliffe ... 235
Justin Verlander ... 238
Ron Villone ... 239
Adam Warren ... 241
John Wetteland ... 241

Section Six: Management ... **245**

Mike Borzello ... 247
Bruce Bochy ... 248
Brian Butterfield ... 248
Bill Evers ... 249
Terry Francona ... 252
Joe Girardi ... 253
Mike Harkey ... 254
Jim Leyland ... 255
Bill Livesey ... 256
Mitch Lukevics ... 259
Joe Maddon ... 260
Bob Melvin ... 261
Mark Newman ... 262
Juan Nieves ... 263
Herb Raybourn ... 264
Larry Rothschild ... 266
Glenn Sherlock ... 266
Mike Scioscia ... 267
Joe Torre ... 268

Career Statistics ... *270*
Acknowledgements ... *273*
Photo Credit ... *276*

FOREWORD

IF YOU'VE EVER studied the best major league pitchers, either from a seat at the ballpark or on television, when a batter swung and missed, you, as a decent ballplayer in your day, might have muttered, "I could've hit that one." And maybe you could have.

But maybe not. Probably not. And if that pitcher was Mariano Rivera, almost certainly not.

Page after page in *Facing Mariano Rivera*, you will read how he not only baffled the best major league hitters with his cut fastball, he often shattered their bats. Of all the gifts he received in his 2013 farewell tour, he said his favorite was a rocking chair constructed of broken bats from the Minnesota Twins. "If you're a left handed hitter," says an opponent who later would be a Yankees teammate, "you almost have to look for an outside pitch and pull it, because if it's middle in, it's going to break your bat." If only David Fischer could have interviewed some of those shattered bats.

No need to tell you here the most successful hitter against baseball's greatest closer, but even *he* acknowledges, "It was never a comfortable at bat." Another hitter who once swatted fifty home runs (none off Rivera), analyzes that "His cutter has four-seam fastball spin and then it cuts—it cuts late … and he learned to throw a two-seam fastball that broke in on righties."

For all of the hitters' testimony, perhaps the most authoritative comments are from his Yankees' teammates. From the outfielder who says, "He was the Devil when I was playing against him, but when I came here, he became God because he's on our side." From the right-handed pitcher who says, "His arm slot is the same every pitch." From the bullpen catcher who says, "I don't think he ever threw a ball that ever bounced in my twelve years of catching him in the bullpen. He would pitch up and down, and in and out, but never in the ground."

And as much as all these opposing batters dislike trying to hit that cut fastball, they praise him for never "showing up" any of them. "Once you get to know Mariano," one says, "you respect him more as a person than as a player." As challenging and frustrating as facing him was, they seem to enjoy having had the opportunity. And now the opportunity in these pages to describe what it was like.

—Dave Anderson

INTRODUCTION

DURING HIS ILLUSTRIOUS career, Mariano Rivera faced over five thousand batters, from Brady Anderson to Gregg Zaun; from stars like David Ortiz, who faced him thirty-four times, to neophytes like Bill Selby, who faced him twice. The list of batters included in this book run the gamut from Hall of Famers like Roberto Alomar, who managed to hit .455 (5 for 11) against him, to All-Stars like Alex Rios, who didn't have a hit in 15 plate appearances, to Jason Smith, a lifetime .212 batter who inexplicably hit .600 (3 for 5) against Rivera.

"I don't think I owned him," says Smith. "I was very lucky."

The success or (more often than not) failure rate when facing Rivera for each player interviewed for this book has been documented to the best of my ability. Some players will boast of their personal accomplishments against Rivera, while others can only laugh at themselves for their futility against him. Whatever the case, each of the speakers' unique achievements, either positive or negative, are recognized under the heading labeled "Mo Cred," as in credibility.

Whatever the results compiled by individual batters, this much is true: If there was one relief pitcher in the last two decades who personifies the word "closer," a stadium full of baseball experts would pick Rivera. Few, if any, relief pitchers enjoyed the immensely positive reputation for finality that Rivera earned with the Yankees. As manager Joe Girardi said: "I love when he comes into the game. You feel like it's over."

Finality is a subject often cited by the nearly 150 baseball people who spoke to me about Rivera. I conducted the interviews during the 2013 season, while Rivera was still an active player; hence, the recollections of the players are spoken in the present tense. One of the first ballplayers I spoke with was Mike Sweeney, who compares Rivera's entrance music to the soundtrack of a horror movie, because "you hear that music and you know what's going to happen," says Sweeney. "Mariano will finish the game and get the save."

The vision of Rivera bursting through the bullpen door was enough to give even the most malevolent opponents serious pause. With the Yankee Stadium sound system blaring Metallica's "Enter Sandman," and the fans raucously cheering in anticipation, Rivera jogged across the outfield grass and strode gracefully to the mound. The music meant that entering the game is Mariano Rivera, the reedy right-handed relief pitcher from Panama with a steely focus and a sense of mental calm so great he could sleep through a thunderstorm. He fires seven or eight warm-up pitches, stares blankly at his target with shark-like eyes, and then gets down to the serious business of recording the three toughest outs in baseball.

More than anyone else, it was Rivera doing his job that propelled the Yankees to be World Series champions five times, as he was on the mound to record the final out in four clinching Series games in 1998, 1999, 2000, and 2009. October after October, the 6-foot-2, 185-pounder held precarious leads the Yankees had scratched together. He literally attacked rival hitters with one pitch: an unsolvable cut fastball that has been called a combination of thunder and location. That pitch, more than any other subject, was a recurring theme among the pitchers and position players who participated in this project. All of the batters I spoke to, particularly those hitting left-handed, had vivid memories of frustrating plate appearances that more times than not ended with them holding a piece of their own broken bat.

Sometimes a ballplayer's time was limited or our time together cut short, resulting in a briefer interview than I had anticipated. Many of these players sincerely apologized for not being able to devote more time to talking about Rivera, though their comments are just as insightful and revealing. In these instances, I have set off the text in a special box titled "Mo Respect," an appropriate moniker to express the admiration they feel toward the last major league baseball player to wear No. 42.

The ballplayers represented in this book told many amusing stories and had an uncanny memory for game situations, pitch sequences, base runners, the name of the umpire behind the plate, and similar details that occurred in games played many years ago. Time and again, I was amazed by a player's instant recall and unusual ability to provide the play-by-play for a regular season game occurring in the last decade that had little or no impact on the league's pennant race. While this book is based on their memories, I do provide footnotes to occasionally set the record straight, to elaborate on their stories, and to place game events in historical context.

Rivera's historical impact on the Yankees' success, especially in the postseason, couldn't possibly be any greater. Twelve people have walked on the moon but only eleven have scored an earned run off Rivera in the postseason. His lifetime postseason earned run average of 0.70 in 141 innings is the major league record. During the Yankees, memorable 1998 season, Rivera did not give up a run in ten postseason appearances. He did the same again during eight appearances in 1999, when he was the World Series Most Valuable Player. More impressive still, his record 42 postseason saves, including 11 in the World Series, are 24 more than his next closest competitor, Brad Lidge (18), which explains why Rivera's teammates could act as if they were about to inherit the family trust fund when he entered the game.

"He wants the ball in big situations and [is] not afraid of anyone," says Derek Jeter. "You won't see anyone like him again."

Rivera retired as the king of all closers. Final inventory figures for his career will show that all other relief pitchers will be shooting at his mark of 652 saves for a long time to come. But Mariano Rivera's contributions go beyond mere numbers, impressive though they happen to be. It's the form as well as the substance that makes Rivera a star in the grand old Yankee tradition: humble, gracious, and poised. The fact that he's also a spiritual man made him all the more valuable as an inspiration to his teammates and to his opponents. Those to whom I spoke lauded Rivera for his comportment, sportsmanship, classy demeanor, and for his professionalism. To a man, everyone admired him as a human being, respected him as a competitor, and marveled at the high level of performance he sustained for a storied franchise in a pressure-cooker environment.

Many of the interviews in this book took place in the days following the 2013 All-Star Game, which will long be remembered for the touching moment when Rivera entered the game.

He stood alone on the mound as his American League teammates and National League opponents remained in their respective dugouts, allowing Rivera to soak in the two-minute standing ovation from the adoring crowd. Those I spoke to cite this unprecedented tribute bestowed upon Rivera as being one of the most emotional moments they've ever experienced while watching a baseball game. Rivera's ability to rehabilitate from a serious knee injury resulting in surgery that limited his 2012 season to just nine appearances and to come back to finish his final season at the top of his game is also a common recurring theme that speaks to Rivera's character.

Hollywood scriptwriters could not have conjured the storyline any better. The son of a fisherman who grew up playing baseball on a beach in Panama with a milk carton for a glove, a tree limb for a bat, and rolled-up fishing net for a ball, would come to America and go on to become the greatest closer of all time. Five years after his retirement, Rivera should become the first player to win unanimous election to the Hall of Fame, proving how revered he is among his peers in the game.

Truly dominant pitchers come along only rarely. Rarer still are those who embody attributes that any parent would want his son or daughter to have.

I sincerely hope you enjoy this tribute to Mariano Rivera.

Section One: Infielders

Roberto Alomar

Second base

Playing Career

San Diego Padres, Toronto Blue Jays, Baltimore Orioles, Cleveland Indians, New York Mets, Chicago White Sox, and Arizona Diamondbacks from 1988 to 2004

Career Statistics

2,379 games, 2,724 hits, 210 home runs, 1,134 runs batted in, .300 batting average, .371 on-base percentage, .443 slugging percentage

Roberto Alomar facing Mariano Rivera (regular season)

5-for-11, 3 extra-base hits, 1 run batted in, 2 walks, 3 strikeouts, .455 batting average, .500 on-base percentage, .727 slugging percentage

Mo Cred

Alomar, a Hall of Famer, struck out and grounded out facing Rivera as a member of the Orioles in the 1996 American League Championship Series, won by the Yankees in five games.

Roberto Alomar

Year	Date	Result			
1996	4/30	Pop out		5/3	Sacrifice bunt
	6/28	Single			
	7/13	Walk	2001	6/2	Strikeout (Swinging)
	9/19	Double			
Postseason	10/9	Strikeout (Swinging)		6/25	Ground out
	10/12	Ground out	2003	6/22	Strikeout (Swinging)
1998	6/17	Double		6/28	Sacrifice fly (1 RBI)
	9/20	Double			
1999	6/1	Single		6/29	Ground out
2000	5/1	Walk		8/28	Strikeout (Swinging)

S EEING MARIANO MEANT, ninety-nine percent of the time, the game was over. Mentally, guys thought it was over when he came into a game.

First of all, he's very confident. I admired his approach. He said, "If you're going to beat me, you're going to beat me with my best pitch."

7

That's what made him so different than all the others. To me, it's amazing how he did it, with only one pitch.

He's a great student of the game, and I think the older he got, the better he got. He started throwing cutters backdoor, and started throwing cutters inside.

Mariano set the standard for closers, and so many people admire him. He's just so good for baseball. For him to close this long, at this level, is just ridiculous.

Mo Respect

David Adams

Adams was Rivera's teammate with the Yankees in 2013.

The one thing that sticks out most to me is how electrifying the crowd gets and how loud the Stadium gets every time he comes out to the mound. As soon as his song comes on the loudspeaker, and he jogs through the gate, it's just like a big boom. That's the one thing that is electrifying to me.

Mike Blowers

Third base

Playing Career

New York Yankees, Seattle Mariners, Los Angeles Dodgers, and Oakland Athletics from 1989 to 1999

Career Statistics

761 games, 591 hits, 78 home runs, 365 runs batted in, .257 batting average, .329 on-base percentage, .416 slugging percentage

Mike Blowers facing Mariano Rivera (regular season)
0-for-3, 2 strikeouts

Mo Cred

Rivera struck out Blowers on three pitches in the decisive game of the 1995
American League Division Series.

Mike Blowers

Year	Date	Result
1995	8/25	Strikeout (Swinging)
	8/25	Strikeout (Looking)
Postseason	10/6	Strikeout (Swinging)
	10/8	Strikeout (Looking)
1998	8/4	Fly out

I SAW HIM COMING out of the bullpen and turned around to walk back to the dugout to ask [coach] Lee Elia for a scouting report. He had a pretty good fastball, mid-90s, with a little late cut to it. I watched him warm up and didn't think much of it. Certainly, I didn't realize he was going to become the greatest closer ever, a Hall of Famer.

Just before I went to the plate, [outfielder] Vince Coleman came out and asked me what I was going to do. He told me, "He's a young guy who isn't going to be sure of the situation. Why don't you take one?"

The first pitch was 93 [miles an hour] right down the middle. I kicked myself for taking it. Every fastball he threw was a little harder. It's the only at-bat I have regret about. Not so much what I would have done with it; I don't feel badly about that. I just wish I would have given myself a chance. That first pitch wasn't his best fastball. Then he put me away.*

I've always appreciated what he's done and what he's about. A lot of guys have been great pitchers, Hall of Fame pitchers, but very few have

---

*The Yankees and Mariners were tied at two games apiece in the best-of-five 1995 A.L.D.S. The Mariners had tied the game at 4-4 with two outs and the bases loaded when Yankees manager Buck Showalter summoned Rivera, a rookie, to face Blowers, who had hit 23 home runs and driven in 96 runs that season. Rivera struck out Blowers on three pitches, though the Mariners would win 6-5 in eleven innings. Rivera had also struck out Blowers in the eighth inning of Game Three. Rivera struck out Blowers four times in five career at-bats, including the postseason.

handled themselves the way he has. That little skip-hop he does coming through the bullpen door, then he comes jogging in, I'll miss that.

Mo Respect

Aaron Boone

Boone's walk-off home run in the eleventh inning of Game Seven of the 2003 American League Championship Series defeated the Boston Red Sox, 6-5, making Rivera the winning pitcher and sending the Yankees to the World Series.

My lasting memory of Mariano Rivera is him collapsing on the mound at the end of Game Seven of the 2003 A.L.C.S. after he had gone three innings and shut down that great Red Sox offense. To see him completely overcome with joy is something I'll always remember.

I think he's arguably the most revered athlete in history. There are a ton of people who love him. That speaks to his character, his grace, and the way he's carried himself throughout his entire career. To have a guy like that who plays for the Yankees—he's revered, whether you're friend or foe. I always tell people he's exactly like how you think he is: humble, graceful, and kind. But underneath it all, he's also the ultimate competitor.

Mike Bordick

Shortstop

Playing Career

Oakland Athletics, Baltimore Orioles, New York Mets, and Toronto Blue Jays from 1990 to 2003

Career Statistics

1,720 games, 1,500 hits, 91 home runs, 626 runs batted in, .260 batting average, .323 on-base percentage, .362 slugging percentage

Mike Bordick facing Mariano Rivera (regular season)

6-for-26, 2 extra-base hits, 1 run batted in, 3 walks, 3 strikeouts, .286 batting average, .323 on-base percentage, .362 slugging percentage

Mo Cred

Bordick's .804 OPS, which is on-base percentage plus slugging percentage, is third best among hitters with at least 24 plate appearances against Rivera, trailing only Rafael Palmeiro (1.050) and David Ortiz (.936).

Mike Bordick

Year	Date	Result		Date	Result
1995	5/28	Single		6/25	Pop out
	5/28	Single		7/2	Fly out
	6/6	Single		9/28	Strikeout
	6/6	Line out			(Swinging)
	9/1	Walk	2000	5/7	Fly out
1996	5/31	Fly out		7/24	Walk
	9/2	Ground out		7/26	Pop out
1997	9/6	Fielder's choice	2001	5/4	Fly out
1998	5/21	Strikeout		5/12	Grounded into
		(Swinging)			DP
	9/20	Fly out		6/6	Walk
1999	4/13	Triple	2002	4/4	Fly out
	4/15	Strikeout		6/3	Double (1 RBI)
		(Looking)		9/28	Single

INEVER REALIZED THAT [statistic]. It's funny because I only remember one hit. It was a triple to left-center. He sped up my bat with a slider. It was one of the highlights of my career. It might have been the only slider he ever threw.*

I don't think that he's changed very much, and why should he, after all those innings, all those clutch situations? Now sometimes he'll mix in a two-seamer that sinks. He's just so comfortable on the mound. His velocity is in the low 90s now, but he's still very effective. He's able to locate. He's so smart. He's something of a grand master. He knows what he wants to do and he executes perfectly almost all of the time.

---

*Rivera entered the game in a non-save situation with the Yankees leading 6-2 at Yankee Stadium, on April 13, 1999. With two outs and nobody on base in the top of the ninth inning, Bordick tripled on an 0-2 pitch and scored an unearned run on a passed ball.

Robinson Cano

Second base

Playing Career

New York Yankees and Seattle Mariners since 2005

Career Statistics

1,374 games, 1,649 hits, 204 home runs, 822 runs batted in, .309 batting average, .355 on-base percentage, .504 slugging percentage

Mo Cred

Cano was Rivera's teammate with the Yankees from 2005 to 2013 and was a member of the 2009 World Series championship team.

WHEN YOU'RE IN the minor leagues, and you see guys up in the big leagues who are the best in the world, you might be afraid to say hello to them. But Mariano was a guy who was always coming up to guys and would say, "Hey, how you doing?"

That's one of the best things about him; you always feel comfortable around him. You don't feel like this is Mariano Rivera and you have to be careful or don't want to bother him. His door is always open. He's always available for whatever you want.

We went to dinner one time in Anaheim. He's a guy who is always around his family and [yet] he takes the time to take a rookie out to dinner and that really meant a lot to me. I remember we went to Benihana. That was one of my best days in baseball because I got to go out with Mariano and I was just a rookie.

To be able to spend time with him and ask questions really meant a lot. I asked him questions about baseball and how he can stay in the game so long and how he can stay so humble. Those kinds of things that you want to ask the guy. He picked up the tab, of course. I would have no chance to pay [when] with him.

Two things about Mariano: He's the greatest closer in the game and one of the best teammates I ever had.

Eric Chavez

Third base

Playing Career

Oakland Athletics, New York Yankees, and Arizona Diamondbacks since 1998

Career Statistics

1,571 games, 1,460 hits, 257 home runs, 894 runs batted in, .268 batting average, .342 on-base percentage, .476 slugging percentage

Eric Chavez facing Mariano Rivera (regular season)
5-for-16, 1 extra-base hit, 1 walk, 3 strikeouts, .313 batting average, .353 on-base percentage, .375 slugging percentage

Mo Cred

Chavez spent two seasons as Rivera's teammate while playing for the Yankees in 2011 and '12.

FACING MARIANO IS what you would expect it to be. You just knew you were going to get a cutter and there was a pretty good chance that if you were a left-hand hitter he was going to break your bat. If I faced him [around] fifteen times, I'd probably say he broke five or six bats. You pretty much knew when you went up there you better be taking a bat you're not too fond of because he was probably going to break it.[*]

---

[*]Chavez also faced Rivera in the 2000 and 2001 American League Division Series. He was 0-for-4 with two strikeouts and made the final out of the 2000 series.

Eric Chavez

Year	Date	Result
1999	4/6	Strikeout (Swinging)
2000	5/30	Single
	8/27	Ground out
Postseason	10/6	Strikeout (Swinging)
	10/8	Foul out
2001	4/28	Strikeout (Swinging)
Postseason	10/13	Strikeout (Swinging)
	10/15	Fielder's choice
2002	4/23	Strikeout (Swinging)
	8/11	Pop out
2003	8/1	Single
	8/3	Single
2004	5/5	Pop out
	8/4	Double
2005	5/6	Single
	5/15	Line out
2007	4/15	Ground out
	6/29	Pop out
2008	6/12	Walk
2010	4/21	Fielder's choice
2013	4/17	Fielder's choice

When he was young, he was your typical 96 miles an hour with a huge cutter. It was puzzling how a ball could move so much. When you go back and look at his career and what he's done with that one pitch, I don't think there's a greater achievement in this game than that. To go through major league hitters and dominate them for all these years, it's one of the greatest feats I'll ever look back on. I

Jeff Conine

Year	Date	Result
1998	5/12	Fly out
1999	4/15	Double (1 RBI)
	6/27	Line out
2000	5/6	Walk
	7/24	Fly out
2001	5/6	Walk
	5/13	Home run (3 RBI)
	6/6	Strikeout (Looking)
	6/7	Ground out
	7/4	Sacrifice fly (1 RBI)
	9/23	Ground out
2002	4/3	Single
	4/18	Strikeout (Looking)
2003	6/30	Ground out
	7/23	Single
Postseason	10/21	Single
	10/25	Ground out
2006	4/23	Ground out
	8/4	Single

Mo Respect

Jeff Conine

Conine was 5-for-14 with 1 home run and 5 runs batted in facing Rivera during the regular season, and 1-for-2 in the 2003 World Series.

There wasn't any particular set plan that I had against him. My focus was to try to get a ball in the strike zone and get a barrel on it. That was basically my approach. You know what's coming every single time and it's still that difficult to hit. Countless times you see him come in and nobody ever gets the bat on the ball.

honestly believe that, too. I don't think people realize how incredible it really is. It will never be duplicated—ever.

I think something I've taken from Mo as his teammate is if you have a routine that works for you, then you definitely should stick with it.

Carlos Delgado

First base

Playing Career

Toronto Blue Jays, Florida Marlins, and New York Mets from 1993 to 2009

Career Statistics

2,035 games, 2,038 hits, 473 home runs, 1,512 runs batted in, .280 batting average, .383 on-base percentage, .546 slugging percentage

Carlos Delgado facing Mariano Rivera (regular season)

8-for-21, 1 extra-base hit, 1 run batted in, 2 intentional walks, 4 strikeouts, .381 batting average, .435 on-base percentage, .429 slugging percentage

Mo Cred

Delgado was walked intentionally twice by Rivera, tying him with Edgar Martinez, Evan Longoria, and Paul Sorrento for most times intentionally walked by Rivera.

SEVEN SINGLES AND one double? I don't call that exactly great success against a guy, but I'm happy for it. Probably the softest 8-for-21 in my career, but I'll take it.

Carlos Delgado

Year	Date	Result		Date	Result
1996	6/4	Strikeout (Swinging)		9/5	Double
			2002	4/9	Fly out
	9/6	Line out	2003	7/13	Ground out (1 RBI)
	9/14	Ground out			
1997	5/20	Single		9/4	Strikeout (Swinging)
	9/20	Foul out			
1999	4/24	Strikeout (Swinging)	2004	7/22	Single
				7/26	Single
	4/25	Single	2006	5/19	Intentional walk
	9/14	Single			
	9/15	Foul out		5/20	Ground out
2000	9/13	Foul out	2007	6/16	Single
2001	4/19	Ground out	2008	6/28	Strikeout (Swinging)
	7/21	Single			
	8/30	Intentional walk			

He always had a good fastball, but once he had that [cutter], he became tougher. The ball just explodes on you. That's the difference between hitting the ball and getting jammed. I always found that the cutter got in on me. I kept hitting the ball on the label. I could never square him up.

What made him so effective is his cutter is so hard [that] by the time you see it, you don't have time [to react]. Your hands can't go to where a ball isn't.

Mark DeRosa

Infield

Playing Career

Atlanta Braves, Texas Rangers, Chicago Cubs, Cleveland Indians, St. Louis Cardinals, San Francisco Giants, Washington Nationals, and Toronto Blue Jays from 1998 to 2013

Career Statistics

1,241 games, 975 hits, 100 home runs, 494 runs batted in, .268 batting average, .340 on-base percentage, .412 slugging percentage

Mark DeRosa facing Mariano Rivera (regular season)
1-for-5, 0 extra-base hits, 3 strikeouts, 1 walk, .200 batting average, .333 on-base percentage, .200 slugging percentage

Mo Cred

DeRosa was a huge Yankees fan while growing up in New Jersey in the late 1980s and early 1990s.

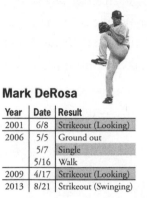

Mark DeRosa

Year	Date	Result
2001	6/8	Strikeout (Looking)
2006	5/5	Ground out
	5/7	Single
	5/16	Walk
2009	4/17	Strikeout (Looking)
2013	8/21	Strikeout (Swinging)

I REMEMBER THE FIRST time I walked into the batter's box at Yankee Stadium, in 1999, to Bob Sheppard announcing my name in that voice, it was just awesome. I went to games as a kid and I remember him saying: "Dahn ... Mat-ting-ly"—and to hear him say my name, it was like, man, I've arrived.

My first at-bat against Mariano was in the Stadium when I was with Atlanta in 2001. [New York manager] Joe Torre calls him in from the bullpen, and the music ["Enter Sandman" by Metallica, which is Rivera's entrance song] starts playing, and I'm like, "This is awesome. I'm going to get to face Mariano!" I remember looking into the stands where my dad and my brother were sitting in the family section. My brother is trying to psych me up, he's yelling, "Let's go! You can do it!"

Next to him is my dad, who has his head buried in his hands, like, "Oh no, my son's about to strike out to end the game."

I remember watching Mariano warm up like it was yesterday. I'm thinking, man, I've watched this guy forever. I think I can get to that [cutter]. I step in the batter's box, and I'm confident, I'm ready. The first pitch I think is going to hit me square between the ribs, so I close my eyes. I open them and the umpire says: "Strike one."

Now I'm thinking, oh no, I'm going to strike out. I tried to act cool, like the big leaguer I am, pretending I've seen a pitcher like this before. But in the back of mind I knew it was only a matter of time before I'm going back to the bench.*

---

*DeRosa struck out on three pitches against Rivera with the Yankees ahead of the Atlanta Braves, 7-4, with one on and two out in the ninth inning at Yankee Stadium, on June 8, 2001. It was Rivera's 183rd career save.

I finally did get a hit off him, a few years later with Texas, but it didn't mean anything as far as the game was concerned. I don't remember the exact situation. The hit I got was a line drive up the middle. I'm pretty sure he was just closing out a game to get in some work. You have moments during your career where you really take it in for a second. I was running down to first, and I'm like, this is awesome. I just got a hit off one of the greatest pitchers to ever take the mound. That's a pretty cool moment for me.[*]

Robert Eenhoorn

Infield

Playing Career

New York Yankees and Anaheim Angels from 1994 to 1997

Career Statistics

37 games, 16 hits, 1 home run, 10 runs batted in, .239 batting average, .260 on-base percentage, .328 slugging percentage

Mo Cred

Eenhoorn spent four seasons as Rivera's minor league teammate with Fort Lauderdale, Albany, and Columbus from 1992 to 1995.

AT FORT LAUDERDALE [in 1992] we would race just to kill time and pitchers never joined in—except Mariano. He would outrun

---

[*]DeRosa singled to center off Rivera leading off the bottom of the ninth inning of a game won by the Yankees 8-5 in Texas. Rivera pitched the ninth in a non-save situation, entering with a four-run lead, allowing only an unearned run, on May 7, 2006.

everybody on the team. He was the best athlete and it really wasn't close.

He only said something when he had something to say. Mariano was observant. There is so much time to mess around, but Mariano was always watching, picking up information, and learning.

I remember facing him in batting practice; you knew fastballs were coming and I still couldn't catch up with them.

Matt Franco
First base

Playing Career

Chicago Cubs, New York Mets, and Atlanta Braves from 1995 to 2003

Career Statistics

661 games, 261 hits, 22 home runs, 117 runs batted in, .267 batting average, .349 on-base percentage, .391 slugging percentage

Matt Franco facing Mariano Rivera (regular season)
1-for-2, 0 extra-base hits, 2 runs batted in, 1 walk, .500 batting average, .667 on-base percentage, .500 slugging percentage

Mo Cred

Franco's two-run single off Rivera in the bottom of the ninth inning gave the Mets a 9-8 walk-off win over the Yankees at Shea Stadium on July 10, 1999.

IT WAS A storybook scenario and I happened to get a good pitch to hit and I did my job, and hit a line drive and we won the game. I

Matt Franco

Year	Date	Result
1998	6/26	Walk
1999	6/4	Ground out
	7/10	Single (2 RBI)
2000 (Postseason)	10/25	Strikeout (Looking)

felt great. I wasn't nervous. It was the highlight of my career.[*]

That hit made the career, right there. I remember every moment like it was yesterday. Everybody went crazy. I got back to our clubhouse and someone, I think it was Jay [Horwitz, the Mets' media relations director], said: "The fans are waiting for you! Go back out there!"

And so I went out and took a curtain call.

[Mariano] lives with that hard, cut fastball. He gets lefties with it time after time. You see it every night on TV. I just told myself I wasn't going to get beat by that pitch. He threw one 92 miles per hour on the outside part of the plate. I was not looking for that pitch. He threw some great pitches on the outside part of the plate, exactly where I wasn't looking.

The pitch just before [the winning hit] was a close call. My heart stopped for half a breath. The Yankees sure thought it was strike three. I'm thinking, "It's Mariano, man, and Mo *always* gets that call. Who the heck am I? Matt Franco doesn't get that call." But I did, though I'm not sure how, and then I got the hit and we won.[**]

My friends will sometimes say in a good-natured way that my [lifetime] batting average [of .267] is not that good, and I say, "Yeah, but

---

[*]The Yankees hit six home runs, including Jorge Posada's two-run shot in the eighth inning that gave them a 7-6 lead. Enter Rivera, at the height of his brilliance, to pitch the ninth. At that point, the Yankees had won 124 consecutive games in which they held a lead after eight innings. Rickey Henderson started the rally with a walk, and Edgardo Alfonzo doubled to center. After John Olerud grounded out, Rivera intentionally walked Mike Piazza, and Franco, pinch-hitting for Melvin Mora, lined a 1-2 pitch to right to score the tying and winning runs.

[**]With two outs and the bases loaded, and the count 0-2, pinch hitter Franco was frozen by Rivera's cut fastball that appeared to blaze over the outside corner of the plate. Plate umpire Jeff Kellogg called it a ball, and Franco laced the next pitch into right field for a two-run, game-winning single.

when your at-bats are against Mariano Rivera, Robb Nenn, and all those closers, it's pretty good." Being a major league player was pretty cool.

Nomar Garciaparra

Shortstop

Playing Career

Boston Red Sox, Chicago Cubs, Los Angeles Dodgers, and Oakland Athletics from 1996 to 2009

Career Statistics

1,434 games, 1,747 hits, 229 home runs, 936 runs batted in, .313 batting average, .361 on-base percentage, .521 slugging percentage

Nomar Garciaparra facing Mariano Rivera (regular season)
7-for-18, 3 extra-base hits, 3 runs batted in, 3 strikeouts, .389 batting average, .389 on-base percentage, .611 slugging percentage

Nomar Garciaparra

Year	Date	Result		Date	Result		Date	Result
1996	9/28	Strikeout (Swinging)		9/9	Strikeout (Looking)		9/7	Fly out
1997	6/1	Triple (1 RBI)	2003	5/28	Single (2 RBI)	Postseason	10/11	Ground out
1998	9/8	Single		7/6	Fielder's choice		10/14	Ground out (1 RBI)
1999	5/20	Single		7/7	Single		10/16	Strikeout (Looking)
	5/27	Pop out		7/25	Double	2004	7/23	Ground out
Postseason	10/14	Single		8/30	Fly out		7/24	Double
	10/17	Ground out		8/31	Strikeout (Swinging)	2009	7/26	Ground out
2000	6/14	Ground out						
	9/8	Fly out						

Mo Cred

Garciaparra, a two-time American League batting champion, was 1-for-5 facing Rivera in the postseason.

HE'S GOING TO go down as one of the best closers, if not the best closer, in baseball. He set a standard for aspiring closers.

I moved closer to the mound against him. It probably increases velocity, but I was more worried about the late break. His cutter would break so late.

Not every one of them cut. It wasn't like every single one of them moved the exact same distance. I was more worried about the break than the velocity, so I thought if I moved up [in the batter's box] I could reduce that late break.

Jason Giambi

First base and Designated hitter

Playing Career

Oakland Athletics, New York Yankees, Colorado Rockies, and Cleveland Indians since 1995

Career Statistics

2,234 games, 2,002 hits, 438 home runs, 1,436 runs batted in, .278 batting average, .400 on-base percentage, .519 slugging percentage

Jason Giambi facing Mariano Rivera (regular season)

3-for-12, 0 extra-base hits, 1 run batted in, 2 walks, 3 strikeouts, .250 batting average, .357 on-base percentage, .250 slugging percentage

Mo Cred

Giambi played with the Yankees for seven seasons as Rivera's teammate from 2002 to 2008.

Jason Giambi

Year	Date	Result
1995	9/1	Strikeout (Looking)
	9/1	Strikeout (Swinging)
1996	5/21	Fielder's choice
	8/23	Single
	9/2	Fielder's choice
1997	4/5	Single
	4/11	Pop out
	7/28	Ground out
1999	4/6	Single (1 RBI)
	8/11	Foul out

Year	Date	Result
	8/30	Walk
2000 Postseason	8/8	Walk
	10/4	Ground out
	10/6	Ground out
	10/8	Fly out
2001 (Postseason)	10/11	Double play
	10/13	Ground out
	10/15	Single
2009	4/22	Fielder's choice
2013	6/4	Strikeout (Swinging)

WE BROKE INTO the big leagues almost at the same time. I spent a lot of time facing him when I played for the [Oakland] A's. The things that made him so successful from Day 1 were presence and preparation. Even when he was younger he was so good with the location of his pitches. He had that cutter that ran up on you at 93, 94 miles per hour. He had other pitches, too, but the cutter was his bread and butter. He was throwing saw blades up there, chewing up bats. The amazing thing is 17 years later the cutter is still his bread and butter. He runs it in on you and ties you up. I don't know if you're going to see a guy like that come around anymore, especially a guy who does it with just one pitch. You go up there looking for one pitch and you still can't hit it.[*]

I was a teammate of his for a long time in New York. He's incredible. There's no better closer, in my opinion, than Mariano. The guy is like ice. I was there [in New York] for seven years and I can only count maybe one or two times that I can remember that he had a blown save.

---

[*]Giambi also faced Rivera six times in the postseason. He was 0-for-3 in the 2000 American League Division Series, and 1-for-3 in the 2001 A.L.D.S., both won by the Yankees.

And you were so shocked that he blew a save. It was incredible. And what really stands out is he did this playing in the American League East. That's where you find out what kind of player you are, the A.L. East, and that's where he spent his entire career. And what he does in the postseason, there's no way to put it into words, how dominating he was. Talk about a guy who makes a difference in a game. Early in his career he was getting two-inning saves, so it's like you're playing seven-inning baseball [games].

When I was a designated hitter, I'd go into the clubhouse between innings to stay loose and watch videos. Mariano wouldn't go to the bullpen until the later innings. We'd start talking and he was never uptight. He was asking me about hitters and what they think about in [certain] situations. He was always looking for something he could use [to his advantage], something that would give him an edge on a hitter.

With most guys if you interrupt their routine they stress out. Not Mariano. He's always relaxed. He likes to stretch and get a massage before the game. With most guys, they keep a routine, like they want their massage at 1:03 p.m. If Mariano walks in and someone is on the table, it doesn't bother him. He waits and nobody feels uncomfortable, like they are disrupting him.

Every day in batting practice, he would go out to center field to shag fly balls after he got done running. He takes shagging fly balls seriously. People don't know what a great athlete he is. We always told him he was our center fielder if anyone went down.

We used to tease Bernie Williams that if Mariano got bored pitching he was going to take Bernie's job from him.

He's an incredible human being. I don't think there will ever be anybody like him again. It's a sad day when he retires. We became really close in New York and I wish him all the best.

Ozzie Guillen
Shortstop and Manager

Playing Career

Chicago White Sox, Baltimore Orioles, Atlanta Braves, and Tampa Bay Rays from 1985 to 2000

Career Statistics

1,993 games, 1,764 hits, 28 home runs, 619 runs batted in, .264 batting average, .287 on-base percentage, .338 slugging percentage

Ozzie Guillen facing Mariano Rivera (regular season)

3-for-12, 1 extra-base hit, 1 walk, .250 batting average, .308 on-base percentage, .333 slugging percentage

Mo Cred

Guillen struck out facing Rivera in the 1999 World Series. He was the manager of the defending world champion White Sox when Rivera earned his 400th career save in 2006.

Ozzie Guillen

Year	Date	Result
1995	7/4	Walk
	7/5	Ground out
	7/6	Ground out
1996	5/3	Fly out
	5/12	Single
	8/8	Single
	8/12	Pop out
	8/14	Ground out
1997	4/19	Ground out
	4/26	Ground out
	7/17	Fielder's choice
1998	6/22	Double
	6/24	Double play
1999 (Postseason)	10/26	Strikeout

GOD BLESS MARIANO. He goes out and he's the closer for two innings sometimes. You don't see that too often. Mariano keeps doing the same thing he's been doing for the last 19 years, whatever he's been in the league. It's amazing what he can do.

One word: Hall of Fame. On the field and off the field, he's a Hall of Famer. Young players look up to him. The way he is, the way he performs on the field and the way he treats people, I think Mariano is the perfect baseball player.

25

I had a great time at the All-Star Game. We got to see the best closer ever, Mariano Rivera. He has broken my bat before and probably hundreds of others during his career. It was amazing to see him go out like that. I actually shed a couple of tears.

One of the things I love about this game is that even though we all know Rivera is the best ever, he's still been beaten and walked off on. That's why this game is so special; you never know what's going to happen.

Scott Hatteberg
First base and Catcher

Playing Career

Boston Red Sox, Oakland Athletics, and Cincinnati Reds from 1995 to 2008

Career Statistics

1,314 games, 1,153 hits, 106 home runs, 527 runs batted in, .273 batting average, .361 on-base percentage, .410 slugging percentage

Scott Hatteberg facing Mariano Rivera (regular season)
1-for-13, 1 run batted in, 2 walks, .077 batting average, .200 on-base percentage, .077 slugging percentage

Mo Cred

Hatteberg is a prominent character in the Michael Lewis novel, Moneyball, *due to his high on-base percentage.*

THINKING ABOUT FACING Mariano Rivera still gives me nightmares. He was the one closer that I ever faced who didn't have that lightning stuff. He wasn't like a black mamba type of snake, he was

Scott Hatteberg

Year	Date	Result
1997	6/1	Single
	6/1	Pop out
	6/2	Fly out
	9/16	Line out
	9/16	Fly out
2000	6/20	Pop out
2001	4/14	Ground out
	5/28	Ground out
2002	4/24	Ground out
	8/9	Ground out
2003	5/10	Ground out
2004	8/4	Walk
		Walk
2005	5/6	Reached on error (2 RBI)
	5/15	Ground out

a constrictor—he slowly sucked the life out of you, and then the lights went out. It didn't seem like a violent at-bat, it just seemed like you had no chance.

I had different grades of success facing him—bad and worse! As a lefthander, I just hoped to save my bat. That was it. If I didn't break my bat, it was a pretty good at-bat for me, and I was happy. I didn't do squat off him. Nobody I knew really did anything off him. The only guy I ever saw do anything off him was Manny Ramirez; he seemed to do a good job facing him. Other than Manny, I didn't see anybody sniff that guy.*

Mariano just chewed up lefthanders. He was pretty darn good against righties, but lefties just had no chance against that cutter. I remember being at a FanFest in Oakland. Ken Macha was our manager, and people at the FanFest were asking questions. One fan asked me, "Is there any question you'd like to ask your manager?" The first question that popped into my mind was, "Why the hell do we keep pinch-hitting lefthanders against Mariano Rivera?" Macha just looked at me and he laughed, but he didn't have any answer for me.

I remember getting one hit, and I broke my bat in 50,000 pieces and the ball barely slinked over into right field. Other than that, I seriously don't think I ever got another hit. I choked up, I stood in front of the box, I pulled off, I took pitches, I swung early; I tried everything. Really the best ball I ever hit I think was a line drive over their dugout. You couldn't do anything with that cutter but pull it foul. The two

---

*Facing Rivera, Ramirez was 8-for-39 with 1 home run, 9 runs batted in, 3 walks, 13 strikeouts, 1 sacrifice fly, 3 hit by pitches, .205 batting average, .273 on-base percentage, .282 slugging percentage. Ramirez's 9 RBIs are the most of any batter against Rivera.

times I walked, that was probably part of my new plan of not swinging at anything!*

Playing in Boston, we faced him a lot. At the time we were pretty good, but the Yankees were really good. They got the best of us more often than not. As a Red Sox you were completely brainwashed, you were trained to hate the Yankees, but he's one of those guys who [is] hard to hate. He was so good, and so classy, that you couldn't hate him. You really respected the guy, obviously, not only for his amazing talent, but he seemed like a quality guy. I don't know him at all, but to do what he did for so long on the big stage, you have to be impressed by him. If you're going to go 0-for-a-century, he's a pretty good guy to do it against.

Okay, I was 1-for-13. Oh perfect. Geez, that's better than I thought it was. The hit was early in Mariano's career, and it didn't change much

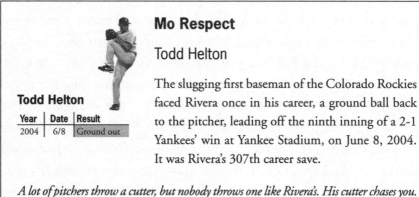

Mo Respect

Todd Helton

The slugging first baseman of the Colorado Rockies faced Rivera once in his career, a ground ball back to the pitcher, leading off the ninth inning of a 2-1 Yankees' win at Yankee Stadium, on June 8, 2004. It was Rivera's 307th career save.

Todd Helton

Year	Date	Result
2004	6/8	Ground out

A lot of pitchers throw a cutter, but nobody throws one like Rivera's. His cutter chases you. It's the nastiest thing I've ever seen. You know it's coming, you adjust for it, and you still can't hit it. Even when you know what it's going to do, you can't make your bat swing.

---

*Hatteberg got a pinch-hit bloop single off Rivera in the bottom of the ninth inning of a game the Red Sox trailed 5-4. Nomar Garciaparra followed with a triple to score Hatteberg with the tying run. Hatteberg faced Rivera again in the bottom of the tenth inning and popped out to the second baseman. The Yankees went on to win the game 11-6 in fifteen innings at Fenway Park in Boston, on June 1, 1997. Rivera was not involved in the decision.

after that. Nothing changed much when it comes to Mariano: Same song, same act, same slender dude, taking the mound and throwing the same pitches—the guy is a broken record. Speaking of records, I hate that song "Enter Sandman."

Derek Jeter

Shortstop

Playing Career

New York Yankees since 1995

Career Statistics

2,602 games, 3,316 hits, 256 home runs, 1,261 runs batted in, .312 batting average, .381 on-base percentage, .446 slugging percentage

Mo Cred

Jeter and Rivera have been teammates on the Yankees since 1995 and together helped the team win five World Series championships in 1996, 1998, 1999, 2000, and 2009.

HE IS THE greatest closer, no disrespect to anybody else. You know what he's done in the regular season, and more importantly, what he's done in the postseason is unmatched. There are a lot of great closers that have played the game—once again, not to be disrespectful—but I would take Mo over everybody.

You can add up all the players that ever played the game, and Mo has been as consistent as anyone. He's done it in the regular season, he's done it in the postseason, he's done it in spring training, he's done it in the minor leagues. He's done it everywhere he's been.

It goes without saying what he's meant to this organization. A lot of people have been spoiled: Yankees fans have been spoiled; baseball fans watching him; us as his teammates. We don't take him for granted. But I think a lot of people may, because he comes in, they assume [the game is] over. The only time you [in the media] talk to him is when he doesn't come through. We've all been spoiled. People will realize it when he's no longer here.

It's pretty impressive what he's been able to do. So he deserves all the accolades he gets. He did something no one's ever been able to do. The impressive thing is he's done it in the postseason, too. He wants the ball in big situations and [is] not afraid of anyone. He has a lot of confidence in his ability and it shows. That's what separates him from everyone else. You won't see anyone like him again.

First of all, it's not one pitch. He throws a cutter, he throws a two-seamer, and he throws a four-seamer. It's one speed in terms of hard, but Mo has perfected the fastball and I'm not surprised by it. I've been playing with him since I've been 18 years old and he's been doing it since then. Nothing he does surprises me.

We've been close for a very, very long time. Our relationship goes beyond just on the field. He's like a brother. Any time you play with someone that long, there's a connection there. He's been the exact same person he was since the first day I met him.

I think our personalities are similar, that's why we get along so well. We're similar in terms of what the goal is—and that's to win. The goal is to come here every single day and do your job and pretty much stay on an even keel.

I know how important it is to him to come here and do his job. He takes a lot of pride in doing his job and he's done his job better than anyone else. It's impressive. Mo's been doing this for a long time. He's doing things that no one's ever done. And you probably won't see it again.

There are so many things that we have been through together. You're talking about 21 years since the minor leagues. Mo was a starter in the minor leagues. When he was coming off [elbow] surgery [in August of

1992] I used to count his pitches at short [at Class A Greensboro in 1993]. I used to run up there and say, "Look, man, you are wasting too many pitches. You have to start throwing more strikes."

He would be on [a short pitch count] when he first was coming back. And this wasn't the days where they had pitch counts on the scoreboard. So I would count his pitches at short. He would say, "Okay, okay, okay."

He worked hard at everything he does, but he worked extremely hard at his rehab, too [from a torn ACL in 2012]. It's not an easy thing to come back from.

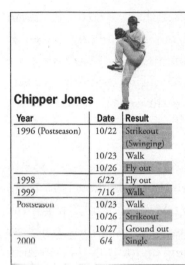

Mo Respect

Chipper Jones

The former switch-hitting third baseman of the Atlanta Braves, who was 1-for-2 with a walk facing Rivera in the regular season, and 0-for-4 with two walks in World Series competition, describes the cutter:

It's like a buzz saw. It just eats you up, especially if you're a left-handed hitter. You know it's coming, but that doesn't really help you much.

Chipper Jones

Year	Date	Result
1996 (Postseason)	10/22	Strikeout (Swinging)
	10/23	Walk
	10/26	Fly out
1998	6/22	Fly out
1999	7/16	Walk
Postseason	10/23	Walk
	10/26	Strikeout
	10/27	Ground out
2000	6/4	Single

Eric Karros

First base

Playing Career

Los Angeles Dodgers, Chicago Cubs, and Oakland Athletics from 1991 to 2004

Career Statistics

1,755 games, 1,724 hits, 284 home runs, 1,027 runs batted in, .268 batting average, .325 on-base percentage, .454 slugging percentage

Eric Karros facing Mariano Rivera (regular season)
0-for-2

Mo Cred

Karros won the 1992 National League's Rookie of the Year award.

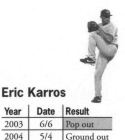

Eric Karros

Year	Date	Result
2003	6/6	Pop out
2004	5/4	Ground out

IT'S FUNNY BECAUSE I credit Mariano with helping me out early in my career. It was in spring training in 1995. That's when we had that abbreviated spring training coming back late because of the strike [which started in August 1994 and caused cancelation of the World Series].

I was coming off an average 1994 season—I was not real good in '94—and I don't know what I'm going to do [to improve], so I was toying around with my stance. I'm facing Mariano, and I've got the Andres Galarraga open stance, so open that I'm facing the pitcher. At the time Mariano is a young guy, he's setting up for [John] Wetteland, but he's also a starter then, too.

So I've got that open stance, and Mariano runs a fastball inside and—BOOM—I get hit right in the sternum. I'm hit right in the sternum with one of Mariano's best fastballs and I'm gasping for air, I couldn't breathe for anything.

The bottom line is that I closed the stance, no more open stance for me. And that year I had one of my best statistical years, I got some Most Valuable Player [award] votes, and I played a few more years after that. So I credit Mariano for making me realize there's going to be no open stance for me.

Mo Respect

Ryan Klesko

The left-handed hitting first baseman of the Atlanta Braves faced Rivera in the final inning of the 1999 World Series. Rivera broke Klesko's bats three times in a span of four pitches, generating two foul balls and a weak pop out to second base as the wood shattered.

That pitch is just wicked. I had never seen anything like it. You can't help but laugh. I couldn't believe it. It was like a 97 miles per hour Wiffle Ball that has no rotation. I told Chipper [Jones], If he breaks one more of my bats, I'm going to have none left.

Corey Koskie

Third base

Playing Career

Minnesota Twins, Toronto Blue Jays, and Milwaukee Brewers from 1998 to 2006

Career Statistics

989 games, 936 hits, 124 home runs, 506 runs batted in, .275 batting average, .367 on-base percentage, .458 slugging percentage

Corey Koskie facing Mariano Rivera (regular season)
0-for-6, 0 extra-base hits, 2 walks, 2 strikeouts, .000 batting average, .250 on-base percentage, .000 slugging percentage

Mo Cred

Rivera retired Koskie with one pitch to earn the shortest save of his career, on August 7, 2005, at Toronto.[*]

Corey Koskie

Year	Date	Result
2000	7/28	Walk
	9/1	Ground out
	9/3	Strikeout (Swinging)
2001	5/9	Walk
2003 (Postseason)	10/2	Fly out
2004 (Postseason)	10/5	Ground out
	10/6	Double (1 RBI)
	10/9	Pop out
2005	4/21	Fly out
	8/7	Fly out
	9/16	Line out
	9/25	Strikeout (Swinging)

I ONLY HAD SIX [regular season] at-bats in my career against Rivera, but it feels like I faced him more. I did face him in the postseason, too; maybe it seems like more at-bats because they're always in big situations.

Most everything I hit off Rivera was a broken bat blooper or an infield dribbler. I got one solid hit off him. I was with the Twins and we were playing the Yankees in the 2004 American League Division Series. We were up one game to none [after] Johan Santana pitched a phenomenal game in Yankee Stadium.[**] In Game Two we're down by two runs when Rivera comes into the game in the top of the eighth inning with runners on first and second base. Justin Morneau singles and we scored one run. So now we're down by one run. There are runners on first and third with one out, and I came up to face Rivera.

I remember it being a long at-bat. He throws me cutter after cutter after cutter. But then with [three balls and] two strikes he threw

---

[*]The Yankees were winning by four runs, with two men on base and two outs. With the tying run on deck, making it a save situation, Rivera entered the game to face Koskie, who flied out to left field on Rivera's only pitch. It was Rivera's 365th career save. The only other time Rivera ever had a one-pitch save was against the Los Angeles Angels of Anaheim, when he induced Erik Aybar to pop out to shortstop Derek Jeter to preserve the victory, on June 4, 2011. It was Rivera's 574th career save.

[**]Johan Santana pitched eight shutout innings and Joe Nathan pitched a scoreless 9th as the Twins defeated the Yankees, 2-0, in Game One of the 2004 American League Division Series at Yankee Stadium.

a sinker away. I was able to hit the ball the other way and it ended up bouncing over the left-field wall for a [ground-rule] double. The runner on third scored and the runner on first [pinch-runner Luis Rivas] would have scored if the ball hit the wall and stayed in play. Had the ball gone another six inches and hit the base of the wall we would have taken the lead. But instead, the ball hit the ground and bounced over the fence, and the runner [who had started out] on first got called back to third base. We had now tied the game and had runners on second and third with one out. Rivera struck out the next guy, and after that got a broken-bat ground ball to the second baseman to get out of [the jam]. We went into extra innings, and in the top of the twelfth inning, we score and go ahead. But in the bottom of the twelfth the Yankees scored a couple of runs to win the game. It was a great game; it just didn't go our way.[*]

You knew what pitch Mariano Rivera was going to throw; a cutter that breaks in to left-handed hitters. I still had trouble hitting it. You start to swing at the pitch and the next thing you know, the ball explodes your bat. I tried multiple things hoping to figure out a way get the barrel [of the bat] on one of his pitches. I tried choking up, and then I tried using a shorter bat. Nothing worked. My normal bat was thirty-four and a half inches long and [weighed] thirty-two ounces. But against left-handed pitchers, and knuckleballers like Tim Wakefield, and Mariano Rivera—against pitchers where you want to wait as long as possible before you commit to swinging—I used a shorter bat that was thirty-three inches and thirty-one ounces.

---

[*] After Koskie's game-tying ground-rule double, Rivera struck out Jason Kubel swinging and induced Cristian Guzman to ground out to first base to end the threat. Minnesota's Torii Hunter hit a solo home run off New York's Tanyon Sturtze with two outs in the top of the twelfth, but Joe Nathan of the Twins surrendered two runs in the bottom of the twelfth to take the 7-6 loss. The Yankees won the next two games to win the series.

A shorter bat forced me to keep my front shoulder closed and let the ball travel deeper. The idea was to wait, and with the shorter, lighter bat I felt my swing was quicker. It was a great bat. Then I used it once against Rivera and on the second pitch, he broke it. Ninety percent of the time he'd break your bat. That's why when you're facing Rivera no teammate ever let you use his bat.

I have an autographed baseball collection, and since I have trouble asking a pitcher for an autograph most of the balls have been signed by hitters. I don't ask pitchers because they're trying to take money out of my pocket. I don't like to say to a pitcher: "I think you're awesome, can you sign this ball for me."

But one of the pitchers I did ask was Rivera. He's a class guy and the ultimate professional.

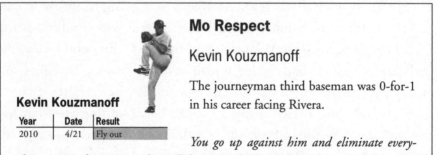

Mo Respect

Kevin Kouzmanoff

The journeyman third baseman was 0-for-1 in his career facing Rivera.

Kevin Kouzmanoff

Year	Date	Result
2010	4/21	Fly out

You go up against him and eliminate everything except the cutter and it still doesn't work. He challenged you with that pitch and you think the pitch is right there. You swing, and it's not there anymore.

Biggest thing is that he not only has that special ability but he has been able to stay healthy for such a long period of time. He's been able to regularly take the ball and get the job done.

Tino Martinez

First base

Playing Career

Seattle Mariners, New York Yankees, St. Louis Cardinals, and Tampa Bay Rays from 1990 to 2005

Career Statistics

2,023 games, 1,925 hits, 339 home runs, 1,271 runs batted in, .271 batting average, .344 on-base percentage, .471 slugging percentage

Tino Martinez facing Mariano Rivera (regular season)

2-for-11, 0 extra-base hits, 1 run batted in, 4 strikeouts, .182 batting average, .182 on-base percentage, .182 slugging percentage

Mo Cred

Martinez teamed with Rivera to win four World Series championships with the Yankees in 1996, 1998, 1999, and 2000.

HE SHUT ME down [when I was with Seattle]. I was always happy when they took him out of the game. I didn't know who he was at first, or how good he was going to be. When he came out of a game we always talked about what kind of great stuff that guy had. And, obviously, he became a great closer.[*]

Then to be a teammate of his for all those years was incredible. He's a total professional. The guy was the best closer ever, and he does it with one pitch. Without Mo, we'd have one, maybe two, World Series [wins], but we wouldn't have four, that's for sure.

The best memory I have of him is in '96, the year we won our first World Series. He pitched the seventh and eighth inning of every

---

[*]Martinez faced Rivera twice in Game Two of the 1995 American League Division Series; he grounded out and flew out.

Tino Martinez

Year	Date	Result
1995	6/11	Ground out
	6/12	Single
	8/25	Strikeout (Swinging)
	8/26	Fly out
	9/5	Fly out
	9/6	Strikeout (Swinging)
Postseason	10/4	Ground out
	10/5	Fly out
2003	6/15	Double play
2004	4/14	Ground out
	5/28	Strikeout (Swinging)
	7/9	Single (1 RBI)
	7/20	Strikeout (Swinging)

postseason game, in the playoffs and World Series. It was the first time I've ever been on a team where after six innings if we have the lead the game was over. And it was all because of Mo. Every postseason game, Mo closed out the seventh and eighth and was dominating, and [John] Wetteland came in and closed out the ninth. If we were ahead after the sixth inning, we knew the game was over, and the other team knew it, too.

It's funny, back then, we loved Wetteland, and he did a great job for us. But we always asked Mo if he could pitch the seventh, eighth *and ninth*! He was that dominant. He shut guys down. It's comforting to have him on your team, because when he comes in, the other team knows the game is over. It's a bad feeling for them, and a great feeling for you. He was a luxury for us to have.

He dominates the game but he doesn't show anybody up. He closes games the right way. You don't see any emotion at all. That's what I love about him the most. He'll strike out three guys, or break their bats, then shake hands, because I did my job, and the game is over. He acted that way, like it's his job, shutting teams down, and winning ball games. He's a good example for young kids to watch, and other closers as well. He has the type of attitude that you can't hate him. You don't think: "I can't stand this guy, let's get him."

You don't feel that way at all because of the way he handles himself on the mound. Instead, you think: "Oh boy, here comes Mariano. He's got great stuff. Here we go again."

He's a great teammate, not just doing his own job, but the way he affects the rest of the team, as well. He teaches the bullpen guys, day in and day out. He's always talking to the young guys that come up, teaching them how to go about their business, how to prepare, how to work out in the weight room, how to get ready for the game. He didn't just talk to pitchers; he would also be talking to hitters.

I'm going to remember how funny it was to see all these big grown men, six foot five inches tall and 250 pounds, hitting balls off the handle of their bat that barely get out of the infield. But I'm also going to think about how we'll never, ever see another guy like him again.

Lou Merloni

Infield

Playing Career

Boston Red Sox, San Diego Padres, Cleveland Indians, and Los Angeles Angels from 1998 to 2006

Career Statistics

423 games, 294 hits, 14 home runs, 125 runs batted in, .271 batting average, .332 on-base percentage, .384 slugging percentage

Lou Merloni facing Mariano Rivera (regular season)

0-for-0, 1 walk, 1.000 on-base percentage

Mo Cred

Merloni is one of fifteen players who walked in their only career at-bat facing Rivera.

I GUESS THE MOST important stat in baseball is on-base percentage, right? So I drew my eight-pitch walk. Listen, I had my one moment against Mo, and then I got out of there. It was beautiful!*

---

*Merloni walked against Rivera in the bottom of the eighth inning of a 10-7 Yankees' win at Fenway Park, on August 30, 2003. It was Rivera's 273rd career save.

Lou Merloni

Year	Date	Result
2003	8/30	Walk

You knew you were in trouble [when Mo came in the game]. The competitive side of you said, "We're going to get this guy today." But the bottom line is, more times than not, you're walking back into that locker room knowing you just lost a game.

He's pitched eighteen years and there's never a blip in the radar. You could make the case he's the most dominant pitcher of all time. He would shut you down. It was one pitch, the cutter. But it's eighteen years of perfect location. He throws nothing in the middle of the plate. He'll paint down and in to a lefty, or he'll paint away to a lefty. Then away to a righty, or [he throws] at your hip and it'll come back and hit the inside corner. Every single pitch isn't the same. The cutter varies; this time maybe it's a little cutter, the next time, maybe he cuts it a little bit more.

He has [ninety-six] appearances in the postseason—and in [fifty-eight] games he went multiple innings. In other words, if your team got to the seventh inning [trailing], you started the eighth inning and you knew Mariano Rivera was out in the bullpen sitting on your neck. You either get to somebody real quick or he was coming in to shut the door, and so you didn't like your chances. When you look at the success the Yankees had, if you ask me if there was one person who was most responsible—Mariano Rivera.

He's been special. I remember playing against him back in 2002 and 2003, and thinking, multiple appearances, two innings closing, how many years can he do this? That was in '02 or '03, and here we are in 2013. It's amazing he's been able to withstand it for so many years.

Doug Mientkiewicz

First base

Playing Career

Minnesota Twins, Boston Red Sox, New York Mets, Kansas City Royals, New York Yankees, Pittsburgh Pirates, and Los Angeles Dodgers from 1998 to 2009

Career Statistics

1,087 games, 899 hits, 66 home runs, 405 runs batted in, .271 batting average, .360 on-base percentage, .405 slugging percentage

Doug Mientkiewicz facing Mariano Rivera (regular season)
0-for-5

Mo Cred

Mientkiewicz spent a season with the Yankees as Rivera's teammate in 2007.

You were 0-for-7 against Rivera in your career, including the postseason, making you one of eleven batters who are exactly 0-for-7 against Mariano.

Doug Mientkiewicz

Year	Date	Result
1999	5/5	Ground out
	5/6	Ground out
2001	5/9	Double play
2003 (Postseason)	10/2	Ground out
2000 (Postseason)	10/4	Line out
2004 (Postseason)	10/17	Sacrifice bunt
2006	4/11	Line out
	5/28	Ground out

SO, I HAVE company then? It's not just me? Awesome.

Did you ever change your approach facing Rivera?

When I got to Boston in 2004, I started using Billy Mueller's bats. I didn't want to break my good ones—my gamers, I'd call them—because I knew I was going to break them.

You pinch hit just after Bill Mueller tied the score with a ninth-inning single

41

in Game Four of the 2004 American League Championship Series. Told to sacrifice, you laid down a bunt, but the pitch hit your finger, and the umpires should have called a foul ball. It was so cold, and it hurt so bad going down the line that I wasn't going to show it. If it's a foul ball, I have to face him again. I was like, No way. I'm just running to first. I don't care if my nail is falling off and I'm bleeding all over the place. If I had to do that again, I don't think that's humanly possible.

Do you have any advice for a batter facing Rivera for the first time?

If you swing at the first one and foul it off, do not even attempt to swing at the second because it's going to be the one that's basically called the "neck ball." It's the one that rides up and in on you. And if you swing—not only do you miss it—you get hit in the Adam's apple, and you embarrass your family.

Kevin Millar

First base

Playing Career

Florida Marlins, Boston Red Sox, and Toronto Blue Jays from 1998 to 2009

Career Statistics

1,427 games, 1,284 hits, 170 home runs, 699 runs batted in, .274 batting average, .358 on-base percentage, .452 slugging percentage

Kevin Millar facing Mariano Rivera (regular season)
6-for-21, 2 extra-base hits, 1 home run, 2 runs batted in, 1 strikeout, .286 batting average, .348 on-base percentage, .476 slugging percentage

Mo Cred

The Yankees were three outs away from sweeping the Red Sox in the 2004 American League Championship Series when Millar, leading off the bottom of the ninth inning, drew a base on balls facing Rivera. Millar was replaced by pinch runner Dave Roberts, who stole second base and scored the game-tying run on Bill Mueller's single. The Red Sox went on to win that game and, improbably, the series, before sweeping the Cardinals in the World Series to capture Boston's first championship in 86 years.

Kevin Millar

Year	Date	Result
1999	6/11	Fielder's choice
2001	7/14	Double
2003	5/27	Home run (1 RBI)
	5/28	Fielder's choice
	7/6	Fly out
	7/25	Strikeout (Swinging)
	8/30	Fielder's choice
	9/7	Single
Postseason	10/11	Fly out
	10/14	Fielder's choice
	10/16	Pop out
2004	4/24	Foul out
	7/1	Double play
	7/24	Single (1 RBI)
	9/17	Walk (Hit by pitch)
Postseason	10/12	Pop out
	10/13	Strikeout (Swinging)
	10/17	Walk
2005	5/27	Single
	9/11	Single
2006	8/4	Fly out
2007	8/15	Ground out
	9/19	Fly out
	9/28	Walk (Hit by pitch)
2008	5/22	Line out
	5/27	Ground out
	7/29	Fly out
	8/22	Pop out
2009	5/14	Ground out

I DON'T EVER GET tired of hearing from Red Sox Nation about 2004. It's not daily that I'm asked about 2004, but it still happens all the time.

Red Sox fans still come up and say, "Thank you guys for getting that monkey off the Nation's back," and Yankees fans come up and say, "Millar, you bum, we're sick of hearing about 2004," though they don't always put it that politely.

That whole Series changed everything in Boston forever. The Red Sox could win twenty more World Series, and that team will still be remembered not only for what we did, but how we did it.

What Dave Roberts [did] was a pivotal moment in changing the history of the franchise: He came off the bench on a freezing night, had to dive back [into first base] a couple of times as Rivera threw over, and then he stole the base by, what, the length of a hand? It was close, man. It couldn't have been closer. Mariano is tough as heck to steal on, and [Jorge] Posada made a great throw with [Derek] Jeter nearly stealing an out with that sweep tag that he does. Dave deserves all the credit in the world for pulling that off, in that circumstance, against those guys, with all of Red Sox Nation on his shoulders.

Dave had a great career, was a regular with the Padres and Giants, and yet it's this one amazing play that has given him a place in baseball history that will always be his. Then Bill Mueller raps a single up the middle off Rivera, who was and still is death on lefty hitters even more than righties. If Bill doesn't get that hit, maybe Dave gets stranded at second, and history is different. [Mueller] was the unsung hero, and it wasn't the first time he beat Rivera.

I remember all the details like it happened yesterday. It's funny, but I actually enjoyed facing Rivera. I was probably the only one, but I'm a little crazy. But he's a fastball pitcher, and comes right at you, and I was a fastball hitter, so I always felt like he was going to challenge me. Honestly, I was literally thinking, man, I could hit a home run here. He was trying to pound me in, and if he came in too far or left that cutter out over the plate, I was thinking I was going to homer.

I had a pretty good idea what they were going to try to do—come up and in and get me to chase one out of the strike zone. It was a pretty good approach on their part, because I couldn't resist those high heaters. And ball four really wasn't that close, which sort of surprised me, because once it got to three balls I thought they'd come after me a little more. It's not like I was Manny [Ramirez] or Papi [David Ortiz] and needed to be pitched around. I'm proud that it was a disciplined at-bat, though, because what we needed was a base runner. Though a homer would have been pretty cool, too!

For me, personally, Mariano wasn't the toughest pitcher I ever faced, because stuff wise, there's other pitchers out there that gave me a harder time. Like Roy Halladay, with a 95 [miles per hour fastball] and a curveball and cutter, and Andy Pettitte, I couldn't get a ball out of the infield against him for years. But Mariano Rivera in that spot in the game, yes, he's extremely tough, because you only get to see him once. Starters you get to see three or four times. Mariano Rivera came in and he had electric stuff, he has an electric arm. Everything he threw was very smooth and easy; it just hopped out of his hand at 95 [m.p.h.] in his prime.*

He is truly the most unbelievable professional; he's classy, just a great human being. When he's on that mound he's the best this game has ever seen. To dominate this game with one pitch, the fastball-cutter, is unbelievable. He has impeccable location. Wherever [Yankees' catcher Jorge] Posada put that glove, Rivera hit it. If [Posada] was setting up inside to a right-handed batter underneath the hands, that ball was looking like it was going to hit you right in your ribs at 95 [m.p.h.]— that made you freeze as a hitter, and then the ball would come around and catch the inside part of the plate.

Mariano has the ability to put that ball on the outside corner, but the ball starts in the middle [of the plate] where it looks like a strike, and next thing you know, as a right-handed batter, you're swinging and you're hitting the ball on the end of your bat. And he saws off left-handers at will. His control was impeccable. What makes Mariano Rivera so great is not only that he dominates the game with that one pitch, the cutter, but also his control. He puts that ball where he wants to every single time he threw it.

*Millar faced Rivera six times in the postseason: He was 0-for-3 in the 2003 A.L.C.S., including a fly out to end Game Three; and he was 0-for-2 with a walk in the 2004 A.L.C.S., including a strikeout swinging to end Game Two.

Bill Mueller

Infield

Playing Career

San Francisco Giants, Chicago Cubs, Boston Red Sox, and Los Angeles Dodgers from 1996 to 2006

Career Statistics

1,216 games, 1,229 hits, 85 home runs, 493 runs batted in, .291 batting average, .373 on-base percentage, .425 slugging percentage

Bill Mueller facing Mariano Rivera (regular season)

5-for-11, 1 extra-base hit, 1 home run, 3 runs batted in, 1 walk, 2 strikeouts, .455 batting average, .500 on-base percentage, .727 slugging percentage

Mo Cred

Mueller hit a run-scoring single off Rivera to tie the score in the ninth inning of Game Four of the 2004 American League Championship Series.

THAT'S WHY YOU'RE talking to me. It is shocking. That's how dominant he's been over the years, especially in the playoffs. He's one of the most special guys in the history of the game. I was never comfortable against him. I never felt good against him. I never felt like I had the advantage.[*]

I went up there trying to keep things as simple as possible, [to make] a positive out, really. It's so difficult to think you're going to have success against such a great pitcher. It wasn't anything more than that. He

---

[*]Mueller was 1-for-6 against Rivera in the postseason. In the 2003 American League Championship Series, Mueller grounded out to second base three times: leading off the bottom of the ninth inning of Game Five; and leading off the top of the ninth and in the eleventh inning of Game Seven. In the 2004 A.L.C.S., Mueller was 1-for-3 against Rivera. He grounded into a double play in Game One, hit the clutch single in the bottom of the ninth of Game Four, and grounded out to first in the bottom of the eighth inning of Game Five.

Bill Mueller

Year	Date	Result
2003	5/21	Ground out
	5/28	Single (1 RBI)
	7/6	Single
	8/30	Strikeout (Swinging)
Postseason	10/14	Ground out
	10/16	Ground out
	10/16	Ground out
2004	4/18	Ground out
	4/24	Pop out
	7/24	Home run (2 RBI)
	9/24	Ground out
Postseason	10/12	Double play
	10/17	Single (1 RBI)
	10/18	Fielder's choice
2005	4/5	Single
	4/6	Walk
	5/27	Strikeout (Looking)
	7/17	Single

was so dominant. To have that success, I guess, I could say I'd rather be lucky than good.

I special-ordered a half-dozen Rawlings bats that were shorter and lighter than my usual [Louisville Slugger] model. I saved them for Mariano. I couldn't get too attached to them, either, because there was a good chance he was going to break them. If for some reason those bats didn't come in, I had to choke up [on my regular bat]. I just used the lightest bat I had. More than anything, it was probably a boost for my mental confidence.

Now, I work as a scout for the [Los Angeles] Dodgers. If you asked me to

Mueller Time

Bill Mueller [pronounced Miller] faced Rivera a total of eighteen times in his career, with all at-bats coming during the height of the intense Yankees–Red Sox rivalry from 2003 through 2005. Including postseason, Mueller batted .353 against Rivera. He was 6-for-17 with one walk.

Mueller delivered two of the most memorable hits Rivera allowed in his career.

Mueller hit a walk-off, two-run home run against Rivera for an 11-10 Boston comeback win at Fenway Park, on July 24, 2004. Mueller's long ball was the thirty-ninth career home run allowed by Rivera, and the second walk-off home run (Bill Selby, Cleveland Indians, July 14, 2002).

Then, with the Red Sox on the brink of elimination in Game Four of the 2004 American League Championship Series, Mueller's ninth-inning single off Rivera scored Dave Roberts with the tying run.

Rivera has appeared in ninety-six postseason games, and Mueller is one of three men to deliver a game-tying hit against Rivera in a Yankees' postseason loss. Sandy Alomar Jr. (Cleveland Indians, 1997 A.L.D.S., Game Four) and Tony Womack (Arizona Diamondbacks, 2001 World Series, Game Seven) are the others.

file a report on him it would be an easy one to write, that's for sure. Perennial All-Star. Stud.

Lyle Overbay
First base

Playing Career

Arizona Diamondbacks, Milwaukee Brewers, Toronto Blue Jays, Pittsburgh Pirates, Atlanta Braves, and New York Yankees since 2001

Career Statistics

1,354 games, 1,212 hits, 138 home runs, 596 runs batted in, .270 batting average, .352 on-base percentage, .438 slugging percentage

Lyle Overbay facing Mariano Rivera (regular season)
2-for-12, 0 extra-base hits, 4 strikeouts, .167 batting average, .167 on-base percentage, .167 slugging percentage

Mo Cred
Overbay was Rivera's teammate with the Yankees in 2013.

AS HIS TEAMMATE, now the only thing I have to worry about is getting out of the way of a broken bat! I see [opposing batters] go through what I went through, and I don't wish that upon anybody. It's a luxury not having to worry about that cutter anymore. It's very nice to be on Mariano's side. It's exciting to hear that song "Enter Sandman" and know the game is going to be over, because now, I'm on the winning side.

He's very confident, yet he's also very quiet. You can see he has a presence that can be very dominant. He's there for everyone. He takes care of the young Latino players. He helps out the young pitchers, too. Not

Lyle Overbay

Year	Date	Result
2006	4/19	Strikeout (Looking)
2007	5/30	Ground out
	7/16	Strikeout (Looking)
	9/12	Single
	9/21	Strikeout (Looking)
2008	4/1	Strikeout (Looking)
	4/3	Fielder's choice
	6/4	Ground out
	8/29	Fielder's choice
2010	7/4	Single
	8/4	Ground out
	9/28	Ground out

a lot of guys have time to help, or want to, but Mariano is willing to spend time in the bullpen and discuss [pitching]. Look what he's done for David Robertson, who has taken advantage [of Mariano's tutelage] and now he's throwing a cutter, too.

Mariano's cutter is different. It's weird, how much his cutter breaks in the last four feet. You swing, and the ball ends up being another four inches farther inside than you expected, and your bat snaps in two pieces. It was a constant battle to make adjustments. I would cheat by stepping in the bucket, then I backed off away from the plate and dove in, other times I'd eliminate the inside pitch. I even tried choking up on my bat. Nothing worked. I always got jammed. I thought about turning my bat around! Maybe I should have tried holding the bat by the barrel, because I hit it off the handle every time!

When I was with Toronto we faced the Yankees a lot because we were in the same division. I remember one hit [helped us] tie a ballgame [when] we were down one run. That was the only at-bat that I felt I had a chance to connect because, that day, his cutter wasn't cutting like usual and he didn't have good velocity, either. He apparently had one bad day in eighteen years. It's amazing that he can [throw] just one pitch for eighteen years and not have to adjust like everyone else in this game. It doesn't make sense.[*]

Facing Mariano Rivera was no easy task. Not only are his pitches deceptive, his location is consistent. That's why he's still dominating,

---

[*] The Toronto Blue Jays were trailing the Yankees, 6-5, at Yankee Stadium, on July 4, 2010, when Overbay led off the top of the ninth inning against Rivera. With the count one ball, two strikes, Overbay hit a ground ball single through the first base hole into right field, and eventually scored the tying run. The Yankees went on to win 7-6 in ten innings. Overbay also homered earlier in that game.

because of location. He pitches up and in, right under your hands for a lefty, or down and away on a lefty, and down and in on a righty. He can hit the [catcher's] glove every time.

Dustin Pedroia

Second base

Playing Career

Boston Red Sox since 2006

Career Statistics

1,016 games, 1,218 hits, 99 home runs, 493 runs batted in, .302 batting average, .370 on-base percentage, .454 slugging percentage

Dustin Pedroia facing Mariano Rivera (regular season)

1-for-12, 0 extra-base hits, 1 run batted in, 3 walks, 5 strikeouts, .083 batting average, .250 on-base percentage, .083 slugging percentage

Mo Cred

Pedroia, hitless in his first 13 at-bats against Rivera, finally broke through with a ground ball single up the middle in the ninth inning of a 4-1 Yankees win at Yankee Stadium, on May 31, 2013. It was Rivera's 627th career save.

HE'S NO FUN to hit against. Hey, I'm still not sold it's his last year. He's dealing.

Mariano is first-class. There's a reason why the Yankees have won as much as they have and been so successful. It's because of the way they carry themselves, the way they prepare. He's a Hall of Fame player and person.

The All-Star Game was awesome. I'll never forget that. I was just standing right there watching. That's one of the coolest things I've seen

Dustin Pedroia

Year	Date	Result
2007	4/27	Walk
	5/23	Strikeout (Looking)
	8/29	Ground out
	9/16	Walk
2008	7/6	Strikeout (Swinging)
	7/25	Ground out
	9/28	Strikeout (Swinging)
2009	4/24	Strikeout (Looking)
	9/26	Strikeout (Swinging)
2010	4/6	Fly out
	4/7	Ground out
	5/18	Fielder's choice
2011	8/7	Sacrifice fly (1 RBI)
2013	4/4	Walk
	5/31	Single
	8/18	Ground out

playing baseball in my life. It looked like he was kind of uncomfortable but it was pretty cool. I had goose bumps the whole time. I'm sure a lot of people did.

The next inning, he's was just standing there on the rail and I was right there, and he said, "That was one of the coolest things I've ever seen," and I was like, "Coolest thing *you've* seen?" Just getting a chance to talk to him for a little while is awesome. He said, "Enjoy it. It goes by fast." He's a first-class guy.

He deserves everything. What he's done over the course of his career is pretty special.

Mark Reynolds

Third base and First base

Playing Career

Arizona Diamondbacks, Baltimore Orioles, Cleveland Indians, and New York Yankees since 2007

Career Statistics

988 games, 797 hits, 202 home runs, 568 runs batted in, .233 batting average, .329 on-base percentage, .464 slugging percentage

Mark Reynolds facing Mariano Rivera (regular season)
1-for-8, 0 extra-base hits, 5 strikeouts, .125 batting average, .125 on-base percentage, .125 slugging percentage

Mo Cred

Reynolds was Rivera's teammate with the Yankees in 2013.

Mark Reynolds

Year	Date	Result
2007	6/12	Strikeout (Swinging)
2010	6/23	Strikeout (Swinging)
2011	4/24	Strikeout (Looking)
	7/31	Fly out
	8/29	Strikeout (Swinging)
	9/5	Single
2012	4/11	Ground out
2013	6/4	Strikeout (Swinging)

SURE, I REMEMBER the first time facing Mariano. It was my rookie year. I'm 23 years old. I go up there and I'm [thinking], I'm going to sit on a cutter away and see what happens.

So I get up on the plate, he throws me a front-door cutter, and I jump out of the way, but it's called a strike. Then I back off the plate, and I guess he notices it, because he throws me a cutter away, another called strike. Now I'm just like, "Aw, crap." And then he throws another cutter away and I swing and miss.[*]

I was like, Well, I guess I'm in the big leagues. This guy's pretty good.

Kevin Seitzer

Third base

Playing Career

Kansas City Royals, Milwaukee Brewers, Oakland Athletics, and Cleveland Indians from 1986 to 1997

Career Statistics

1,439 games, 1,557 hits, 74 home runs, 613 runs batted in, .295 batting average, .375 on-base percentage, .404 slugging percentage

---

[*]Reynolds struck out on four pitches leading off the top of the ninth inning against Rivera. The Yankees defeated the Diamondbacks, 4-1, at Yankee Stadium, on June 12, 2007. It was Rivera's 421st career save.

Kevin Seitzer facing Mariano Rivera (regular season)

3-for-6, 0 extra-base hits, 1 run batted in, 2 strikeouts, .500 batting average, .429 on-base percentage, .500 slugging percentage

Mo Cred

Seitzer, who led the American League with 207 hits as a rookie in 1987, witnessed Sandy Alomar Jr.'s famous home run in the 1997 postseason.

Kevin Seitzer

Year	Date	Result
1995	8/1	Foul out
	9/26	Single
1996	4/17	Single
	7/4	Strikeout (Looking)
	7/20	Single
1997	6/27	Strikeout (Looking)
	6/29	Sacrifice fly (1 RBI)

MY LAST SEASON in the big leagues was in 1997 with Cleveland. I was in the dugout when Sandy Alomar Jr. hit that clutch home run off Mariano. Our bench erupted. Obviously, we were ecstatic. That would be a normal reaction no matter who's pitching. Whether it's Mariano or Joe Nobody on the mound, a hit that big, in that situation, in such a big game, is definitely pretty cool.

You have to keep everything in perspective. Mariano wasn't yet the dominant force he'd become; he was just getting himself established as a closer. Still, I'm sure Sandy feels pretty good about himself. For me, it was just as big a deal then as it is now, not because of who Mariano became, but because of the timing of when the home run happened, in a really big game, in an important spot.[*]

When I first faced Mariano Rivera [in 1995] he threw a four-seam fastball. The ball had good life, with a little skip to it, but it wasn't a big deal because you saw the ball real good out of his hand.

---

[*]With the Indians four outs from elimination, Alomar's solo home run off Rivera over the right-field fence tied the score with two outs in the eighth inning of Game Four of the American League Division Series at Jacobs Field in Cleveland. The Indians went on to win that game to even the series at two games apiece, and then the next day won Game Five to eliminate the Yankees from the playoffs. This was Rivera's first playoff series as the Yankees closer, having replaced the 1996 World Series Most Valuable Player, John Wetteland, in that role.

Then, the next year, all of a sudden, he's got the cutter. I remember facing him for the first time when he threw the cutter, and I said to myself, "Oh crap."

You need intense mental training to hit the cutter because you have to trick your brain. Your eyes see the ball at a certain spot, and that's the spot you swing at, but the ball is not there by the time contact happens. You have to tell yourself, See it here, but hit it there. Mariano's command of the cutter was excellent. He could put the ball wherever he wanted; that's what makes the pitch such a good weapon for him. He basically can make the plate feel like it's three feet wide—and no batter can cover that much distance.

I didn't really change my game plan against Mariano or against anybody. My game is hitting the ball up the middle, and taking the outside pitch to the opposite field. It makes me feel good [to learn] I was 3 for 6 against him, but striking out twice in six plate appearances is extremely high for me because I was a contact hitter. The RBI was probably a broken bat blooper in a game that didn't mean anything and he was just getting in some extra work because he hadn't thrown for a few days. [Laughs.] Obviously the guy is the best of all time and he's going to be a first ballot Hall of Famer. He's the ultimate professional. It makes me feel pretty good that I got to play against somebody of that caliber.

Bill Selby

Infield

Playing Career

Boston Red Sox, Cleveland Indians, and Cincinnati Reds from 1996 to 2003

Career Statistics

198 games, 96 hits, 11 home runs, 48 runs batted in, .223 batting average, .279 on-base percentage, .360 slugging percentage

Bill Selby facing Mariano Rivera (regular season)

1-for-2, 1 extra-base hit, 1 home run, 4 runs batted in, .500 batting average, .500 on-base percentage, 2.000 slugging percentage

Mo Cred

Selby hit a walk-off grand slam home run off Rivera to beat the Yankees on July 14, 2002; it was the first walk-off Rivera allowed in his career.

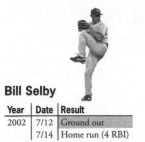

Bill Selby

Year	Date	Result
2002	7/12	Ground out
	7/14	Home run (4 RBI)

YOU DON'T HAVE to ask me what was the highlight of my career! Whenever somebody hits a walk-off home run off Mariano, I'll get so many texts my phone blows up. Friends say, "I saw your name on *Sports Center* on some list about Mariano Rivera."

It was such a surreal moment, and it's lasted a long time. I still get to re-live it because a lot of people ask me about it. At the time when it happened, I'm thinking, wow I just hit a home run that won the game. But now that the dust had cleared, and it turns out that was the first walk-off home run Mariano ever gave up, I'm forever linked with the greatest closer of all time. Some people might have an ego and want to talk about it all the time, but I just have to laugh, because he's still playing and I've been a coach [at Northwest Mississippi Community College] for the past eight years.

My mind started working while I was walking to the plate. I faced Mariano for the first time two nights before. The first at-bat was nothing dramatic like the next one. I pinch-hit with the game on the line and grounded out to first base. You don't need an advance scouting report for Mariano. It's not a secret. If you're a left-handed batter like me, he's going to pound you inside and break your bat. Facing him two nights before helped me. I got to see how his ball moves in a game

55

situation. His cutter is a little different than a lot of cutters I've faced; it had a riding effect to it, it appeared to rise. It was like a 95 miles per hour slider that went up—it's hard to explain. After the first at-bat, I spoke to our hitting coach, Eddie Murray, about the approach to have, and he suggested I choke up and get off the plate a little bit, to try to get inside of the ball, and that's what I tried to do. So I was seeing the same guy I saw two nights before, but the approach I tried worked better.[*]

I got the count to two balls and no strikes right out of the gate. I was thinking the bases are loaded, a walk ties the game, and so I'm going to take a pitch, which is a strike. When the count got to two and two, I didn't want to take a big swing and get jammed. I hit a line drive down the right-field line, but it went foul by a foot or two. I remember walking back to the batter's box, thinking I just squared up that cutter, a lot of people in that situation would have been upset because that was their chance. I told myself to slow down, slow down. It's still two and two—it's an even count—so get your mind right back to thinking about what you need to do. He started his motion and I was thinking: "Get your hands inside the ball and let him do the work."

Then baseball happened. That's a saying I like to use—baseball happened—because you can never figure out this game. The wind was blowing in that day. I hit it pretty good, but I hit it really high. I put my head down and started running. I thought, "God if you want it to be a home run, please let it be a home run"; and [the ball] kept carrying and carrying. I was running around second base and [Derek] Jeter was walking off the field. I remember him looking back at me with a little grin, and I kept running around the bases until I got mobbed by my teammates at home plate.[**]

---

[*] The Indians defeated the Yankees, 2-1, in ten innings at Jacobs Field in Cleveland, on July 12, 2002. Rivera blew the save in the eighth inning, and escaped a perilous ninth after walking two batters before retiring Selby on a ground out to first base unassisted for the third out.

[**] The Yankees had an early 7-0 lead, but the Indians made it 7-4 after seven innings. Rivera entered in the ninth and struggled immediately. After four hits, a fielder's choice, and an intentional walk, the Indians had whittled the deficit to 7-6 with two outs. That's when Selby hit the grand slam for a 10-7 Indians' win.

That was the only walk-off hit I ever had in the major leagues, and the only grand slam I hit in the majors. I still have the ball. After the game, the fan that caught it brought the ball down to the tunnel and gave me the ball. He didn't want a thing in return. If I ever had a chance to have Mariano sign that baseball, it would be great. It's on my desk in my office. I also have a picture from the *New York Times* that was framed and sent to me; it's a picture of me running around third base and you can see the fans in the background and I have my fist in the air. It's a special moment preserved forever.

I live in a small town. Around here, I'm known as the—quote, unquote—ballplayer. But I've always been a fan of the game, even when I was playing. I was star struck and I never lost that feeling while I was playing. I don't know if you call it star struck or respect, but when you walk to the plate to face Pedro Martinez or Curt Schilling or Mariano Rivera, the superstars of the game, I remember thinking: "This is an opportunity of a lifetime, this is something you'll talk to your kids about."

You're supposed to be focused on the task at hand, but I knew these at-bats were being etched in my memory. I had a short, sporadic, journeyman career, so these at-bats were special regardless if they're spring training or regular season.

I watched the All-Star Game [at Citi Field in New York on July 16, 2013] on television, and it was a really, really touching moment to see the way baseball presented Mariano an opportunity to say thank you. It was really neat to see. I'm just like any other fan watching baseball, even though I was fortunate to get a chance to play. The respect he's garnered and earned from peers in the baseball world, you got chills watching what they did for him.

Ed Sprague

Third base

Playing Career

Toronto Blue Jays, Oakland Athletics, Pittsburgh Pirates, San Diego Padres, Boston Red Sox, and Seattle Mariners from 1991 to 2001

Career Statistics

1,203 games, 1,101 hits, 152 home runs, 558 runs batted in, .247 batting average, .318 on-base percentage, .419 slugging percentage

Ed Sprague facing Mariano Rivera (regular season)

1-for-9, 1 extra-base hit, 1 home run, 1 run batted in, 2 strikeouts, .111 batting average, .111 on-base percentage, .444 slugging percentage

Mo Cred

Sprague hit a home run off Rivera on July 18, 1998.

Ed Sprague

Year	Date	Result
1995	10/1	Fly out
1996	6/4	Pop out
	6/10	Line out
	9/6	Strikeout (Looking)
1997	5/28	Line out
	7/3	Strikeout (Swinging)
1998	4/27	Pop out
	7/18	Home run (1 RBI)
	9/2	Pop out

IT'S CERTAINLY SOMETHING to say; I hit a home run off Mariano Rivera, the all-time saves leader. I'm proud I got him on that one occasion. I don't have to say it [happened] in a meaningless game, with a 10-2 score, in a non-save situation. I don't have to mention that, and I don't have to talk about the other eight at-bats either!

I cheated [when I hit] the home run. I took a chance that he was going to pound me inside, so I cheated to the inside fastball, and I was fortunate to be able to keep it fair. The Yankees consistently pounded me inside with fastballs. Their scouting report was not to let me extend my arms. So I'm looking inside and banking on getting a pitch on the inside corner of the plate. I stepped in the bucket and hit [the ball] off the left-field foul pole.

I took a chance by stepping in the bucket, but there was not much for me to lose in that situation. It was a non-save situation, and it was a three-and-one count in a 10-2 game. He's coming into the game just to get some work.* Many closers typically aren't at their sharpest mentally in a non-save situation. I remember he got a chuckle out of it. I wasn't having a very good year in '98. He was probably thinking to himself: "I can't believe I gave up a home run to this guy."

I was fortunate to hit it off the foul pole. When you cheat and step in the bucket it's hard to keep the ball fair. I was probably six inches from hooking it foul. Had he thrown me a cutter I probably would have missed it by four feet!

It was never fun facing Mariano Rivera. It usually means game over. It's rare to know what pitch is coming and not be able to square it up. But no matter how many times you faced him, because of his smooth delivery, the ball seemed to get on you a lot faster. He doesn't have overpowering velocity like some other closers; he has tremendous location. Your only hope is to get a mistake pitch that's in the middle of the plate. Still, the ball might miss your barrel. That's Mariano's greatest gift—he misses barrels. When you get non-barrel contact, there's not going to be a lot of strong hits against you.

Not a lot of hitters have had success against him. I was happy to hit the home run. That [season] was his second year as the closer, so the real appreciation for what he [would accomplish] didn't come until he was able to do it over and over again for a number of years.

---

*Rivera entered the game to pitch the bottom of the ninth inning with the Yankees leading the Blue Jays 10-1 on July 18, 1998. Rivera surrendered a lead-off home run to Mike Stanley, recorded two outs, and then allowed the home run to Sprague on a three-one count before getting the final out.

Jason Smith

Second base and Shortstop

Playing Career

Chicago Cubs, Tampa Bay Rays, Detroit Tigers, Arizona Diamond-backs, Colorado Rockies, Kansas City Royals, Toronto Blue Jays, and Houston Astros from 2001 to 2009

Career Statistics

278 games, 122 hits, 17 home runs, 60 runs batted in, .212 batting average, .248 on-base percentage, .361 slugging percentage

Jason Smith facing Mariano Rivera (regular season)

3-for-5, 0 extra-base hits, 1 strikeout, .600 batting average, .600 on-base percentage, .600 slugging percentage

Mo Cred

Smith, a career .212 hitter, batted .600 against Rivera.

Jason Smith

Year	Date	Result
2005	5/26	Single
2007	7/25	Single
	8/3	Strikeout (Looking)
	8/5	Fly out
	9/9	Single

I'M NOT WALKING around telling people I'm three-for-five off Mariano Rivera. When I'm joking around with my friends, that's when I'll brag about it. When my buddies come over to watch the game, we'll be sitting on the couch, and if we happen to be watching the Yankees, and Mariano comes in [the game], that's when I might say: "I want you all to know I'm three-for-five off Mariano Rivera!"

I don't think I owned him. He probably does not remember me, and he probably does not have a book on me. Those hits are all broken bat singles. I was very lucky. I'm sure you've seen my career stats. They're not going to vote me into the Hall of Fame anytime soon!

Facing Rivera is not a whole lot of fun, especially being a left-handed batter. You know what the outcome [of your at-bat] is going to be. It doesn't make sense because the match-ups say you want left-handed batters against a right-handed pitcher, but not with Mariano.

I only remember one at-bat: when I was with Kansas City in 2007. It was the bottom of the ninth inning at Kauffman Stadium, and we were getting beat. Everybody in the entire world knows Mariano's going to throw that devastating cutter, so I'm waiting for it. I had nothing to lose. I'm going to do whatever I can to get the good part of the bat [into the hitting zone], so I was stepping in the bucket and trying to get my hands out front so the barrel would hit the baseball. I still got jammed. That's how good his cutter is. I fisted the ball just over the infielder's head. It's a hit, but I can honestly tell you, I never squared him up. I remember not getting the barrel on it. I also remember getting stranded on base.*

Mark Teixeira
First base

Playing Career

Texas Rangers, Atlanta Braves, Los Angeles Angels of Anaheim, and New York Yankees since 2003

---

*Smith singled to right field on a three-and-two count with two outs and the Royals trailing, 6-3, in the bottom of the ninth inning of a game in Kansas City, on September 9, 2007. He then took second base on defensive indifference to get into scoring position, but Rivera retired John Buck to end the game and earn his 438th career save. Smith faced Rivera three other times that season: he singled, on July 25, 2007; struck out looking, on August 3; and flew out to deep center field, on August 5 (career save No. 430). His other hit facing Rivera came as a member of the Detroit Tigers, on May 26, 2005 (career save No. 347).

Career Statistics

1,512 games, 1,588 hits, 341 home runs, 1,113 runs batted in, .278 batting average, .368 on-base percentage, .525 slugging percentage

Mark Teixeira facing Mariano Rivera (regular season)

1-for-9, 0 extra-base hits, 1 walk, 2 strikeouts, .111 batting average, .200 on-base percentage, .111 slugging percentage

Mo Cred

Teixeira played with Rivera on the Yankees' 2009 World Series championship team. His lone hit against Rivera was a single on August 11, 2005.

Mark Teixeira

Year	Date	Result
2004	6/6	Ground out
	8/11	Ground out
2005	7/18	Strikeout (Looking)
	7/20	Strikeout (Looking)
	8/11	Single
	8/13	Ground out
	8/13	Foul out
2006	5/5	Line out
	5/7	Ground out
2008	8/1	Walk

IT WAS PROBABLY a weak broken bat hit somewhere because I faced him when he was throwing 95 miles an hour and at the top of his game. Even though he's low 90s now, he's still at the top of his game.[*]

He's the greatest closer of all time, maybe one of the greatest pitchers of all time. When you talk about the greatest pitchers of all time, people don't think about relievers. But I think we need to put Mo in that conversation of one of the greatest pitchers of all time. Because of what he's done in the postseason and how he closes the door in so many tight games, you can make an argument he's the best of all time. So he's on your side late in the game, you feel good about it.

When Mo makes his pitches, you can't hit them. I remember thinking: "Honestly, how am I supposed to hit that?"

I mean, as a left-handed hitter, you almost have to try to look for an outside pitch and pull it, because if it's middle in, it's going to break

---

[*] Teixeria's only hit against Rivera was an opposite field ground ball single to left field on a three-and-two pitch in the top of the ninth inning with one out and Rivera protecting a 9-8 lead against the Rangers at Yankee Stadium, on August 11, 2005. On the next pitch, Hank Blalock flew out and then Rivera struck out Alfonso Soriano to record his thirty-first save of the 2005 season, and 367 for his career.

your bat. People said don't bring up your good bat because chances are you're going to break it. Facing Mo definitely wasn't fun. The cutter is such a good pitch when he puts it in the right location. That's why he's been so great for so long.

If you haven't heard about Mariano Rivera, you'd dug a hole somewhere and hid in it. He was everything and more, and he could do it all. I'm really happy to be a teammate of his so I don't have to face him anymore.

Mo Respect

Jim Thome

The former Cleveland Indians slugger with 612 career home runs had more walks, 8, against Rivera than any other player. Thome was 3-for-15 with one home run and four strikeouts facing Rivera.

If you have to pick the one guy with devastating stuff, it's him, because of that pitch. He throws enough strikes so that you have to be aggressive. It comes out of his hand and looks like a regular fastball, over the plate, and boom, it's on your knuckles. It moves in on you so late that it's hard to make an adjustment on him, and this game is all about making adjustments.

It's obvious that they've won the world championships they have because of him.

Jim Thome

Year	Date	Result
1995	8/10	Double play
	8/10	Walk
	8/10	Walk
1996	6/16	Strikeout (Swinging)
	6/21	Strikeout (Swinging)
	6/21	Ground out
1997	6/27	Home run (1 RBI)
	6/29	Walk
	7/14	Strikeout (Swinging)
Postseason	9/30	Line out
1998 (Postseason)	10/7	Line out
	10/10	Ground out
	10/11	Foul out
2000	5/1	Double
	5/2	Ground out
	5/3	Walk
2001	6/2	Strikeout (Looking)
2002	7/3	Fly out
	7/14	Intentional walk
2006	7/14	Single
	7/16	Walk
	8/9	Fielder's choice
2007	6/7	Fielder's choice
2008	9/15	Ground out
2010	5/16	Walk (1 RBI)
	5/25	Walk
Postseason	10/6	Pop out
	10/7	Fly out
	10/9	Strikeout (Looking)
2011	4/4	Pop out

Robin Ventura

Third base

Playing Career

Chicago White Sox, New York Mets, New York Yankees, and Los Angeles Dodgers from 1989 to 2004

Career Statistics

2,079 games, 1,885 hits, 294 home runs, 1,182 runs batted in, .267 batting average, .362 on-base percentage, .444 slugging percentage

Robin Ventura facing Mariano Rivera (regular season)

4-for-13, 1 extra-base hit, 3 runs batted in, 2 walks, 2 strikeouts, .308 batting average, .400 on-base percentage, .385 slugging percentage

Mo Cred

Ventura was Rivera's teammate with the Yankees in 2002 and 2003. He currently is the manager of the White Sox.

I REMEMBER OUR SCOUTING report said he had a really good changeup. He never showed it that day. I remember we couldn't touch him. Tim Raines [the leadoff hitter] shattered his bat, and he pretty much told me, "There's no changeup." He had a very painful look on his face.[*]

Mariano's had a great career, he's been a great teammate, and I think he's a good example for a lot of people to follow because he does a lot of good stuff. He's a better person than he is a player.

---

[*]Ventura was batting second for the Chicago White Sox on July 4, 1995, when Rivera pitched eight shutout innings to earn his second big league victory in a 4-1 Yankees win at Comiskey Park, in Chicago. Rivera allowed two hits, both singles to Frank Thomas, walked four and struck out 11 batters.

Robin Ventura

Year	Date	Result
1995	7/4	Fly out
	7/4	Strikeout (Swinging)
	7/4	Line out
1996	5/3	Walk
	5/5	Double play
	5/12	Pop out
	8/7	Line out
	8/12	Single

Year	Date	Result
	8/14	Single
1998	5/26	Walk
	6/1	Double (2 RBI)
	6/2	Pop out
	9/4	Single (1 RBI)
2000	7/7	Foul out
Postseason	10/21	Fly out
	10/25	Pop out
2004	6/19	Strikeout (Swinging)

Mo Respect

Ty Wigginton

The versatile journeyman infielder faced Rivera 12 times. He is 0-for-8 with 3 strikeouts, 1 sacrifice fly, and has been hit by a pitch three times.

You hear about the cutter and that's his pitch, but when you're in his division, when he's going to see you in six series a year, he will mix in a sinker that catches you off guard.

Every player has an off year. Well, every player except Mariano. Just think of the consistency he's had in a job that doesn't usually have a long shelf life. He hasn't just been good. He has been dominant.

Ty Wigginton

Year	Date	Result
2003	6/28	Strikeout (Looking)
2006	4/26	Strikeout (Swinging)
	4/26	Sacrifice fly (1 RBI)
	9/22	Hit by pitch
2007	7/14	Ground out
	7/21	Hit by pitch
2009	4/9	Line out
	5/20	Ground out
2010	6/1	Ground out
	6/3	Hit by pitch
	9/19	Foul out
2011	6/26	Strikeout (Swinging)

Tony Womack
Infield and Outfield

Playing Career

Pittsburgh Pirates, Arizona Diamondbacks, Colorado Rockies, Chicago Cubs, St. Louis Cardinals, New York Yankees, and Cincinnati Reds from 1993 to 2006

Career Statistics

1,303 games, 1,353 hits, 36 home runs, 368 runs batted in, .273 batting average, .317 on-base percentage, .356 slugging percentage

Tony Womack facing Mariano Rivera (regular season)
No at-bats

Mo Cred

Womack hit a game-tying one-out double against Rivera in the bottom of the ninth inning of Game Seven of the 2001 World Series.

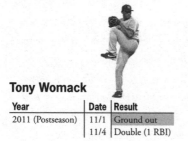

IF YOU LOOK at the videotape after my double, he started blinking his eyes on the mound. You can see clearly that he's blinking quite a bit. He looks fully aware of what was going on. He was put in an unfamiliar situation. That's the first time you got the feeling he was thinking: "Oh man, I've never been in this situation before."*

Tony Womack

Year	Date	Result
2011 (Postseason)	11/1	Ground out
	11/4	Double (1 RBI)

---

*Rivera has allowed three game-tying hits in postseason games the Yankees have lost, but only one, by Womack, occurred in a World Series. The three game-tying postseason hits in Yankees' losses are to Sandy Alomar, Jr. of the Cleveland Indians in Game Four of the 1997 A.L.D.S.; to Tony Womack of the Arizona Diamondbacks in Game Seven of the 2001 World Series; and to Bill Mueller of the Boston Red Sox in Game Four of the 2004 A.L.C.S.

It's a great accomplishment for me, especially against someone like Mariano, who people say is the best closer in the game. The 2-2 count didn't bother me; I was still looking to hit the ball out in front of the plate, because with his cutter, the deeper it gets, the harder it is to hit. If he throws a borderline strike you've got to fight it off. Two strikes didn't change my approach. I still stuck to the game plan. It was a little easier to stick to the game plan against him because you knew he was throwing the cutter. It's not like facing somebody else who throws a curveball and a change-up. His cutter is very hard to hit but I still stuck with the plan because that's all that he was throwing.

I treated Mariano just like any other big league pitcher. It was his good stuff versus my good stuff. That's the way I approached it. See the ball and hit the ball. It wasn't a guessing game. We all knew he had one pitch—a hard cutter that breaks late. I had a game plan to get the bat head out in front, square it up, and drive the ball.

I never changed bats, never changed my batting stance, or moved closer or farther away from the plate against Mariano. Nothing changed. Once you start thinking that way and changing your approach, you get beat. You give the pitcher more credit than he deserves. I never gave the pitcher credit. My job was to get on base. If I had to change because of one pitch a guy throws than I'm giving him the edge. I wanted to stay firm, stand my ground, and take the challenge of his best against my best.

To be remembered for coming through in the clutch, that's great. But fans don't see us play day in and day out. They never see that I averaged 148 games a year. They don't see one year I had 700 at-bats. The average fan doesn't see that. They remember the big moments, the things they see on television to remind them. To be remembered for one hit, that's great, I appreciate it, I'm thankful, and I'm glad I came through. Of all the great players on that Diamondbacks team, would you think it would be me to get a big hit? No, but it was me. If that's how the fans remember me, then so be it. I felt I played a part of that World Series championship team, so it feels special.

Accolades are great, and it means so much doing it in the World Series. Thirty teams started the season and you're the last two teams standing. To succeed in the clutch, and to do it in front of everybody, it ranks right up there. The odds may have been against me to get the hit, but you never know if you can't do anything if you're not put in that situation. Getting that hit tells me that I belonged.

When I was with the Yankees [in 2005], I got to know Mariano as a teammate, not as a person. I was coming to a new team, and he was already established there. We never talked about [the 2001 World Series]. You don't do that. At the time, the Yankees were going for championship No. 26 and I was looking for number one, so I didn't rub it in his face and we didn't talk about it. What happened was in the past and I'm sure he thought the same. The only time anybody [on the Yankees] ever mentioned my hit was when [Derek] Jeter told me that was the longest offseason he ever had. It's a great compliment. I told him, "Look man, you guys had so many championships and I was looking for one. I'm sorry you had a long offseason but I was in the league a while and I had a lot more longer offseasons than you."

David Wright

Third base

Playing Career

New York Mets since 2004

Career Statistics

1,374 games, 1,558 hits, 222 home runs, 876 runs batted in, .301 batting average, .382 on-base percentage, .506 slugging percentage

David Wright facing Mariano Rivera (regular season)

3-for-8, 1 extra-base hit, 3 runs batted in, 1 walk, 1 strikeout, .375 batting average, .375 on-base percentage, .500 slugging percentage

David Wright

Year	Date	Result
2005	5/22	Fly out
	6/26	Ground out
2006	5/19	Single (1 RBI)
	5/20	Strikeout (Swinging)
2009	6/12	Double (1 RBI)
2010	5/21	Ground out
	6/20	Fly out
2013	5/28	Single (1 RBI)

Mo Cred

Wright singled off Rivera in the ninth inning to give the Mets a 7-6 walk-off win at Shea Stadium, on May 19, 2006.

I HAVE THE DISTINCT honor to one day tell my kids and grandkids that I got a walk-off hit against him. Obviously that's one of the highlights for me. It went over Johnny Damon's head in center field. As passionate as New York fans are about the Subway Series, to deliver a walk-off hit against the greatest closer in the game will definitely be a good story for my kids and grandkids one day.[*]

It's a feat in itself to get a hit off of Mo, much less a run, and we were fortunate to be able to get a win against him. I think we surprised ourselves because when you get Mo coming in, it's usually game over. He's been about as perfect as you can be. Anytime you get a chance to steal one against Mo, you better take advantage of it, because that's a once-in-a-career opportunity.

He's first class all the way. The All-Star Game [tribute] was well-deserved for Mariano. I was in the clubhouse when he came in the game. All of a sudden I heard "Enter Sandman" start to play. So I hurried to throw on a sweatshirt and run out there, because I didn't want to miss it. You knew something special was happening. You start to get some positive vibes in the dugout. I was on the top step clapping and cheering as loud as I could.

---

[*] The Mets fell behind 4-0 in the first inning, and also trailed 5-3 and 6-5, but tied in the ninth inning. Wright hit a long drive that barely eluded Johnny Damon for the clutch hit that drove home Paul Lo Duca with the winning run.

I don't feel intimidated too often, but it was intimidating talking to Mo the first time. He's legendary. I had just enough courage to thank him for being an unbelievable ambassador for the game. I kind of had to collect myself, because I was stuttering a little bit. Forget about the numbers. Forget about his body of work. Forget about being the greatest closer of all time. The way he carries himself and the way he goes about his business is special. I told him that every young baseball player should try to follow in his footsteps, because he's a remarkable role model and someone that I look up to.

There are certain players, when you see them, there is a certain awe about them. I think Mariano has that, no matter if you are a Yankee or a Met or a Red Sox, whatever, you just have the utmost respect for guys like that. He's gone out there and dominated and basically can tell you what's coming and you still can't hit it. There are not too many pitchers who have the ability to do that. It's impressive.

Just from the few times I've been around him, he has been nothing but class [and] very nice to me. It just seems like he is a professional the way he goes about his business and the way that he handles himself and the results speak for themselves on the field.

I've always enjoyed watching him pitch. On one hand it's the end of something, obviously great and historic, but on the other hand it's a relief because we play those guys every year and I know how tough of an at-bat it is against him.

Kevin Youkilis

First base and Third base

Playing Career

Boston Red Sox, Chicago White Sox, and New York Yankees since 2004

Career Statistics

1,061 games, 1,053 hits, 150 home runs, 618 runs batted in, .281 batting average, .382 on-base percentage, .478 slugging percentage

Kevin Youkilis facing Mariano Rivera (regular season)

4-for-12, 0 extra-base hits, 1 run batted in, 2 strikeouts, .333 batting average, .467 on-base percentage, .333 slugging percentage

Mo Cred

Youkilis was a member of the archrival Red Sox before joining the Yankees as Rivera's teammate in 2013.

AS A PLAYER, I've always loved facing the best because you're not supposed to get hits, and if you do, it's great. There was one game at Fenway where I got a base hit to start up a rally, and then Jason Bay [hit a homer that] tied it, so that was probably the best memory.*

Kevin Youkilis

Year	Date	Result		Year	Date	Result
2004	9/17	Strikeout (Swinging)			8/28	Fly out
2006	5/10	Fly out			9/28	Ground out
	5/11	Single (1 RBI)		2009	4/24	Single
	8/20	Fielder's choice			8/7	Strikeout (Looking)
2007	4/28	Pop out			9/26	Walk (Hit by pitch)
	6/3	Walk (Hit by pitch)		2010	5/18	Fly out
2008	7/5	Walk (Hit by pitch)		2011	5/15	Single
	7/25	Single				

---

*Youkilis singled through the box, knocking down Rivera, and with two outs in the ninth inning Bay hit a game-tying homer. Then Youkilis hit a walk-off homer in the eleventh off Damaso Marte for a 5-4 Red Sox win at Fenway Park, on April 24, 2009.

Section Two: Outfielders

Brady Anderson
Center field

Playing Career

Boston Red Sox, Baltimore Orioles, and Cleveland Indians from 1988 to 2002

Career Statistics

1,834 games, 1,661 hits, 210 home runs, 761 runs batted in, .256 batting average, .362 on-base percentage, .425 slugging percentage

Brady Anderson facing Mariano Rivera (regular season)

6-for-20, 2 extra-base hits, 1 walk, 1 strikeout, .300 batting average, .333 on-base percentage, .400 slugging percentage

Mo Cred

Anderson hit 50 home runs in 1996 to set the Baltimore Orioles' single-season record.

❙REMEMBER GETTING A hit off Rivera at Camden Yards in [what was to be] my last at-bat against him, and it helped us win a ball game. The next day, two young [Orioles] players, Jay Gibbons and Chris Richard, both also left-handed batters, asked how I was able to hit him, as if I had some secret, which I clearly didn't. I had to laugh because Mariano saws me off as much as the next guy. To have three left-handed hitters talking about how you hit a right-handed pitcher who just throws fastballs, that's unheard of.*,**

---

*With a 6-5 lead in the bottom of the ninth inning, Rivera allowed back-to-back singles to Tony Batista and Anderson, and after a sacrifice bunt moved the runners into scoring position, surrendered a two-run single to Jerry Hairston in a 7-6 loss to the Orioles at Camden Yards, on September 21, 2001.

**Gibbons was 3-for-23 facing Rivera; Richard was 0-for-8 facing Rivera.

Brady Anderson

Year	Date	Result
1996	4/30	Fly out
	6/28	Ground out
	6/28	Fielder's choice
	7/11	Strikeout (Swinging)
	7/13	Double
Postseason	10/9	Ground out
	10/12	Strikeout (Swinging)
1997	9/6	Fielder's choice
1998	5/21	Line out
	7/4	Single
	9/20	Pop out
1999	4/13	Fly out
	4/15	Double
	6/27	Ground out
	7/2	Ground out
2000	5/7	Single
	7/24	Foul out
	7/26	Fly out
	10/1	Ground out
2001	5/3	Walk
	5/4	Fielder's choice
	5/13	Single
	9/21	Single

That particular at-bat I had crept up in the box about one foot. I once saw [Roberto] Alomar hit a line drive down the left-field line off Mariano. Robby was one of those hitters, like Tony Gwynn and Wade Boggs, whose front foot was ahead of home plate when they took their batting stance. My front foot was behind the plate in my usual stance, but against Mo in that particular at-bat I stood forward in the box and stood away from the plate a bit. The strategy worked fine that at-bat, but if you do that and Mo catches you, then he'll throw the cutter outside. It was a decision I made for that game and it happened to work.*

An at-bat against Mariano is an at-bat you can't figure out. It's strange because you knew what pitch was coming, and you knew it was going to cut in on your hands. You'd tell yourself to see the ball a long time, to pull your hands in, and still, when you're grounding out weakly to end the game, you just shake your head in disbelief. He never pitched around me; as a closer, he was never in a situation to pitch around me. I knew I was going to get a fastball and he could still jam me in a way that I couldn't figure out.

I'll tell you how unusual and unique this guy is. As I was laying in bed one night before facing the Yankees the next day, I considered if

---

*Alomar was 5-for-11 facing Rivera; Boggs was 1-for-4 facing Rivera; Gwynn was 1-for-1 facing Rivera in the 1988 World Series.

it was humanly possible to swing at a spot not where you thought the ball *was*, but where you thought the ball would *be*. As a hitter, you're trained to hit the ball on the barrel of the bat, but with Mariano, I thought, maybe I should swing a few inches over to the right from where the ball actually is.

[My Orioles' teammates] Rafael Palmeiro and Roberto Alomar had a bat they called Stumpy. It was a bat [they used] just for Rivera. I used to crack-up laughing when I saw Stumpy. It had a big barrel, but it was a super short bat. It was thirty-two inches long. I used a thirty-four inch, thirty-three ounce bat, and I thought, what the heck, I'm going to try Stumpy. I still couldn't get the cutter off my hands. Stumpy didn't work.

You get tired of getting jammed and you're determined not to get jammed against him. So when I was in the batter's box he forced me to do different things. If I cheated inside he would throw the cutter outside, and when I'd be looking outside, he'd throw the cutter in. He has a great idea of how to pitch. He's phenomenal. What he does is hard to describe. Even now when I watch him on television I have a hard time figuring it out.

A lot of guys throw cutters, but this is one pitcher who you cannot scout, you can't talk to other hitters about him, because until you face him, you don't know how different his cutter is. His pitch does not have the same spin as other cutters. His cutter has four-seam fastball spin and then it cuts—it cuts late. With Mo, it's unusual when every single hitter in the line-up knows what pitch is coming and knows he's not going to walk you; it makes for a different kind of game.

I liked our battles; it was fair competition. I remember we got to Mo and beat him a couple of other times at Yankee Stadium—once scoring three runs in the ninth inning—but all closers are going to blow a few saves if you face a team often enough. I fared pretty well against him. You're proud of every hit, but if you saw some of those at-bats I had against him, there were some pretty weakly hit balls. I had good numbers against him, but it doesn't tell the whole story. If you add in the postseason, then I'm 6-for-22 facing Rivera.[*],[**]

For a while, right-handed batters had a better chance against him. But Mo figured that out, and he learned to throw a two-seam fastball that broke in on righties. I remember Cal [Ripken Jr.] coming back to the dugout really pissed off, saying: "Great, now he's got a two-seamer."

I recently saw him diffuse Evan Longoria on television. He threw one cutter away just to show it to him. Then he threw three two-seamers in on his hands, making one of the best hitters in baseball look helpless. When I saw that at-bat, I thought, he shouldn't retire. I hope he doesn't. He certainly has at least another year, maybe two, in him. I'm hoping he'll reconsider. He's one of the unusual athletes in that you want to beat him, but you certainly respect him, and we'll miss him when he's gone.[***]

I've admired him for a long time. He's one of my favorite players to watch, and I hope he pitches a few more years. He's a pro. There's a lot to like about him. I like the way he walks onto the mound and the way he leaves the mound. I like his demeanor. I like that he saves his best performances for the postseason. He's arguably the best postseason pitcher ever.

---

[*]Albert Belle hit a two-out, two-run single in a three-run ninth inning off Rivera as the Orioles beat the Yankees 7-6 at Yankee Stadium, on May 7, 2000. Charles Johnson singled leading off and Anderson singled with one out. Delino DeShields' single pulled the Orioles to 6-5 and B.J. Surhoff's ground out advanced the runners. Belle then lined a single to center.

[**]Anderson faced Rivera twice in the 1996 American League Championship Series; he grounded out in the eleventh inning of Game One and struck out in Game Four.

[***]Ripken is 3-for-13 facing Rivera; Longoria is 4-for-16 with two home runs facing Rivera.

Garret Anderson

Left field

Playing Career

Anaheim Angels, Atlanta Braves, and Los Angeles Dodgers from 1994 to 2010

Career Statistics

2,228 games, 2,529 hits, 287 home runs, 1,365 runs batted in, .293 batting average, .324 on-base percentage, .461 slugging percentage

Garret Anderson facing Mariano Rivera (regular season)

3-for-19, 0 extra-base hits, 1 run batted in, 1 walk, 3 strikeouts, .158 batting average, .200 on-base percentage, .158 slugging percentage

Mo Cred

Anderson is the Angels' franchise leader in hits and runs batted in. He was the Most Valuable Player of the 2003 All-Star Game.

DIDN'T HAVE A lot of success off him, but I liked facing him because, from a hitting standpoint, you knew what you were getting. I knew he was going to throw me a cutter inside. He's destroyed so many left-handers' bats over the years, so I backed off the plate. You can't cover the whole plate; you have to pick a spot. I picked the inside corner, and if he throws it there, that's your best chance to have success. I would give him the outside part of the plate. If he could hit the outside corner I'd tip my hat to him.

The three hits I had off him were probably broken bat singles. The only hit I remember was a topper down the first base line that jumped over the first baseman's head. All those hits were probably before he was the Mariano we know now, before he learned to throw the cutter. When he came up as a starter, he got hit around pretty good, because

Garret Anderson

Year	Date	Result
1996	5/17	Double play
1997	4/8	Single
	8/21	Fielder's choice
1998	7/30	Single
	8/25	Ground out
	8/26	Ground out (1 RBI)
1999	6/18	Walk
2000	4/4	Ground out
	8/13	Ground out
	8/18	Strikeout (Swinging)
2001	8/4	Pop out
2002 (Postseason)	10/1	Line out
2003	7/31	Fly out
2005	7/30	Ground out
	7/31	Double
Postseason	10/4	Fly out
2006	8/27	Line out
2007	7/7	Pop out
	8/20	Single
	8/22	Strikeout (Swinging)
2008	8/1	Strikeout (Swinging)
2010	6/27	Fly out

he didn't have that pitch yet. Once he started throwing the cutter, it was a 180-degree difference.

His approach to pitching is very simple; he has a devastating pitch and he uses that to his advantage. You knew he was throwing a cutter, but you didn't know how quick the cutter moved until you were standing [in the batter's box]. His ball is very hard to track. You can't track it the same as you can a normal fastball, it almost disappears on its way there and then it's on you. I faced guys who threw harder, but their ball doesn't get there as quick as his ball. You see the ball moving but you don't realize how much it's really moving. It's an illusion to some degree. You almost had to guess where the ball would end up. I would bring my hands in and try to get the bat on the ball. I didn't try to do too much. I wasn't trying to drive the ball; all I was trying to do was make contact. The cutter isn't designed to make you swing and miss; he wants you to hit that pitch, because he knows it's moving so much you're not going to get good wood on it.

I remember watching the 2001 World Series at a friend's house. I was dumbfounded that Arizona could come back and win the seventh game [beating Rivera]. That's when he was on top of his game. My friend didn't know about Mariano. He said, "What's the big deal? Relievers blow games."

I said, "You don't understand, that doesn't happen to this guy."

I can't put into words how great he is. A lot of little things had to happen for the Diamondbacks to win the game—a throwing error on a bunt—it was a freak game.

Yankee Stadium was my favorite place to play. I'm sorry they tore it down. I loved playing against the Yankees in that stadium. Those fans got to their feet for all their players. When Mariano Rivera was coming into a game they blasted the music, they made sure you knew he was coming in. I loved their fans, how they stood up and made a lot of noise for their stars.

My last season in Anaheim in 2008 I bought a No. 42 jersey and asked Mariano to autograph it for me. There's a handful of guys I got signed jerseys from, guys I respected for how they approach the game. Mariano is someone I respected as a professional and a great player, nothing more than that.

Frank Catalanotto
Left field

Playing Career
Detroit Tigers, Texas Rangers, Toronto Blue Jays, Milwaukee Brewers, and New York Mets from 1997 to 2010

Career Statistics
1,265 games, 1,113 hits, 84 home runs, 457 runs batted in, .291 batting average, .357 on-base percentage, .445 slugging percentage

Frank Catalanotto facing Mariano Rivera (regular season)
3-for-11, 0 extra-base hits, 1 run batted in, 1 strikeout, .273 batting average, .250 on-base percentage, .273 slugging percentage

Mo Cred
Catalanotto set the Toronto Blue Jays franchise record for most hits in a game, going 6-for-6 against the Chicago White Sox, on May 1, 2004.

FACING **MARIANO RIVERA** was a nightmare for me. It seemed like every at-bat was the same. Mariano would always feed me the cutter inside. It had such [a] late break. All left-handed hitters are worried about that cutter inside. It's a psychological thing. You have to pick one side of the plate [because] there is no way you can cover both sides of the plate against him. I looked inside. If he painted the outside corner, I tipped my hat to him.

I took a different approach against Mariano [beginning] in 2002, when I was playing on the Texas Rangers with Rafael Palmeiro. Rafael hit Mariano very well.[*]

Rafi told me to move way up in the batter's box. I thought he was crazy. By moving closer, I'm making a 95-miles-per-hour pitch look like 100 [m.p.h.]. He said, "No, because he's got such great late break, you want to hit the ball before it breaks, so move up as far as possible."

That [advice] helped me. By making that adjustment, I got the bat on the ball better the next few times I faced him.

In 2004, I smartened up and ordered a shorter bat to use just for [at-bats against] Mariano Rivera. I normally used a thirty-three inch, thirty-one ounce bat. I had the clubhouse manager order me a bat that was thirty inches long and thirty ounces. The most solid ball I ever hit off Rivera was using that short bat in a game in Toronto when [Blue Jays outfielder] Vernon Wells hit a big walk-off home run.[**]

Frank Catalanotto

Year	Date	Result
1999	7/6	Sacrifice fly (1 RBI)
	7/8	Single
2000	4/17	Ground out
	4/19	Ground out
2001	8/20	Fielder's choice
	8/23	Single
2003	7/13	Ground out
2004	7/22	Ground out
	7/26	Foul out
2005	4/30	Strikeout (Looking)
	8/25	Ground out
2006	7/20	Single

---

[*]Facing Rivera, Palmeiro was 8-for-24 (.333 batting average) with 2 home runs (.583 slugging percentage), 3 runs batted in, and 6 walks (.467 on-base percentage).

[**]Wells hit a walk-off home run off Rivera to give Toronto a 5-4 victory in eleven innings, on July 20, 2006. Catalanatto had led off the inning by hitting a line-drive single to right field after being down in the count no balls and two strikes. Catalanatto was then thrown out attempting to steal second base on a failed hit-and-run attempt. On the next pitch, Wells hit the game-winning homer.

By moving up in the [batter's] box and swinging the shorter bat, I was hoping to get some good wood on the ball. Sure enough, in the two or three at-bats against Mariano after I got that bat, I didn't crush the ball, but I hit it well enough.

Bubba Carpenter

Outfield

Playing Career

Colorado Rockies in 2000

Career Statistics

15 games, 6 hits, 3 home runs, 5 runs batted in, .222 batting average, .323 on-base percentage, .556 slugging percentage

Mo Cred

Carpenter was Rivera's minor league teammate with Albany-Colonie and Columbus in 1994 and '95.

WHEN I PLAYED with Mariano he was a starter. When it came to getaway day we wanted Mariano to pitch, because he got on the mound and he got after it. He either got outs quick, or he got hit quick. He didn't mess around. He got after it. He wasn't the Mo that you see now. When he was a starter he didn't have that cutter. As soon as he learned that cut fastball, the rest is history.

His numbers weren't really good [in the minor leagues]. But even when he was bad, he looked good being bad. His body language, his demeanor, everything about him was professional. You could just tell that one of these days he was going to be what he ended up being. He had that look. The way he carried himself, his attitude on the mound, everything about him was the Mariano that we see now.

You could just tell [he was going to be a major league player]. There are two people I played with that I say that about: Derek Jeter and Mariano Rivera. Jeter could go 0-for-4 and make two errors and he looked really good doing it. You walk away saying: "Wow, Jeter's a good player."

I could go 0-for-4 and make two errors and you'd say: "Bubba Carpenter, he's not good."

It's the same with Mariano. He could give up five runs in five innings and look good doing it. There's something about him, the way he carries himself, it just says professionalism. He didn't get on the mound and fist pump or anything like that. You knew he had confidence.

Thinking back, Mariano was a top ten prospect in Columbus, but he wasn't one of the top prospects. Some of those guys get labeled a top prospect and you don't see it. But Mariano you could just tell. I was big on what's inside of guys. I call it the ABCs: attitude, balls and character. You look at Mariano and that's him. You just talk to him about pitching and you knew that everything about him exudes success.

In the minor leagues, showing up to the field day to day for work, you just knew at some point he was going to be the man. Whether you knew he was going to be a Hall of Famer, I don't know about that, but you could tell he was going to be successful. He was destined to be really good. How good, I couldn't have told you back in the day. But you see certain players and you just know, and that was the case with Mo, you just knew.

He wasn't a big talker. We would hang out, but Mo didn't go out to sports bars after the game like a lot of us. Mo's quiet. The funniest thing I remember was Mariano trying to teach Jeter [to speak] Spanish. Jeter kept screwing it up; he would constantly butcher words. I was taking college Spanish classes at the time during the off season when I came home, so I didn't know a lot of Spanish, but I knew enough to know Jeter was getting it all wrong. Mo was real patient with him, and eventually, Jeter would get it right.

I was so bummed out when Mo retired. I felt like a part of me was retiring. It's been great to be able to say I played with him in the minor leagues, but with him retiring, it was sad for me. I hate to see him go, but I'm glad he's going out like he is, in my opinion, as the best of all time—while he still is Mariano. Going out healthy and on top, it's fun to watch him. I've been a Yankees fan since I was a little boy, and anytime Mo comes in the game, whatever we're doing at that time, we all stop and watch him pitch. It's fun to see him dominate.

He's the one person in the game that I don't think I've ever heard anyone say anything bad about, and that's a testament to him. I've never once heard anything bad said about Mariano.

Johnny Damon
Outfield

Playing Career

Kansas City Royals, Oakland Athletics, Boston Red Sox, New York Yankees, Detroit Tigers, Tampa Bay Rays, and Cleveland Indians from 1995 to 2012

Career Statistics

2,490 games, 2,769 hits, 235 home runs, 1,139 runs batted in, .284 batting average, .352 on-base percentage, .433 slugging percentage

Johnny Damon facing Mariano Rivera (regular season)
5-for-29, 0 extra-base hits, 2 runs batted in, 3 walks, 2 strikeouts, .172 batting average, .250 on-base percentage, .172 slugging percentage

Mo Cred

Damon played with the Yankees as Rivera's teammate from 2006 to 2009 and was a member of the 2009 World Series championship team.

MARIANO IS DEFINITELY the best closer of all time, probably the best pitcher of all time, too. You know what pitch you're getting from him, you get ready for that pitch, he throws you that pitch,

Johnny Damon

Year	Date	Result
1996	4/11	Single
	4/22	Pop out
	7/27	Pop out
	8/2	Fielder's choice
	8/5	Fielder's choice
1997	5/2	Fielder's choice
	5/10	Single
	8/4	Ground out
	8/14	Pop out
2000	4/14	Reached on error
	8/3	Ground out
	9/4	Walk
2001	4/27	Ground out
	4/29	Ground out
Postseason	10/11	Triple
	10/13	Foul out
2003	5/21	Ground out
	7/6	Single
	7/7	Ground out
	7/25	Strikeout (Swinging)
	8/30	Walk (1 RBI)
Postseason	10/11	Ground out
	10/16	Fielder's choice
2004	4/18	Fly out
	4/24	Walk
	7/1	Ground out
	9/17	Single (1 RBI)
Postseason	10/13	Strikeout (Looking)
	10/17	Reached on error
	10/18	Single
	10/20	Ground out
2005	4/5	Fly out
	4/6	Single
	4/13	Ground out
	7/14	Strikeout (Swinging)
	7/16	Line out
	7/17	Ground out
	9/11	Ground out
	10/1	Ground out
2011	5/17	Ground out

and then your bat's breaking. It's no fun. That's what makes him special; you knew what pitch was coming and you still couldn't make good contact.

I don't think too many guys have had great success off him. I definitely did not. I started to get a little bit better towards the end of my career, but still, a little bit better, like hitting .150, is not good. What I tried to do was take the cutter away by moving towards him. Normally my back foot is against the back line of the batter's box, but against Mo, I would straddle the plate so I'm closer to the pitcher. It makes the fastball seem harder, but hopefully I can get to that cutter before it moves too much. Later in my career, I started to make better contact, but he still made firewood out of my bat.[*]

He's done so many great things throughout the years. He not only racks up the saves, and racks up the World Series rings, but he actually goes and teaches the young kids how to grip the cutter, how to get better, how to approach the game. You always see how focused he is, he pays attention to every hitter and every situation. There's a different approach to attacking a hitter who's hot, and a different approach to a hitter who's not. Mariano is always paying attention.

---

[*]Damon was 2-for-8 facing Rivera in the postseason. He was 1-for-2 (a triple) in the 2001 A.L.D.S. with Oakland; 0-for-2 in the 2003 A.L.C.S. with Boston; and 1-for-4 (a single) in the 2004 A.L.C.S. with Boston.

The comeback against the Yankees in 2004 is a series that will always be dear to me, and to Red Sox Nation, because of how close we were to being done. Most of us actually felt like we were done. In baseball there's a never-say-die attitude. But when Mariano steps on the mound you know your chances are very slim.

No, he and I never discussed that series. I have too much respect for the game, and for him. When somebody is successful, there's somebody who fails. Pitchers can make the nastiest pitch, but hitters can get lucky sometimes, hit a blooper that falls in, and that could be the difference in a game, that could be a series. That's why I never showed anybody up, or pimped a home run, because I know with success there's a failure and I would never want a pitcher to show me up after a strikeout or after a season-ending, playoff-ending performance.

When we had the lead in Game Six of the 2009 World Series and Mariano came in, we felt very safe. You never want to get overexcited because you know this game of baseball can love you and it can rip your heart out. When Mo closed the door, it was special; it was another defining moment of my career. Winning that World Series was special

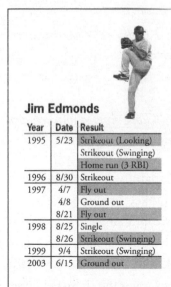

Mo Respect

Jim Edmonds

The flashy center fielder hit the first home run ever allowed by Rivera. Edmonds struck out his first two at-bats facing the rookie Rivera and then hit a three-run homer in the bottom of the fourth inning of a 10-0 Yankees' loss to the Angels at Anaheim Stadium, on May 23, 1995. Rivera, making his major league debut, fanned the first two hitters he faced but then got hit hard and did not escape the fourth inning.

Jim Edmonds

Year	Date	Result
1995	5/23	Strikeout (Looking)
		Strikeout (Swinging)
		Home run (3 RBI)
1996	8/30	Strikeout
1997	4/7	Fly out
	4/8	Ground out
	8/21	Fly out
1998	8/25	Single
	8/26	Strikeout (Swinging)
1999	9/4	Strikeout (Swinging)
2003	6/15	Ground out

I do remember that. He was throwing hard. I always thought he'd be good.

because to do it with that core of players like Jeter, Pettitte, Posada, and Rivera—the winningest players of our generation—it actually made my move from Boston even more satisfying.

Darin Erstad
Outfield and First base

Playing Career

Los Angeles Angels of Anaheim, Chicago White Sox, and Houston Astros from 1996 to 2009

Career Statistics

1,654 games, 1,697 hits, 124 home runs, 699 runs batted in, .282 batting average, .336 on-base percentage, .407 slugging percentage

Darin Erstad facing Mariano Rivera (regular season)
5-for-12, 0 extra-base hits, 3 RBI, 3 strikeouts, 1 walk, .417 batting average, .462 on-base percentage, .417 slugging percentage

Mo Cred

Erstad is a two-time All-Star, a three-time Gold Glove Award winner, and member of the Angels' 2002 World Series championship team.

THE BEST AT-BAT I ever had against Mariano was an eleven-pitch battle in 1998. It's the ninth inning at Yankee Stadium, we're losing by a run, and [Norberto] Martin got a two-out single. He's on first base and I get down in the count no balls, two strikes, and then I foul off some tough pitches and work myself back into the at-bat. I get [the count] to three-and-two and hit a soft line drive down the right-field line. I broke my bat again, but I got a hit, and Martin scored from first and we tied the game. It was during a pennant race, and it's in the ninth inning

Darin Erstad

Year	Date	Result
1997	4/8	Single
	4/15	Foul out
	8/21	Single
1998	8/26	Single (1 RBI)
1999	6/20	Single (1 RBI)
	9/4	Strikeout (Swinging)
2000	4/3	Walk
	8/18	Fielder's choice (1 RBI)
2001	8/3	Pop out
2002 (Postseason)	10/1	Single
2003	7/31	Strikeout (Swinging)
2005	7/30	Strikeout (Swinging)
	7/31	Single
Postseason	10/4	Single (1 RBI)
2006	4/9	Ground out

in Yankee Stadium, so that was an electric moment.[*]

I relished those situations. Any time you're facing the best, during those moments when everybody's senses are heightened, that's the greatest challenge, and that's why you're playing the game. Yankee Stadium is the greatest place to play of any venue that I've ever played in. There's so much electricity in the stadium, and you can feel the ghosts of the past. To get to play in Yankee Stadium and bat against Mariano Rivera, oh my goodness, that's what it's all about.

Mariano Rivera should be one of the wonders of the world. Every person that loves baseball should get the chance to stand in [the batter's box] against him and see what his cutter looks like, because it defies what a baseball is supposed to do. When he throws a cutter, being a left-handed hitter, the ball gets halfway there and then it seems to explode out of a cannon sideways at you. Until you get in there and get your bat blown in half, you really don't believe it. There's no way you can explain that pitch to somebody, until you get in the batter's box, and see it with your own eyes.

All of us [professional baseball players] get paid because we know how to hit a baseball, and for a guy to throw one pitch and be that successful, it defies all the laws of the game. A pitcher can throw a straight ball 110 miles per hour, and major league hitters who know it's coming are going to catch up to it. But Mariano has the ability to create deception

---

[*]Manager Joe Torre called for Rivera in the eighth inning with the Yankees leading the Angels, 6-4, in the second game of a doubleheader, on August 26, 1998. This was only the second time in Rivera's career that he had been summoned to notch a potential six-out save. Although Rivera botched the save, he did get the victory when Derek Jeter singled in Jorge Posada in the ninth inning for a 7-6 Yankees win.

with the pitch, to make it feel like it explodes on you. God gave him an unbelievable gift, and he's used that gift to [reach] the highest level.

You don't forget your at-bats against Mariano. I'm proud of how I did against him. Most of those hits I got early. My first five at-bats against him I got three hits, but I had six broken bats in five at-bats. I got jammed and hit bloopers that dropped in [safely]. I remember one at-bat in the first game of the 2002 playoffs. It was late in the game, and the Yankees were winning by a few runs. I hit a soft, broken-bat line drive between first and second. I'm standing on the base and [Yankees' first baseman] Jason Giambi said, "How do you hit him?"

I said, "I don't really hit him. He breaks my bat every time. I just get lucky."*

When I was playing with the Angels, the left-handed batters had a philosophy of moving farther away from the plate against Mariano. I credit Orlando Palmeiro** for coming up with the idea. By moving away from the plate, you're literally turning the inner third of the plate into the middle or outer third of the plate. This worked a couple of times; we got some big hits off him. The most memorable time we got to Mariano was when we made a comeback from five runs down and Mo Vaughn hit a home run off him and we tied the game.*** We knew the odds were

---

*Erstad singled to short right field against Rivera in the ninth inning but Rivera retired the side to earn the save in the Yankees' 8-5 victory over the Angels in Game One of the 2002 American League Division Series, on October 1, 2002. The Angles won the next three games to take the series, then dispatched the Minnesota Twins in the A.L. Championship Series en route to capturing the franchise's first World Series championship.

**Orlando Palmeiro was 2-for-11 facing Rivera during his career with the Angels, Cardinals and Astros from 1995 to 2007.

***The Angels came back from a five-run deficit to beat the Yankees, 9-8, in Yankee Stadium on August 18, 2000. Trailing 8-3, the Angels loaded the bases with one out in the top of the ninth inning when Rivera entered the game. After runs batted in by Erstad and Palmeiro made the score 8-5, Vaughn hit a three-run home run to tie the score. Erstad hit the game-winning home run off Mike Stanton in the top of the eleventh inning. Erstad also saved the game for the Angels in the bottom of the tenth inning by making a spectacular diving catch in left-center field with two outs and the winning run on third base.

stacked against us, but we were a resilient team that could swing the bats. For that [comeback] to happen the baseball gods were on our side that day.

The year after I retired [in 2010], my wife, Jessica, and I organized a charity golf tournament to help the Orange County Child Abuse Prevention Center. I bought a couple of Rivera jerseys and I asked the visiting clubhouse guy to see if he'd sign the jerseys for us. I'm sure he gets asked all the time to sign memorabilia, and he could have easily said no, but he didn't, he said yes, and signed the jerseys. The guy is a Hall of Famer that could be requesting money for his signature but out of the goodness of his heart he did it. I'll remember that more than anything else he did on the field. That's the kind of person he is. You read all the great stories about him, you hear of his reputation as one of the most selfless people, and that's the truth. He helped us raise a lot of money for our charity.

Lew Ford
Outfield

Playing Career
Minnesota Twins and Baltimore Orioles from 2003–2007, 2012

Career Statistics
519 games, 425 hits, 35 home runs, 176 runs batted in, .268 batting average, .345 on-base percentage, .399 slugging percentage

Lew Ford facing Mariano Rivera (regular season)
0-for-2, 1 strikeout

Mo Cred
Ford faced Rivera more times in the postseason than in the regular season.

Lew Ford

Year	Date	Result
2003 (Postseason)	10/4	Strikeout (Swinging)
2004	8/19	Strikeout (Looking)
	9/29	Ground out
Postseason	10/5	Strikeout (Swinging)
	10/9	Pop out

I THINK I STRUCK out the first five times I faced him [including at-bats in spring training games]. I wasn't a guy that struck out a lot, so it was really frustrating. I remember thinking: "Just put the ball in play, just one time."*

That's really not what you want to be thinking when you're going up to bat—just put the ball in play. But he's one pitcher that I did not even get the ball in play in against him.

I remember getting the ball in play once. I hit one off my fists right back to him, a little slow roller, and he got me at first [base]. I think that's the only ball I ever put in play against him.

It's almost like [he's] a freak of nature. There's no one else like him; he's a really special player.

Mo Respect

Brett Gardner

Gardner was Rivera's teammate on the Yankees from 2008 to 2013, and was a member of the 2009 World Series championship team.

The biggest moment was being able to stand out in center field behind him in the 2009 World Series. When you're a little kid, you grow up dreaming of playing in the big leagues. I don't know if I can ever say I grew up dreaming of being in the World Series in Yankee Stadium in center field with Mariano Rivera on the mound, so it doesn't get any better than that. It's something you never forget. It's almost surreal. Growing up a little kid in South Carolina, I never really dreamed I'd be able to be a part of that, so it's really nice to be able to call him a teammate.

---

*Ford faced Rivera three times in the postseason as a member of the Twins. He struck out in Game Three of the 2003 American League Division Series, won by the Yankees in four games. In the 2004 A.L.D.S., also won by the Yankees in four games, Ford struck out in Game One and popped out to second base in Game Four.

Luis Gonzalez

Left field

Playing Career

Houston Astros, Chicago Cubs, Detroit Tigers, Arizona Diamondbacks, Los Angeles Dodgers, and Florida Marlins from 1990 to 2008

Career Statistics

2,591 games, 2,591 hits, 354 home runs, 1,439 runs batted in, .283 batting average, .367 on-base percentage, .479 slugging percentage

Luis Gonzalez facing Mariano Rivera (regular season)
0-for-2

Mo Cred

Gonzalez got the winning hit off Rivera in Game Seven of the 2001 World Series.

IT'S WEIRD BECAUSE every time I go somewhere, somebody talks about that hit. I played for eighteen years in the major leagues, hit over 350 homers, fifteenth all time in doubles with 596, and everybody always says: "You're the guy who got the bloop single off Mariano Rivera."

But when they say "to win the World Series" that means a lot.

Getting an opportunity to go to the plate in Game Seven in the World Series and to face the greatest reliever of all time, that was the highlight of my career, by far. If you look at Mariano's reputation and his numbers in the postseason, to be able to come back

Luis Gonzalez

Year	Date	Result
1998	4/24	Ground out
	4/25	Pop out
2001 (Postseason)	10/30	Strikeout (Looking)
	10/31	Ground out
	11/4	Strikeout (Swinging)
	11/4	Single (1 RBI)

93

in the ninth inning against him, that is something that never happens. That Yankees team had won so many championships, and they'd been in that situation before, and usually, when those guys got a team down, they closed the door, they put the nail in the coffin.

Believe me, we knew we had a tough task at hand. Although we were swimming against the current, we still had fight in us. [First baseman] Mark Grace kept saying: "C'mon guys, you gotta believe, you gotta believe." That was our motto the whole season. Our ball club was filled with veteran guys that were all journeymen. We were guys who played for three or four different organizations, guys that played many years in the major leagues, but didn't stick with one team. So the adversity didn't bother our guys. This was just the mountain we had to climb over, which was named Mariano Rivera.

The ninth inning started with swirling winds and rain, stuff that doesn't normally happen in Arizona. There were a lot of strange things going on in that game; the strangest of all was Mariano not closing that game out. After Grace singled to start the ninth, Mariano threw the bunt away. When does Mariano ever make a throwing error? The grass was wet from the rain, which is rare. Mariano picked up a wet ball. I told you there were strange things going on. On the next bunt, he makes a great play. Then Tony [Womack] doubles, and we tie the game.

Now there's base runners on second and third, and [Craig] Counsell is up with one out. I'm on deck, thinking: "He was the Most Valuable Player of the [National League] Championship Series, he had been swinging the bat well, and he has a shot at winning this game."

In my mind I was figuring the game would be over with Counsell hopefully getting a hit or getting that runner in from third. When Mariano hit him [with a pitch], I was like, "Oh shoot, here we go." It was a rush.[*]

---

[*]Counsell was named the Most Valuable Player of the 2001 N.L.C.S. In a five-game series win over Atlanta, Counsell batted .381 with eight hits, three doubles, four runs batted in, and five runs scored. In the World Series, Counsell had faced Rivera in games three, four, and five—and grounded out weakly all three times—before being hit by a pitch in the fateful ninth inning of Game Seven.

My mindset in that situation was to try to get something into the outfield. Mariano had already pitched the eighth inning, and I struck out swinging. Seeing him a second time in that game [in the ninth inning] didn't help me. That had no play. Mariano is a guy you could see him a million times and he can get you out every time up. He's a great pitcher—with one pitch—the cutter. He has a psychological advantage on hitters because of the fact that everyone knows how good his cutter is. Being a left-handed batter, the pitch comes in on your hands and eats you up like Pac Man.*

Mariano is so successful with one pitch, but he's got that championship attitude and that winning way about him, and he knows how to win. Plus, the simple fact is, this guy has ice in his veins. If you ask a million people I think there may be less than one percent that thought he wasn't going to close that game out, especially with the lead and knowing his record in postseason play.

[Yankees' manager] Joe Torre brought the infield in. Some people question that. Mariano breaks a lot of bats, and with the bases loaded, I think Joe figured if I got jammed and hit a slow roller, the infielders would not have been able to turn a double play, and the winning run would score. With the infield playing in, if I do hit a slow roller, they have a chance to force the lead runner going from third to home. Joe got exactly what he wanted—the jam shot—but it went over the infielder's head; it wasn't a ground ball.**

You dream about hitting a home run in that situation or a line drive in the gap. I hit 596 doubles in my career. I would have loved to shoot a ball in the gap, but in reality, facing a guy like Mariano, I'll take the

---

*Facing Rivera in the 2001 World Series, Gonzalez struck out looking in the eighth inning of Game Three; grounded out to first in the tenth inning of Game Four; and struck out swinging leading off the bottom of the eighth of Game Seven with Arizona trailing 2-1, before his ninth inning single to win it.

**Gonzalez came to the plate in the bottom of the ninth inning of Game Seven, with the score even at 2-2, the bases loaded and one out. Gonzalez swung at Rivera's 0-1 pitch and hit the game-winning bloop single into left-center field that sealed the first franchise World Series title for Arizona. It was Rivera's first and only loss of his postseason career, and it snapped his record streak of 23 consecutive postseason saves converted.

jam shot that just barely got out of the infield. I'll be honest with you. People say that hit off Mariano was lucky. I'm not disagreeing. Sometimes you'd rather be lucky than good. I never got a hit off him before, and how many consecutive saves did he have? Maybe it was his one time to fail, and my one time to get a hit off him. The stars aligned and I was able to come through. I'm pretty sure that was my final at-bat against Mariano. Baseball is a strange game. They say when you go to the park you'll always see something you've never seen before, so expect the unexpected. That was certainly true on that day.

I never have [spoken to Mariano about the hit]. For the Arizona fans it's a thrill, and a moment I'll never forget in my life, but I have the utmost respect for that guy, and for everything he's ever done for the game. He's not only a great closer; he's also a great person. By no means would I ever say to him, "I got the game-winning hit off you, and the bat is in the Hall of Fame."

I was fortunate. I did run into Mariano in the offseason a few years later. I grew up in Tampa, Florida, and that's where the Yankees have spring training. I went home to Tampa and was walking around at the International Mall, and Mariano was in the mall, too. I said, "Hi, how are you, what's going on?"

I didn't want to bring it up, and I'm sure he didn't either. We were both very cordial, very professional.

Tino [Yankees' first baseman Tino Martinez] and I have spoken about it. He and I played Little League together and we played together in high school. I played second base; he played first. That was another thrill for me, and for our high school coach, to have two players from the same high school on the same field playing for a World Series title. Later on, in the evening after Game Seven, the first message on my phone was from Tino, saying, "Congratulations, it was a hell of a World Series, enjoy the moment, because you don't know how many of these [experiences] you're going to get."

That World Series was unbelievable from start to finish. The drama of being in New York after the tragedy of 9/11, there were a lot of different story lines that were being played out in that World Series. Tino's home run was crazy. After losing those three games in New York the way we did, it was a very quiet plane ride back to Arizona. We were confident, but we were worried at the same time. When you played the Yankees of that era, they had so many great players, and so many unsung heroes on that team, and they all gelled well together and they were good. Those guys knew how to sniff blood and they knew how to win games. We felt like we outplayed them the whole World Series, but good teams find a way to win, and that's what they kept doing. We tried to hit them with a knockout punch but they'd bounce off the ropes and hit us back three or four more times.*

If you look back, it seems one hundred percent of the relief pitchers are never really the same type of reliever after a tough [World Series] loss. You have to be mentally strong and Mariano is. Especially playing in New York City, where if you sneeze the wrong way your picture shows up on the front page of the tabloids. For him to stay out of the limelight says a lot about him as a person. He stepped right in and took over as their closer, and he's been the main guy there for a long time. He's played on some fantastic teams with great players, and he's earned the confidence of his teammates and the fans.

I watched the [2013] All-Star Game at home with my family, and my son was sitting next to me. It was a pretty cool moment to see [the tribute to Mariano]. That just goes to show you, when certain players have an impact on the game, as Mariano has, it's pretty incredible. I was surprised he didn't get emotional on the mound. Although he's been in bigger situations, like the World Series, I can guarantee his heart was pounding a million miles a second. He is truly the ultimate professional. Whether he wins or loses, he has the same reaction. The only time I ever

---

*Just weeks after the September 11 tragedy, the Yankees helped to uplift the spirit of New York with three straight dramatic World Series victories at the Stadium. They won Game Four on Derek Jeter's walk-off home run after a two-out, game-tying homer in the ninth by Martinez. They also took Game Five after a two-out, game-tying homer in the ninth by Scott Brosius.

saw him get emotional was the time he laid on the mound after the Yankees won Game Seven [of the 2003 American League Championship Series] against Boston.[*]

He carries himself with dignity, on and off the field. I respect his demeanor. He doesn't show guys up from the field, he's not pointing up at the sky, or yelling at guys. When you see today's generation of players—relievers with their crazy antics on the mound, and batters who take twenty minutes to round the bases after hitting a home run—and you watch Mariano go about his business, he just gracefully does his job; he doesn't show a lot of flair. I think he's a perfect role model for every pitcher that wants to be a closer. They should follow in his footsteps. He's a true, blue-collar guy, and that's why he has such a strong following among the players who play with him and the players who play against him. All players respect him.

Curtis Granderson

Outfield

Playing Career

Detroit Tigers, New York Yankees, and New York Mets since 2004

Career Statistics

1,187 games, 1,157 hits, 217 home runs, 606 runs batted in, .261 batting average, .340 on-base percentage, .488 slugging percentage

---

[*]Rivera's memorable performance in Game Seven of the 2003 A.L.C.S. against the archrival Boston Red Sox is one for the ages. He entered the game in the ninth inning with the score tied 5-5 and pitched three scoreless innings. Aaron Boone's eleventh-inning walk-off home run propelled the Yankees into the World Series, but Rivera was named Most Valuable Player of the series for earning two saves and recording a win in the decisive contest. As Boone celebrated with teammates at home plate, Rivera ran to the mound to bow his head in prayer, and then buckled with joyous exhaustion.

Curtis Granderson facing Mariano Rivera (regular season)
1-for-4, 1 extra-base hit, 1 home run, 3 runs batted in, 1 strikeout, .250
batting average, .250 on-base percentage, 1.000 slugging percentage

Mo Cred

Granderson hit a three-run home run off Rivera with two outs in the bot-
tom of the ninth inning while playing for Detroit, but it was not enough, as
the Yankees won 8-6, on April 29, 2009. From 2010 to 2013, Granderson
was Rivera's teammate on the Yankees.

Curtis Granderson

Year	Date	Result
2006	5/30	Strikeout (Looking)
Postseason	10/3	Single
2007	8/18	Fly out
2009	4/29	Home run (3 RBI)
	7/17	Fly out

WITH HIM, YOU just hopefully hit it before it cuts and keep it fair. Since I never really watched him on TV much, my first chance to see his ball move as much as it does was in the batter's box. It's hard to get a read on how much the ball is actually moving until you step in the box.

Even playing [center field] behind him, you still can't see [the movement] as much as you can from hitting against him, because a lot of pitches he throws are around the zone and you get a lot of swing and misses. You try to figure out why, because it looked like the batters were right there on it, but it's the deception and the amount of movement the ball has. You can start to understand more why there is a lot of swing and misses when you're facing him.

[His saves record] is absolutely amazing; it's probably going to be something that's never going to get touched ever again. And to get a chance be a part of it as a Yankee, I couldn't have written a better story for myself. He definitely is, no doubt about it, he's a Hall of Famer. He's the all-time saves leader and he's still got plenty more left with the rest of this [2013] season and hopefully the postseason.

He's the guy we want out there. Hopefully when he's coming into the game that means we got the lead and that means we're going to be winning games and hopefully making the postseason.

Gabe Gross

Outfield

Playing Career

Toronto Blue Jays, Milwaukee Brewers, Tampa Bay Rays, and Oakland Athletics from 2004 to 2010

Career Statistics

657 games, 349 hits, 40 home runs, 186 runs batted in, .239 batting average, .330 on-base percentage, .385 slugging percentage

Gabe Gross facing Mariano Rivera (regular season)

3-for-10, 0 extra-base hits, 1 run batted in, 1 walk, 2 strikeouts, .300 batting average, .364 on-base percentage, .300 slugging percentage

Mo Cred

Gross hit a game-ending single in the eleventh inning against Rivera on May 13, 2008.

Gabe Gross

Year	Date	Result
2004	8/26	Strikeout (Swinging)
	9/21	Single
	10/2	Pop out
2005	9/16	Ground out
2008	5/13	Single (1 RBI)
	9/13	Single
2009	6/7	Strikeout (Swinging)
	7/29	Walk
	9/7	Pop out
	10/4	Ground out
2010	4/20	Double play

IREMEMBER THE WALK-OFF very well. It was a tie score in the bottom of the eleventh inning. [Cliff Floyd singled] and Jonny Gomes pinch ran for him. Jonny stole second base. Now, with the winning run on second base and no outs, my objective completely changed. I had to move the runner over to third. I remember thinking: "There is no way Mariano is going to throw me an inside cutter and let me break my bat and ground out to second base and advance the runner."

Because that's what you did against Mariano as a lefty batter. It was a normal occurrence for him to jam you with a cutter, and all you can do is hit a weak ground ball to the right side.[*]

I remember stepping out of the [batter's] box and thinking: "He's got to throw a back door cutter to the outside part of the plate."

I was looking away; I wanted to hook my wrists and pull the ball. Fortunately, he did throw a back door cutter that I'm sure got more plate than he planned, and I was able to do exactly what I wanted. I hit [the ball] back up the middle to center field and Jonny beat the throw home and we won the ball game. It was mid-May and Mariano had not given up an earned run to that point in the season until Jonny scored. The win put us into first place. That fact was not lost upon me at that moment.[**]

It's a big deal any time you beat New York, any time you can beat Mariano, and it was a big deal for the team. Tampa then was not the organization it is today. They had been bottom feeders, finished dead last in the division nine years out of ten and next-to-last in the other year. I had gotten traded from Milwaukee to Tampa earlier that season, on April 22, so I had been around the team for about three weeks. I was battling my brains out trying to prove myself to a new team and establish myself amongst my teammates. Soon after I got to Tampa—and this has nothing to do with me—we won eight or nine straight and we were gaining momentum and a confidence was building to the point where we knew we could beat anybody. It was a magical season. That [2008 Rays] team was the first to win the division, first in the playoffs, first in the World Series. Any year in the big leagues is not a bad year, but that year was special. I had three walk-off hits during my big league

---

[*]Facing Rivera, Floyd was 2-for-8 with 1 extra-base hit, 1 walk, 3 strikeouts, .250 batting average, .333 on-base percentage, .375 slugging percentage. Gomes is 3-for-11, 1 extra-base hit, 3 walks, 4 strikeouts, .273 batting average, .467 on-base percentage, .571 slugging percentage.

[**]Gross drilled a one-and-one pitch from Rivera up the middle to drive in the winning run, to lead Tampa Bay past New York, 2-1, and into first place in the American League East, on May 13, 2008. Rivera absorbed the loss after he allowed his first run in fourteen appearances that season.

career playing parts of seven different seasons, and all three happened that year in about one month's time.

Early in my career I was three-for-six against [Rivera]. Whenever we played the Yankees and I was not in the starting lineup, my manager knew those numbers and would use me to pinch-hit when Mariano came in the game. Trying to get a hit against Mariano when you're in the game and you have a lather going is hard enough. Trying to come off the bench to do it is another objective altogether. Later in my career my numbers against him waned. That walk-off hit *is* a highlight of my career. I don't imagine there are many people who have had RBIs off Mariano in extra innings.*

Facing Mariano is a difficult task not because his cutter is better than anyone else's, it's because he doesn't make mistakes. Whether it's intentional or unintentional, his ball moves so much that you end up swinging at something that isn't a strike. You can't figure out how to hit it. I had a teammate at Toronto, Gregg Zaun, who told me to take pitches until I got two strikes. He didn't want to swing at a pitch five inches off the plate and get jammed and waste an at-bat. So he would take pitches, hoping to get into a good [hitters'] count, to have a better chance to try to hit a strike. He thought his strategy was better than swinging at a pitch that wasn't a strike.**

---

*Besides Gross, five other players have game-ending RBIs in extra innings against Rivera. They are: Keith Lockhart, Royals, 10th inning double, August 2, 1996; Robert Fick, Tigers, 11th inning fielder's choice, June 27, 2000; Manny Ramirez, Red Sox, 10th inning single, April 13, 2001; Vernon Wells, Blue Jays, 11th inning home run, July 20, 2006; David Murphy, Rangers, 10th inning single, August 10, 2010.

**Facing Rivera, Zaun was 2-for-16, 1 extra-base hit, 1 run batted in, 1 walk, 4 strikeouts, .125 batting average, .176 on-base percentage, .188 slugging percentage. (See Zaun entry in catchers' section.)

David Hulse

Center field

Playing Career

Texas Rangers and Milwaukee Brewers from 1992 to 1996

Career Statistics

423 games, 336 hits, 5 home runs, 103 runs batted in, .266 batting average, .307 on-base percentage, .337 slugging percentage

David Hulse facing Mariano Rivera (regular season)
1-for-2, 1 extra-base hit, 1 home run, 2 runs batted in, .500 batting average, .500 on-base percentage, 2.000 slugging percentage

David Hulse

Year	Date	Result
1995	8/1	Home run (2 RBI)
1996	4/16	Line out

Mo Cred

Hulse hit an inside-the-park home run off Rivera on August 1, 1995, the only inside-the-park homer Rivera has allowed.

❚DISTINCTLY REMEMBER THE inside-the-park home run I hit off Mariano. I remember all my home runs. I only had five! But the one off Mariano is particularly memorable. It was his first year [in 1995] and they were all saying, "He's the next up-and-coming kid."

It was a real long at-bat. He kept throwing me pitches away, away, away, and I kept fighting them off, hitting foul ball after foul ball after foul ball. I had to keep battling. He wasn't giving in, and I wasn't giving in, either. That was one of the few battles in my career when I won!*

---

*Hulse's two-run, inside-the-park home run off Rivera came on the eighth pitch of the at-bat, scoring Matt Mieske ahead of him, to give the Brewers a 5-4 lead in the top of the seventh inning. The Yankees scored three runs in the bottom of the seventh as Rivera and the Yankees won the game, 7-5, at Yankee Stadium, on August 1, 1995. The victory was Rivera's fourth career win.

I liked balls middle-away; that was my strength. So Mariano is throwing pitches middle-away, right into my wheelhouse. He hadn't developed a cutter yet, or else he would have sawed me off, being I was a left-handed hitter. Like I said, every pitch was away, and I kept fouling them off. Finally, I catch up to one away, and slap it over third base and down the left-field line. Right out of the [batter's] box I'm thinking double, that the left fielder is going to sprint over to the [foul] line, and come up throwing. But the ball hit the corner of the wall and ricocheted like a shot toward the left-center field gap.

As I'm sprinting to second base, I pick up the third base coach, and he's waving for me to come on. I wasn't expecting him to keep waving me on, but I was flying, and I was pumped to go for three bases. I loved hitting triples, because I could run. My speed is the only reason I made it to pro baseball. After I hit the second base bag, I pick up my coach again, and he was waving me the whole time, so I just kept running. The last thing I remember is rounding second and heading for third. From there, it's like a blur. I remember sliding into home and being safe, but from second on, it was a blur. I don't even know if there was a play at the plate, I just slid, and then ran into the dugout.

Obviously, I remember it like it was yesterday so it ranks up there very highly in my career. In hindsight, people say: "Dang, you hit an inside-the-park home run off Mariano Rivera, the most dominating closer in the game."

I gladly say: "Yes, I did."

But I don't have to tell people the whole story. They don't have to know that it was his first year and he wasn't throwing a cutter yet. As a hitter, that's not how I tell it!

Mike Humphreys

Outfield

Playing Career

New York Yankees from 1991 to 1993

Career Statistics

54 games, 15 hits, 1 home run, 9 runs batted in, .176 batting average, .283 on-base percentage, .259 slugging percentage

Mo Cred

Humphreys and Rivera were minor league teammates with the Columbus Clippers in 1994.

I WAS IN TRIPLE A Columbus the whole year in 1994. What's funny is I don't remember ever playing a game with Mariano at all. I wish I could remember playing with a future Hall of Famer. I would love to see box scores; maybe that would jar my memory.*

I don't understand it. I was looking at Mariano's stats, and it wasn't like he only pitched one game, he pitched six games [for Columbus] that year. I've got no recollection of any of that. I would love to see who he pitched against; I want something to jar my brain.**

My memories of Mariano are from spring training. For three straight years I went to spring training and he always seemed to be coming off injury or having to rehab from an arm problem. I don't remember him pitching in any spring training games, because he was hurt or had been

---

*Humphreys collected 121 hits in 135 games played for the Triple A Columbus Clippers in 1994. He batted .248 with 8 home runs and 51 runs batted in.

**Pitching for the Triple A Columbus Clippers in 1994, Rivera was 4-2 with a 5.81 earned run average. He allowed 34 hits and 10 walks in 31 innings, and struck out 23 batters.

hurt. At the time you're thinking, why do they keep this guy around? Now we know!

He's never been one that's out front or draws attention to himself. The quiet Mariano that everybody knows, that was the type of guy I remember. He wasn't loud in the locker room or anything like that. I just don't remember seeing him out on the field. Obviously, the Yankees saw something in Mariano and thank goodness they did.

That was also the year [1994] that Derek Jeter was coming up. He went through Single A, Double A, and Triple A that year and had incredible stats. We were roommates. It's always been neat to watch him play, and be able to say, "yeah, that was my roommate in spring training in '94."

I remember playing with Jeter, and I played many years with Bernie Williams.*

That '94 Columbus team was a special group—players like Jeter, Williams, [Andy] Pettitte, [Jorge] Posada. You knew that core was going to be together for a long time and be successful. I remember playing with those guys and I enjoyed watching them play on TV. I watch Mariano on TV, but I don't have memories of playing with Mariano.

Torii Hunter

Outfield

Playing Career

Minnesota Twins, Los Angeles Angels, and Detroit Tigers since 1997

---

*Jeter soared through the Yankees' minor league system in 1994. He had a .329 batting average in 69 games for Single A Tampa; .a 377 batting average in 34 games for Double A Albany-Colonie; and a .349 batting average in 35 games for Triple A Columbus.

Torii Hunter

Year	Date	Result
2000	9/3	Walk
2001	5/10	Strikeout (Swinging)
2002	5/17	Strikeout (Swinging)
2003 (Postseason)	10/2	Strikeout (Swinging)
	10/4	Ground out
2004	9/29	Strikeout (Looking)
2005	6/3	Single
	7/28	Strikeout (Swinging)
2006	4/15	Strikeout (Looking)
2008	8/1	Single (1 RBI)
2009	4/30	Single
	9/23	Strikeout (Swinging)
Postseason	10/16	Walk
	10/17	Strikeout (Looking)
	10/19	Fielder's choice
	10/25	Ground out
2010	4/13	Strikeout (Swinging)
2011	6/5	Ground out
	8/9	Ground out
2013	4/7	Strikeout (Swinging)
	8/9	Ground out

Career Statistics

2,091 games, 2,170 hits, 314 home runs, 1,227 runs batted in, .279 batting average, .335 on-base percentage, .466 slugging percentage

Torii Hunter facing Mariano Rivera (regular season)

3-for-14, 0 extra-base hits, 1 run batted in, 1 walk, 8 strikeouts, .214 batting average, .267 on-base percentage, .214 slugging percentage

Mo Cred

Hunter is a five-time All-Star and nine-time Gold Glove Award winner.

MY FIRST HIT [facing Mariano Rivera] was a single to center at Yankee Stadium when I was with the Twins. I got a couple of base hits [off Rivera] with the Angels, but I haven't had much luck lately. He got me to end the game earlier this year.[*]

The first time he threw me two-seamers instead of cutters was in the 2009 postseason. He blew my bat up [with a two-seamer], and I said to myself, "He's not going to do that again."

---

[*]Hunter's run-scoring single to center field in the ninth inning off Rivera gave the Angels a 1-0 victory over the Yankees at Yankee Stadium, on August 1, 2008. Hunter also singled off Rivera in a 7-4 Yankees win over the Angels, on April 30, 2009 (career save No. 487 and the start of Rivera's career-best streak of 36 straight save opportunities converted). Facing Rivera in the regular season and postseason, Hunter was 0-for-his-last-9 with a walk, including a game-ending strikeout in a Yankees' victory over the Tigers, on April 7, 2013, which was Rivera's final appearance in Detroit.

But I faced him again—and he blew me up again.[*]

Even now, hitters hate facing him. When you have a pitcher and hitters talk about him like he's a ghost or a monster that they are afraid to see, that's impressive. I definitely include him as one of the best pitchers of all time.

We spent time together [at charity events] during the All-Star Game in New York [in 2008]. That was the longest conversation I had with him away from the field. He's just a good dude. He talked about his family. His wife was there. He just loves the right stuff. You've got to love a guy like that. Once you get to know Mariano, you respect him as a person more than as a player.

He's such a competitor, and such a good player; you'd think he'd have an attitude. But he's so down to earth. He shook everyone's hand. He had a conversation with everybody. He wasn't standoffish. That opened my eyes that this is a great man. He treats all people the same. He didn't have a bodyguard. He's genuine. He isn't a fake—this is who he is.

That moment [for Rivera at the 2013 All-Star Game] was powerful. For the young players to see a guy who started off in the major leagues when he was 20-something years old and now he's 40-plus, tipping his cap at his last All-Star Game in the last year of his career, everybody's going to get that. The young guys who look at that say: "Man, I want to do that one day."

It motivates all the young guys—it motivates me and I've got a couple years left [to play]. I'm going to be [in that position] one day so for me it was very special. I hope that I can go out like that.

He's been one of the best in the game, so he deserves it. I've seen this guy do some damage in this game. For me as an athlete, a guy that's

---

[*]The Yankees defeated the Angels in six games in the 2009 American League Championship Series. Hunter was 0-for-3 with a walk facing Rivera: he walked in Game One, struck out looking in Game Two, and grounded out weakly in Games Three and Six. Hunter also faced Rivera as a member of the Twins in the 2003 A.L. Division Series, won by the Yankees in four games. Hunter struck out in Game Two and grounded out to end Game Three. Hunter did not face Rivera in the 2004 A.L.D.S., also won by the Yankees in four games.

been playing 17 seasons, I've got to tell you, his craft is unbelievable. I respect the craft. Even though he broke all my bats, he killed me. My [best] bats are all gone but I still admire than man.

Raul Ibanez

Left field

Playing Career

Seattle Mariners, Kansas City Royals, Philadelphia Phillies, New York Yankees, and Los Angeles Angels since 1996

Career Statistics

2,071 games, 1,993 hits, 300 home runs, 1,181 runs batted in, .276 batting average, .338 on-base percentage, .471 slugging percentage

Raul Ibanez facing Mariano Rivera (regular season)
2-for-16, 0 extra-base hits, 4 walks, 5 strikeouts, .125 batting average, .300 on-base percentage, .125 slugging percentage

Mo Cred

Ibanez hit two doubles off Rivera as a member of the Phillies in the 2009 World Series.

THAT WORLD SERIES was my best memory and my worst memory, too. It was tough watching the Yankees celebrate. It felt so close you could touch it. Not to be able to walk away with that victory for the city [of Philadelphia] and for the [Phillies] organization was one of the more difficult times in my career.

When you play this game in your backyard as a kid, nobody is saying: "5-4 game, bases loaded and it's April."

Raul Ibanez

Year	Date	Result
1999	8/6	Ground out
	8/7	Fielder's choice
	8/29	Pop out
2000	4/8	Fly out
	8/30	Ground out
Postseason	10/11	Ground out
	10/13	Line out
	10/17	Fly out
2001	4/2	Walk
	4/11	Strikeout (Looking)
2003	8/20	Single
2004	5/15	Pop out
	8/14	Fielder's choice
2005	5/9	Ground out
	5/16	Walk
	8/29	Strikeout (Swinging)
	8/31	Fly out
2007	9/5	Strikeout (Swinging)
2008	5/2	Strikeout (Looking)
	5/25	Strikeout (Swinging)
2009	5/24	Single
Postseason	10/29	Double
	11/4	Double
2013	6/8	Walk
	6/9	Walk

You're always envisioning being a part of the last team standing, the one that's on the pitcher's mound, celebrating that final victory. That's why you play the game. To have that opportunity is a blessing.

Mo's broken a lot of my bats. He's broken a lot of everyone's bats. He keeps the bat companies in business. The approach, I think, has to be to hit the ball on the barrel. He's obviously missed a lot of barrels in his career. I don't know how many people have figured him out. I don't think many people have figured him out at all.

Not just is he the greatest closer ever, he's one of the greatest human beings I've had the privilege of knowing. He's humble. He's a fierce competitor. He's the kind of man I would want my own son to grow up and be like, and that's the highest compliment I can give a person.

A few years ago, when I was with the Phillies, we played a spring training game in Tampa against the Yankees. After the game, my son [R.J.] wanted to meet Rivera, but Mo was already in his car and getting ready to leave the ballpark.

I said, "Mariano, would you say hello to my son?"

Mo got out of the car and called for my son to come out of my car. My son shook his hand, and Mo said, "Where's the camera? Who has the camera?"

My wife scrambled to grab her camera phone. She took a picture that my son cherishes. That's just a great gesture for a superstar to do that. It made a huge impact on my son and my own life. My son still has the picture. He's very proud of it.

Reed Johnson

Outfield

Playing Career

Toronto Blue Jays, Chicago Cubs, Los Angeles Dodgers, and Atlanta Braves since 2003

Career Statistics

1,190 games, 965 hits, 63 home runs, 380 runs batted in, .282 batting average, .339 on-base percentage, .409 slugging percentage

Reed Johnson facing Mariano Rivera (regular season)
2-for-11, 1 extra-base hit, 1 home run, 2 runs batted in, 4 strikeouts, .182 batting average, .182 on-base percentage, .455 slugging percentage

Mo Cred
Johnson hit a home run off Rivera on June 18, 2011.

Reed Johnson

Year	Date	Result
2003	7/11	Strikeout (Swinging)
2004	7/26	Ground out
2005	8/23	Single (1 RBI)
	9/25	Strikeout (Swinging)
2006	7/20	Line out
	7/22	Pop out
2007	7/18	Fielder's choice
	9/21	Fly out
	9/22	Strikeout (Swinging)
2010	6/27	Strikeout (Swinging)
2011	6/18	Home run (1 RBI)

I HIT A HOME run off Mariano Rivera when I was with the Cubs in 2011. I was leading off the ninth inning, we're down two runs; I was trying to get on base to start a rally. I hit a line drive and I wasn't sure if it was going to be a home run. I knew it had a shot to go out. I was hustling around first base when [the ball] went over the wall. I knew I'd done something—in Wrigley Field, against the Yankees, with Mariano Rivera pitching. The crowd was going crazy; it was a special memory. At the time, in the moment, I didn't hear the crowd. After the game, I watched a replay and listened to the audio. Of course, Mariano ended up doing what he does best, which is finishing the inning and collecting another save.*

He always gets ahead of me by throwing cutters middle-away and then he tries to mix it up by going inside with front-door cutters. There were two strikes on me, and then I fouled off two quality pitches to stay in the at-bat. The first was a fastball up in the zone. On the next pitch, I figured he might run one away from me; he did, and I fouled it off, too. I had a feeling he was going to try to get me [out] with a front-door cutter. He had gotten me on that pitch a few times before. Baseball is about trying to recall what guys have done in the past to get you out. When it's a pitcher like Mariano, the best closer ever, you're not going to forget [your at-bats against him]. Some guys, like [Toronto teammate] Carlos Delgado, keep a book on pitchers.**

Once I got two strikes on me, I was guarding against the front door cutter, the one he starts at your front hip if you're a righty batter. Most times [the right-handed hitter] will give up on that pitch. You have to mentally force yourself to trust the pitch is going to come back over the inside part of the plate. That's a tough plan, but if you can follow through, that's your only shot [to succeed against Rivera]. I was looking for an inside cutter, and I got exactly what I was looking for.

I have the video of that home run on my iPad. At the end of the year, the team will give you a video of all your best hits from that season, so you can look back and see what you were doing right, mechanically. So that video is always going to be there, and the home run is something that I'll remember. I also had a go-ahead base hit off him in the

---

*Johnson led off the bottom of the ninth inning with the Cubs trailing the Yankees, 4-2, at Wrigley Field, on June 18, 2011. Rivera got ahead in the count one-and-two, and then Johnson fouled off two pitches. On the sixth pitch, Johnson connected for a home run to left-center field, cutting the Yankees' lead to 4-3. Then Rivera gave up a single, got a double-play ground ball, and a strike out, to earn his 576th career save.

**Delgado was 8-for-21 (.381 batting average) with one extra-base hit and one run batted in facing Rivera. Rivera has twice intentionally walked Delgado, tying him with Edgar Martinez, Evan Longoria, and Paul Sorrento for most times intentionally walked by Rivera. (See Delgado entry in Infielders' section.)

ninth inning at Yankee Stadium when I was playing for Toronto, but we ended up losing that game. Those two hits are the only at-bats I remember; you want to forget everything else.*

Adam Jones

Center field

Playing Career

Seattle Mariners and Baltimore Orioles since 2006

Career Statistics

946 games, 988 hits, 140 home runs, 481 runs batted in, .279 batting average, .322 on-base percentage, .460 slugging percentage

Adam Jones facing Mariano Rivera (regular season)
3-for-11, 1 extra-base hit, 1 home run, 2 runs batted in, 1 walk, 4 strikeouts, .273 batting average, .333 on-base percentage, .545 slugging percentage

Mo Cred

Jones hit a two-run home run in the ninth inning off Rivera, on July 7, 2013.

THAT WAS THE biggest hit I've ever had in my career, hands down, in terms of who it was hit against—Mariano—and that it was a game-winner. It surprised the hell out of me. I took the first pitch. You can't swing at the first pitch off him, that's a bad idea, because you

---

*Johnson's line-drive single to left field off Rivera scored Orlando Hudson to give Toronto a 4-3 lead in the top of the ninth inning of a game at Yankee Stadium, on August 23, 2005. The Yankees scored two runs in the bottom of the ninth, making Rivera the winning pitcher in a 5-4 walk-off victory.

Adam Jones

Year	Date	Result
2008	4/20	Strikeout (Swinging)
	5/20	Single
	5/27	Strikeout (Swinging)
	5/28	Strikeout (Swinging)
	9/19	Ground out
2009	5/21	Ground out
2010	6/3	Strikeout (Swinging)
	9/17	Pop out
2011	4/24	Walk
	5/18	Single
2013	4/12	Fly out
	7/7	Home run (2 RBI)

don't know if he's going in or out, and you're going to guess wrong, and ground into a double play. I was taking to see how he'd work me. He threw a first pitch two-seam fastball inside [for strike one]. I said, "Okay, look inside."

You have to pick a side of the plate against Mariano. The next pitch was in the same spot. I cleared my hips, I didn't over-swing, and I put the barrel on the ball. I felt it leave my bat, and I'm thinking: "Get up; you better get up."

When I saw the ball clear the fence, inside, I was as happy as a two-year-old that you give a sugar cane to. I showed no emotion rounding the bases, but I'm telling you, inside, if I could have showed emotion, I would have been jumping up and yelling like we just won the championship.*

I know he's blown some saves this year, but it wasn't like Mariano didn't have it that day. What does that mean? Those words don't even formulate together. That's not even a sentence that you can write. That's almost illegal in the game of baseball to write that Mariano didn't have it that day. You always give credit to a hitter. It's hard enough to hit a baseball. Like Ted Williams said: "You try to hit a round ball with a round bat and square it up."

He's still having a pretty damn good year. The only reason he's retiring is because he hates to travel, not because he can't do it anymore. He's tired of all the travel. Traveling ain't easy, man. You think it's nice planes and fancy hotels, but it's not all that. You'd rather have your own bed, not so many different hotel beds.

---

*With one on and one out in the ninth inning, Jones drove an 0-1 pitch into the bullpen in left-center field for a two-run homer off Rivera to give the Orioles a 2-1 victory at Yankee Stadium, on July 7, 2013. It was the 67th home run surrendered by Rivera, who had converted 41 consecutive save opportunities at home. His last failure had been on September 26, 2010, against Boston.

The first thing I think about when I hear that music, "Enter Sandman," that song he comes out to, my thing is: "Does he even know that song? He doesn't know that damn song! Mo ain't going home and listening to Metallica!" You know when he comes in the game there's a 99.9 percent chance the game is over. I can't give it 100 percent because there's always a chance, as you've seen, you never know how baseball works. But you're facing the most dominating relief pitcher, arguably the most dominating pitcher, period, in the history of baseball. And he throws one pitch—the cutter—the same pitch every time, and you can't hit it, because he can put it wherever he wants. That's the crazy part.

I know I didn't have success against him at the beginning, but who does? You say I started off one for eight [facing Rivera]. I didn't know my numbers. He's not an uncomfortable at-bat. He's not going to have one slip out of his hand and come up and in. I felt I had good at-bats against him, just couldn't do no damage. You say I'm two for my last three with a walk, including the homer? That's legit. I'm getting more mature as a hitter. I've tried to have better at-bats, especially late in the game. I want to thrive in late-inning situations, because that's the time in the game when I can help my team the most. When a closer comes in, I have to raise my level of play, especially when Mariano comes in. It's not about raising your level; your level is already raised; your heart is pumping when you're facing him.

Since Buck Showalter came along [as the Orioles' manager] he's helped me, and he's helped everybody feel more confident. He never doubts his players. He gives you that extra vote of confidence that you're going to get the job done. Since we know that as a team, we go up to the plate in any situation with the most confidence, because we feel our manager has our back, our fans have our back, so let's go out there, give it our all, and get the job done.

After [hitting the home run off Rivera] I saw Buck kick his leg up, which was the funniest thing ever. We've played that [video] clip over and over. You don't ever see Showalter show emotion. Even after the biggest hits, he's stone faced. That's Showalter. But he knew the situation, he knows baseball, and you don't get many opportunities to get Mariano to blow a save, so that was unbelievable.

Mark Kotsay
Outfield

Playing Career
Florida Marlins, San Diego Padres, Oakland Athletics, Atlanta Braves, Boston Red Sox, and Chicago White Sox from 1997 to 2013

Career Statistics

1,914 games, 1,784 hits, 127 home runs, 720 runs batted in, .276 batting average, .332 on-base percentage, .404 slugging percentage

Mark Kotsay facing Mariano Rivera (regular season)
0-for-7, 2 strikeouts

Mo Cred
Kotsay was the final out of Rivera's 290th career save.

I DO RECALL BEING rung up on a fastball off the plate away when I was playing with Oakland to make the last out of a game. The ball was far enough away for a hitter to say it's a ball, and close enough for the pitcher to say it was a quality pitch.

The home plate umpire who rung me up was Bill Welke. The next day, I was running out to center field and I ran right by him and said: "That pitch was a ball."

Umpires are really reluctant to say, "Yeah, you're right." But he said: "I was caught up in the moment."

Mark Kotsay

Year	Date	Result
1998	6/6	Ground out
2004	4/29	Strikeout (Looking)
	5/5	Fielder's choice
	8/4	Fly out
2005	5/6	Strikeout (Looking)
2006	6/11	Ground out
2008	8/28	Fly out

So it does help to be Mariano Rivera.*

It's definitely not fun trying to hit off him. In my 17 seasons as a major league baseball player the most difficult at-bats that I had were against Mariano. I don't know if I ever got a ball to the outfield. When you don't have success, you try to forget those at-bats. The only advice I ever gave a teammate [facing Rivera]: "Good luck."

I tried everything. I tried a smaller bat; I tried moving up on the plate; moving up in the box; moving back in the box. He might have won the battle against me even before the at-bat! But you have to make adjustments to compete at our level; if you're not willing to make changes you won't stay around very long. I even tried moving while he was in the windup, coming towards the plate, to give him a different look, but nothing seemed to work. No matter how far you got off the plate the ball still found the inside portion of the label of your bat.

He didn't have a fear. That's what makes him so great. He never pitched around a hitter. He never gave you the impression that he didn't have his best stuff. As a hitter you can look at a pitcher's eyes and tell that he doesn't have "it" per se, or on certain days you can tell from the first hitter that the pitcher doesn't have a feel for his best pitch. Most guys have two pitches, and if one isn't working, you can eliminate it. But Mariano consistently threw one pitch. It was well known for my seventeen years that he threw one pitch—you had to hit the cutter. There's not anyone else in the game you could say that about.

He approached everyone very similar, in that he was going to attack you and throw his cutter. He was throwing 93 or 94 miles per hour on a plane with cut and it was difficult to square up. That's why you

---

*Kotsay struck out looking at a one-two pitch from Rivera to make the final out in a 7-5 Yankees' win in the Bronx, on April 29, 2004. Rivera came on in relief of Tom Gordon in the eighth inning with two outs and runners on first and third and got Bobby Crosby to ground out to second to end the threat.

never saw him make a drastic change. He never had to reinvent the wheel. Later in his career he did start throwing a back-door cutter to left-handed hitters and he threw to both sides of the plate a little more than early in his career.

If I was a switch-hitter I would have hit right-handed against him instead of left-handed. In my opinion, he would be easier to hit right-handed than left. He was so dominant coming inside to a left-handed hitter. If I was to ever manage, I would not pinch-hit a left-handed hitter against Mariano.

When the game is on the line, he never faltered. He had the ability to dominate at the highest level consistently throughout his career. The title he's been given is one well deserved. He was a master at his craft.

Paul O'Neill
Outfield

Playing Career
Cincinnati Reds and New York Yankees from 1985 to 2001

Career Statistics
2,053 games, 2,105 hits, 281 home runs, 1,269 runs batted in, .288 batting average, .363 on-base percentage, .470 slugging percentage

Mo Cred
O'Neill teamed with Rivera to win four World Series championships with the Yankees in 1996, 1998, 1999, and 2000.

HE CAME UP as a starter [in 1995] and he threw the ball pretty well. All of a sudden he made the transition into setting up for

John Wetteland. As a player out on the field, you were actually more comfortable when Mariano was in there [pitching] than you were Wetteland, because Wetteland would work out of a mess, whereas you'd have an easy seventh and eighth inning with Mariano. It's hard to say you expect to see someone become the greatest at his craft, but you saw it coming, you saw he was special.

I do agree he was [the most valuable player of our successful Yankees teams]. If you look at how [manager] Joe Torre used him in the midst of those World Series championship years, bringing him in for the eighth and ninth innings, that shows how important it is to have a good closer in big games, because so many of those games end up close. He's won so many games for us, so I don't think [calling him our most valuable player] is slighting anybody else.

I took a couple of swings off him in spring training once and it was a horror story for me as a left-handed batter. I took a couple of swings, got jammed, and walked out of the [batting] cage. I was at the point in my career when I didn't need to frustrate myself in early March. He threw the cutter inside to all left-handers. He fooled around with back-door pitches and then he learned a two-seam fastball when he needed something to get Edgar Martinez out. Basically, he threw one pitch his whole career and that pitch has been thrown by other people but never mastered the way Mariano has.

Humble is a good word [to describe him] and it's a great tribute to him. He really has not changed in all the years I've known him. He's a very good teammate, he loves to win, and he's very determined. A lot of times people misrepresent what intensity is. He's one of the most intense competitors you'll ever see, but he didn't show up people. He [competed] in such a mild-mannered way that he made it look easy, and believe me, those last five or six outs in a World Series game are anything but easy.

Jay Payton

Outfield

Playing Career

New York Mets, Colorado Rockies, San Diego Padres, Boston Red Sox, Oakland Athletics, and Baltimore Orioles from 1998 to 2010

Career Statistics

1,259 games, 1,157 hits, 119 home runs, 522 runs batted in, .279 batting average, .323 on-base percentage, .425 slugging percentage

Jay Payton facing Mariano Rivera (regular season)
2-for-12, 1 extra-base hit, 3 runs batted in, 1 walk, 2 strikeouts, .167 batting average, .231 on-base percentage, .333 slugging percentage

Mo Cred

Payton is the only player to hit a World Series home run off Rivera. The blast occurred in the ninth inning of Game Two of the 2000 Series.

Jay Payton

Year	Date	Result
2000	7/7	Fly out
	7/8	Strikeout (Swinging)
	7/8	Reached on error
Postseason	10/21	Fly out
	10/22	Home run (3 RBI)
	10/25	Fly out
2001	7/7	Ground out
2006	6/9	Double play
2007	6/28	Fielder's choice
	9/28	Triple (3 RBI)
2008	4/20	Single
	5/27	Walk
	7/29	Line out
	8/22	Ground out
	8/24	Strikeout (Looking)
	9/21	Ground out

WE WERE DOWN 6-2 when I hit a three-run home run off Rivera to put us within one run. It's the most memorable highlight of my career. It would've been better had I hit a five-run home run to give us the lead and we go on to win the game. Kurt Abbott came up after me and Mariano struck him out [looking] to finish the game. That could have been a big win for us. Losing Game One was tough, when Timo Perez didn't run [hard and was thrown out at home plate] on Todd Zeile's [double]. To me, that made a huge difference in the series. Had we been able to win that game, and even come back to [win] Game Two we might have been able to turn things around.[*]

That World Series game [when I hit the homer] was the game of the Roger Clemens-Mike Piazza [incident]. The whole New York vs. New York atmosphere gave [the series] all the fuel and fire that it needed, but the history between those guys added to it. The atmosphere [in the ballpark] was unbelievable. It seemed like every celebrity from New York came to those [World Series] games. Everybody who was anybody was there, from P. Diddy [Sean Combs] to J.Lo [Jennifer Lopez]. They came to watch us play, but we were sitting in the dugout looking into the stands and pointing out all the celebrities. Later on, I told Mike that I wished he'd [have] thrown some punches at Clemens. [The Mets] might've been better off with a rumble and Mike getting tossed out of the game along with Clemens, who went on to be dominating [that night]. I would've taken our chances losing Mike, if Clemens got tossed, too; [so] we could've gotten into their bullpen.[**]

I was a rookie in 2000. I had played a little in 1998 and '99, but 2000 was my first full season in the big leagues, so I was classified as a rookie. I was a highball hitter; I liked pitches up and away and that's the way [Rivera] pitched me. He didn't know me, there wasn't a scouting report on me yet, so when he threw me a cutter up and away, right where I liked it, he played right into my hands. I let the ball get deep and I hit

---

[*]Game One of the first Subway Series since 1956 was scoreless when Perez singled in the top of sixth inning off Andy Pettitte. With two outs, Zeile hit a ball inches shy of being a home run, but the ball bounced off the top of the left-field wall and back onto the playing field. Perez thought the ball was a home run and slowed down enough on his way around second base that he was thrown out at home plate. The Yankees went on to win the game in twelve innings and ultimately took the series in five games.

[**]In the top of the first inning, Clemens fired the barrel of Piazza's broken bat in the direction of the Mets' catcher. The incident aroused heated public debate in light of Clemens' beaning of Piazza in July. Clemens, who was not ejected, went on to pitch eight shutout innings, allowing just two hits, before the Mets rallied for five runs in the ninth, but fell a run short and lost, 6-5.

it just right. I didn't think it was gone right away off the bat. I didn't hit a ton of home runs in my career to know that feeling! But I was able to get enough of the good part of the bat on the ball to have it go over the wall in right field. The short porch at Yankee Stadium definitely helped me out.

Being in that situation is something you think about your whole life. As a kid you play pick-up games in your backyard against your buddies, and you imagine it's the ninth inning of the World Series and the game is on the line. You dream about that [situation] but you don't think it will ever really happen. It was a surreal moment. I got to live out a real-life dream. The home run is something you don't think about at the time, but now that I'm a bit older and get a chance to reflect [on my career], I never had a moment quite as big as that one. Had we won the game it would have been a much bigger moment.

It's an honor to get an opportunity to play in the World Series, and to hit a home run in the World Series is not something everyone gets to say they did. It's a special moment, and on top of that, to hit a home run in the World Series off Mariano Rivera, who has a gazillion saves, and is quite possibly the best closer to ever put on a uniform in the history of baseball, well, that is special. I know I'm on a short list of players who have hit a postseason home run off Mariano. There are only two people on that list—Alomar and me.[*]

I dealt with so many injuries and went through so much emotionally just to get to the big leagues—two Tommy John [elbow] surgeries, two shoulder surgeries—that I wouldn't let the pressure of the moment phase me. I didn't think about where I was, or worry about being overwhelmed by playing in the World Series. I had confidence in myself. No, I have not seen a replay of the homer yet. My mom has everything on video. She's transferring everything from VCR to DVD, and one day, I'll watch the old films. That's one game, even

---

[*]Sandy Alomar Jr. hit a game-tying home run off Rivera in the eighth inning in Game Four of the 1997 American League Division Series; Cleveland won the game and the series in five games. This was Rivera's only blown save in the playoffs until 2001.

though it's a special moment, I haven't looked back and revisited yet. When I do watch it, I'm sure something in my mind will click and I'll realize what I did was special.

I know I didn't have great numbers against Rivera. There are two hits that I remember, so at least I have two positive at-bats on my side! The only other big hit I got off him was when I was with Baltimore. He came in to close out a game, and I hit a bases-clearing triple to tie the score. We went on to win that game, and that helped Boston clinch the pennant that year.[*]

Alex Rios
Right field

Playing Career
Toronto Blue Jays, Chicago White Sox, and Texas Rangers since 2004

Career Statistics
1,455 games, 1,542 hits, 161 home runs, 708 runs batted in, .278 batting average, .324 on-base percentage, .443 slugging percentage

Alex Rios facing Mariano Rivera (regular season)
0-for-16, 4 strikeouts

Mo Cred
Rios has the most at-bats without a hit against Rivera among all active players.

---

[*]Payton's bases-loaded, two-out triple off Rivera tied the game in the ninth inning, and Melvin Mora dropped down an RBI bunt single in the tenth as Baltimore eliminated the Yankees from the postseason for the first time in ten years with a stunning 10-9 comeback win at Camden Yards, on September 28, 2007.

Alex Rios

Year	Date	Result
2004	7/26	Ground out
	8/28	Ground out
	9/21	Fielder's choice
2005	4/21	Ground out
	8/5	Fly out
2006	4/30	Ground out
	9/30	Fly out
2007	7/18	Strikeout (Swinging)
	8/6	Strikeout (Swinging)
2008	8/29	Strikeout (Swinging)
2009	7/3	Strikeout (Swinging)
	8/4	Ground out
	8/28	Pop out
2011	4/27	Fly out
	8/1	Ground out
2013	8/7	Foul out

YES, IT WOULD be nice [to get a hit off Rivera.] It would be very nice. If I get it—and I will get it—I'm going to ask to keep the ball! Unfortunately, I haven't gotten a hit yet. But just facing him is something you should be happy for. I'm glad that I faced him, just so I could say I faced one of the best pitchers ever. He's the greatest. What he's accomplished in this game is unbelievable. I've never had a conversation with him, but I'd like to get to know him better. From what I've heard he's a great man, and a very humble guy. I really admire him for being humble. A lot of people appreciate how he goes about his business. He could be a flashy guy, but he's not. He goes about his business the right way. He does his job, and people appreciate that.

Dave Roberts

Outfield

Playing Career

Cleveland Indians, Los Angeles Dodgers, Boston Red Sox, San Diego Padres, San Francisco Giants from 1999 to 2008

Career Statistics

832 games, 721 hits, 23 home runs, 213 runs batted in, .266 batting average, .343 on-base percentage, .366 slugging percentage

Dave Roberts facing Mariano Rivera (regular season)
0-for-1

Mo Cred

The Yankees led 4-3 in Game Four of the 2004 American League Cham-
pionship Series, and were three outs away from sweeping the Red Sox in
the bottom of the ninth inning in Fenway Park when Kevin Millar drew
a leadoff walk against Rivera, who had worked a scoreless eighth. Boston
manager Terry Francona sent Dave Roberts into the game as a pinch run-
ner. Roberts promptly stole second base, and scored the game-tying run on
Bill Mueller's single. The Sox won 6-4 in 12 innings, and won the next
three games en route to becoming the first major league team to rally from
a 3-0 deficit to win a seven-game series. Then they won the franchise's first
World Series in 86 years.

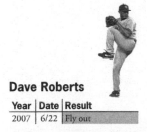

YOU JUST KNEW the game was over
[when Rivera entered]. That was the one
guy in a Yankee uniform you didn't want to
see. Because if you saw him, you knew the
game was over. What he means to the Yankees
and major league baseball—he's a guy who, to

Dave Roberts

Year	Date	Result
2007	6/22	Fly out

a man, commands the most amount of respect. He's done it right. So
for me to have the opportunity to compete against him, it's something
that I cherish.

First and foremost, it's a credit to Mariano being so dominant that
we had to go outside the box and couldn't play it straight as far as a
sacrifice bunt to try to get two hits with one out. We had to go outside
the box and maybe get one hit.

As far as scouting him and looking at tendencies, I just had had a
sequence against him in Yankee Stadium in September where Jorge
Posada went out to the mound and had a meeting with Mariano,
and I felt he told him to hold the ball against me and then go to the
plate. And so I felt, if I ever got a chance to be in the same situation,
his defense against me would be to hold the ball and then quicken

up. So, basically, when I got out there, I tried to calm my nerves as much as possible and wait him out. And so, as he came set, I just knew that after the three throw-overs, just wait him out. And he held and he held, and it felt like an eternity. I stayed relaxed and got a great jump.

A few years later, we did a commercial together for a Macy's [department store] in Miami. It was me, him, Brandon Phillips, and Dan Uggla. It was a Father's Day ad. I was with the Giants then. He's just a pro. He said, "Hey, it's great seeing you, and congratulations again." That's him.

Tim Salmon
Right field

Playing Career
California/Anaheim Angels from 1992 to 2006

Career Statistics
1,672 games, 1,674 hits, 299 home runs, 1,016 runs batted in, .282 batting average, .385 on-base percentage, .498 slugging percentage

Tim Salmon facing Mariano Rivera (regular season)
2-for-14, 1 extra-base hit, 1 walk, 5 strikeouts, .143 batting average, .200 on-base percentage, .214 slugging percentage

Mo Cred
Salmon was the first player ever to get a hit off Rivera.

I KNOW I GOT the first hit against Mariano Rivera. At the time, I really didn't think much of it. He was just another young starting

Tim Salmon

Year	Date	Result
1995	5/23	Single
	5/23	Double
	5/23	Walk
1996	5/18	Fly out
1997	4/8	Strikeout (Swinging)
	4/15	Strikeout (Looking)
	8/21	Strikeout (Swinging)
1998	7/30	Fly out
	8/26	Ground out
2000	4/3	Fly out
	4/4	Fly out
	8/18	Strikeout (Looking)
2001	8/4	Strikeout (Swinging)
	8/26	Fly out
2002 (Postseason)	10/1	Fly out
2006	4/9	Pop out

pitcher. I faced more intimidating pitchers with power who throw hard and you don't see the ball well. But it was comfortable to hit off him, because he wasn't doing anything special. I singled and doubled, and my walk knocked him out of the game. Then the next time I saw him, he was coming out of the bullpen and he was a completely different pitcher. Everyone said, "Remember him as a starter?"

And I said, "No, I don't."

He seemed like two different guys. That was baffling.[*]

Facing him as a starter wasn't nearly as intimidating as facing him as a reliever. As a reliever he was ridiculously filthy. To his advantage, you might face him once or twice a season, so you don't get a good read on his ball. His fastball was lively. The ball jumped out of his hand, sinking and darting. It got on you so quick, and with a cutting action. I swung at the ball anticipating making contact and I would consistently swing and miss. It always surprised me. It was frustrating, like I had a hole in my bat. He was very deceptive, like a magician. To his credit, he transformed into something completely different. I hit him as a caterpillar, but as a butterfly he was untouchable. I never even squared up another ball against him. Any good

---

[*]Salmon was the first player to get a hit off Rivera. It happened in the first inning of Rivera's major league debut, as a starting pitcher against the California Angels at Anaheim Stadium, on May 23, 1995. Salmon singled in the first inning, doubled in the third and walked in the fourth to knock Rivera out of the game, which was a 10-0 Yankees' loss.

Salmon faced Rivera thirteen more times after Rivera's debut. He never reached base again. The next time Rivera faced the Angels was one year later, on May 17, 1996, when he closed out an 8-5 Yankees' win for the first save of his career.

swing was a foul tip or maybe off the end of the bat. I thought I was a good hitter, against everybody else.[*]

When your team has the lead in the ninth inning and then loses it, the repercussions stay with you for a few games. You don't feel secure. When you have a closer like Mariano Rivera, it's no secret; it's an eight-inning game. You had to get to the pitchers before him. When he comes in, you can light the cigar and call it a day. Without a doubt, he's the biggest reason [the Yankees] were the great team they were. They knew Mariano could close the door every night.

A lot of closers grunt and snort and spit, they scowl at you, and throw the ball under your chin, trying to intimidate you, which makes you want to bear down and beat them all the more. Mariano was never like that on the mound. He was pleasant; his demeanor was disarming, it was like facing an old friend. I think that works to his advantage. Hitters don't have that extra motivation you might have against guys you despise who are flaunting their stuff and pointing to the sky and talking trash. Mariano was never about that; he's the complete opposite. He's very well respected because he goes out there and he beats you, and then he shakes hands and walks off the field.

Mike Simms
Right field

Playing Career
Houston Astros and Texas Rangers from 1990 to 1999

---

[*]The 1993 American League's rookie of the year, Salmon is the Angels' all-time leader in home runs (299) and walks (970) and second in hits (1,674), runs batted in (1,016), on-base percentage, and slugging percentage. He was also a member of the Angels' 2002 World Series championship team.

Career Statistics

330 games, 163 hits, 36 home runs, 121 runs batted in, .247 batting average, .323 on-base percentage, .464 slugging percentage

Mike Simms facing Mariano Rivera (regular season)

1-for-3, 1 home run, 1 run batted in, 1 strikeout, .333 batting average, .333 on-base percentage, 1.333 slugging percentage

Mo Cred

Simms hit a solo home run off Rivera on August 14, 1998, the twentieth homer allowed by Rivera.

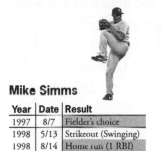

Mike Simms

Year	Date	Result
1997	8/7	Fielder's choice
1998	5/13	Strikeout (Swinging)
1998	8/14	Home run (1 RBI)

FAINTLY REMEMBER IT. I'm kidding! It's most definitely a highlight for me. It was 1998, the Yankees were going to the World Series and I do remember it was a big deal. Any time you're facing the premier closer it was a big deal in the sense that you look forward to the challenge of facing the best in a big situation. It was the top of the ninth inning, and being a part-time player, a right-handed hitter, not facing too many right-handers, it was unusual for me to get that chance to face Mariano, but I'm glad I did on that occasion.[*]

I talked to Will Clark and Rusty Greer—and in particular Mark McLemore—about what is was like facing him.[**] Those were my go-to

---

[*]Simms hit a one-two pitch from Rivera over the center field fence in the ninth inning of a Yankees' 6-4 win over the Rangers at Yankee Stadium, on August 14, 1998. Andy Pettitte got the win. Rivera has saved 72 wins for Pettitte, a record for any closer/starter combination.

[**]Clark was 2-for-9 facing Rivera with the San Francisco Giants, Texas Rangers, Baltimore Orioles, and St. Louis Cardinals from 1986 to 2000. Greer was 4-for-15 facing Rivera with the Texas Rangers from 1994 to 2002. McLemore was 5-for-19 facing Rivera with the Anaheim Angels, Cleveland Indians, Houston Astros, Baltimore Orioles, Texas Rangers, Seattle Mariners, and Oakland Athletics from 1986 to 2004.

guys because of their experience in the league, facing so many pitchers, so I went to them to gather information. They said he throws a cutter 95 miles per hour, so be ready to go, and look out over the plate. The pitch before [the home run], he threw a cutter that was up and in. A pitch that is 95 miles per hour and is coming up and in will wake you up right away. I remember leaning back, getting out of the box, and thinking: "Alright, here we go."

I got back in there, and on the next pitch, which he left up and out over the plate, where I was looking, I hit it out to dead center field.

It's cool to be on the list as one of the guys who have hit a homer off him. When you think about how many games he's pitched in, how many innings he's pitched, and how many outs he's gotten in his career, I'm sure those numbers are mind-blowing. I'm in a unique category, to be one of only [67] to homer off him. I was one for three against him in my career, with a home run and a strikeout. That's a good day! It's also a very low range on the cardio scale. You're either walking back to the dugout or jogging around the bases.

Everybody saw the way [baseball] honored him at the [2013] All-Star Game. I was watching on television with my two daughters, and when my oldest daughter saw the situation [in which] Mariano was the only one on the field warming up, she asked me why they were doing that for him. I said because Mariano is the greatest closer ever. You use that term—the greatest—with Mariano. It would be the equivalent of being alive and watching Babe Ruth for the final time. You can argue back and forth about numbers and production, but I don't think anyone's ever going to get more saves than Mariano's 600-plus saves, so you can state as fact that he's the greatest ever.

Matt Stairs

Outfield

Playing Career

Montreal Expos/Washington Nationals, Boston Red Sox, Oakland Athletics, Chicago Cubs, Milwaukee Brewers, Pittsburgh Pirates, Kansas City Royals, Texas Rangers, Detroit Tigers, Toronto Blue Jays, Philadelphia Phillies, and San Diego Padres from 1992 to 2011

Career Statistics

1,895 games, 1,366 hits, 265 home runs, 899 runs batted in, .262 batting average, .356 on-base percentage, .477 slugging percentage

Matt Stairs facing Mariano Rivera (regular season)

2-for-14, 0 extra-base hits, 4 strikeouts, 0 walks, .143 batting average, .143 on-base percentage, .143 slugging percentage

Mo Cred

Stairs smashed a record 23 pinch-hit home runs while playing for more franchises (12) than any other position player in major league history.

FACING THE GREATEST closer ever in the World Series in Yankee Stadium was an honor. I played in Yankee Stadium so many times, and faced Rivera so many times throughout my career, it can overwhelm a young player, but I never was [fazed]. The World Series is different. When the bullpen door opens and the music "Enter Sandman" is playing and you see Mariano make that smooth jog in from left-center field, you do get caught up in the moment.

I was the designated hitter in Game Two [of the 2009 World Series]. I was watching his warm-ups and it seemed like his cut fastball was a little flat. Maybe he did that on purpose, because when I got up to bat, his cutter changed lanes. Instead of going across the plane, now it had

Matt Stairs

Year	Date	Result
1996	8/23	Line out
	9/2	Foul out
1997	4/5	Single
	4/13	Foul out
	7/29	Single
1999	4/6	Ground out
	8/30	Fly out
2000	5/30	Pop out
	5/31	Ground out
	8/27	Strikeout (Swinging)
Postseason	10/6	Pop out
2004	4/30	Strikeout (Swinging)
	5/2	Strikeout (Swinging)
2007	5/30	Ground out
2008	6/4	Strikeout (Looking)
2009 (Postseason)	10/29	Strikeout (Swinging)
	10/31	Ground out
	11/1	Ground out
	11/4	Line out

more of a downhill tilt. I came up with two outs in the ninth inning. He threw a couple of good cutters and stuck me out. I did what I always did—go up swinging, if I get a hit, great, if not, I'm going down swinging. Once again he got the best of me.[*]

In Game Six, I led off the ninth inning and hit a foul home run into the fifth deck. That was the most memorable at-bat I ever had against him. It was a three-and-one count and I was guessing that he would throw a fastball inside. He threw me a cutter inside and I got the head of the bat out, but he puts the ball in a spot where even if you hit it, you can't keep it fair. I didn't have success against Mariano, so that made me feel good about myself. The next pitch was a back-door cutter and I lined out to [Derek] Jeter at shortstop. It wasn't a base hit, but it was a non-broken bat and one of the few times against him when my fingers didn't hurt from getting jammed.

When I think about facing Mariano Rivera, two words come to mind: frustrating and challenging. When I played in Oakland, we joked about how ridiculous he can make [batters] look. I weigh 220 pounds and remember hitting jam-shots not even eight feet in the air. One hit barely made it to the outfield grass; it was a deep drive to shallow third base! All you can do is laugh. It isn't embarrassing because he's so dominating.

---

[*]Rivera picked up a two-inning save to give the Yankees a 3-1 victory over the Phillies in Game Two of the 2009 World Series. Matt Stairs struck out swinging on a two-and-two pitch to end the game with Raul Ibanez on second base as the tying run.

If I was more patient he might have walked me more. But when you're batting in a situation with the game on the line, you open up your strike zone. Cutters on the inner half that you should let go, you swing at, and the pitch ends up near your back thigh. His cutter can be devastating. I swung at one that ended up cutting between my legs. I've seen guys swing and miss and get hit in the stomach with the pitch. At least I never swung and missed at a pitch that hit me!

Ichiro Suzuki

Outfield

Playing Career

Seattle Mariners and New York Yankees since 2001

Career Statistics

2,061 games, 2,742 hits, 111 home runs, 695 runs batted in, .319 batting average, .361 on-base percentage, .414 slugging percentage

Ichiro Suzuki facing Mariano Rivera (regular season)

5-for-13, 1 extra-base hit, 1 home run, 2 runs batted in, 1 walk, 1 strikeout, .385 batting average, .429 on-base percentage, .615 slugging percentage

Mo Cred

Suzuki hit the fifth and final walk-off home run against Rivera on September 18, 2009 in Seattle. He also was Rivera's teammate on the Yankees in 2012 and 2013.

AS A VISITOR you come in here, and when I was playing against him, he was like the Devil. Like a guy that just would get you.

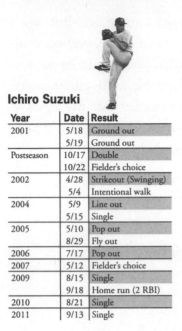

Ichiro Suzuki

Year	Date	Result
2001	5/18	Ground out
	5/19	Ground out
Postseason	10/17	Double
	10/22	Fielder's choice
2002	4/28	Strikeout (Swinging)
	5/4	Intentional walk
2004	5/9	Line out
	5/15	Single
2005	5/10	Pop out
	8/29	Fly out
2006	7/17	Pop out
2007	5/12	Fielder's choice
2009	8/15	Single
	9/18	Home run (2 RBI)
2010	8/21	Single
2011	9/13	Single

He'd have a nice smile and a soft face, but he was just that Devil when I was playing against him. But then when I came here, he became God because he's on our side.[*]

What comes to mind is when I hit a home run off him to win a game in Seattle [in 2009]. I'll never forget it. I wish I could have run the bases again. That home run, to me, is very special. It had an impact on me. Of course, you don't want to face him. But it was that much more gratifying because he's the best.[**]

Pitchers obviously try to throw to places where the batters will have a hard time hitting it; pitchers try to place balls where a hitter doesn't want it thrown. But Mariano would just throw to where you're waiting for the pitch—and you still can't hit it.

A batter has a spot that he wants the ball thrown to. That's where Mariano would throw it. So as a hitter, when you had that ball where you wanted it, and you miss it and make an out, usually, hitters want to make, not excuses, but reasons why you got out that at-bat. But with Mariano, he's so good that you can only just say, "He beat me."

You can't really have reasons why you got out. You just have to say, "He flat-out beat me."

---

[*]Suzuki faced Rivera in the 2001 American League Championship Series as a member of the Mariners and was 1-for-2. He doubled in Game One and grounded out in Game Five. The Yankees won the series in five games.

[**]Suzuki hit the first pitch he saw from Rivera deep over the right field fence for a two-run walk-off home run as the Mariners defeated the Yankees, 3-2, on September 18, 2009, in Seattle.

Nick Swisher

Right field and First base

Playing Career

Oakland Athletics, Chicago White Sox, New York Yankees, and Cleveland Indians since 2004

Career Statistics

1,354 games, 1,220 hits, 231 home runs, 736 runs batted in, .255 batting average, .358 on-base percentage, .462 slugging percentage

Nick Swisher facing Mariano Rivera (regular season)

1-for-5, 0 extra-base hits, 1 strikeout, .200 batting average, .200 on-base percentage, .200 slugging percentage

Mo Cred

Swisher spent four seasons as Rivera's teammate with the Yankees from 2009 to 2012; on September 19, 2011, the Yankee Stadium crowd cheered when he grounded into a double play with two runners on base to end the eighth inning with the Yankees holding a 6-4 lead over the Twins because it meant Rivera had an opportunity to set the all-time record with his 602nd save.

Nick Swisher

Year	Date	Result
2005	9/4	Fly out
2006	5/12	Double play
	6/9	Single
	6/11	Strikeout (Swinging)
2013	6/3	Fly out

I'M TRYING TO get a hit right there. I'm not trying to make an out. But what can I say? Greatest double play of my life! I've never been cheered for grounding into a double play at home, and then the next thing you know, I look up at the bullpen and I'm like, "Oh, that's right." It took me a quick second to figure out what was going on—but then it sunk in real fast.

It was a great day and I'm so happy that I could witness something like that. It was really exciting. He had his family there, he had his kids there—everyone was there. And for all of

135

the games [to achieve a record], it was a make-up game, the crowd was hyped, they were going crazy. It was such a wonderful day. He's gone about his job with such professionalism, and if people didn't believe that he was the best closer of all time, that 602 proves it.

The first time I faced him, I was like, "holy [cow], man, I'm in the box against Mariano Rivera and I'm [hopefully] hitting a missile right here." I think, in general, for someone to go that long in his career throwing one pitch, that's pretty impressive. He's a perfectionist. He knows what he's doing. He has a plan and knows exactly what he's doing every time he goes out there.

It doesn't matter if he's 22 [years old] or 42. It's kind of sad to see a guy going through his last season, but if you had to pick a career, that wouldn't be a bad one to pick. He's the best. His numbers kind of speak for themselves. He's been doing it for so long and he's done it the right way. Congratulations to him. It was an honor for me to play with him for four years and I wish him the best of luck.

B.J. Upton

Center field

Playing Career

Tampa Bay Rays and Atlanta Braves since 2004

Career Statistics

1,092 games, 982 hits, 127 home runs, 473 runs batted in, .248 batting average, .329 on-base percentage, .409 slugging percentage

B.J. Upton facing Mariano Rivera (regular season)
3-for-14, 0 extra-base hits, 1 run batted in, 10 strikeouts, .214 batting average, .214 on-base percentage, .214 slugging percentage

Mo Cred

Upton's 10 strikeouts in 14 plate appearances is the highest strikeout rate of anyone facing Rivera. Manny Ramirez has struck out the most times, 13, but in 44 plate appearances.

What's it like facing Mariano Rivera?

IT'S LIKE GOING to a gunfight with a knife. You know what's coming and you know he's most likely going to throw you a strike—and you still can't get him.

Why is it so difficult to put the ball in play when you know what pitch is coming?

I don't know. If I knew that answer I wouldn't have ten strikeouts in fourteen at-bats against him. You almost have to anticipate where the ball is going to be. You have to trick your eyes because your eyes tell you to swing in a place the ball won't end up. There is no one like him.

Do you remember having even one quality at-bat facing Rivera?

I don't recall any specific at-bats where I was successful. I'm really aggressive so I'm aggressive with everyone I face [and I] just tried to be the same with Rivera.

Was it fun to face one of the greatest pitchers of all time?

No. There was nothing fun about facing Mo. We saw him a lot [when I played for Tampa] and sometimes you just had to shake your head and laugh.

Did teammates give you advice on how to approach your at-bats against Rivera?

When no one has success against a guy no one really wants to talk about it. You just hoped you had the lead after eight [innings]. He's the best to ever do it and I'll miss watching him do his thing on television—but not in person.

Shane Victorino

Outfield

Playing Career

San Diego Padres, Philadelphia Phillies, Los Angeles Dodgers, Boston Red Sox since 2003

Career Statistics

1,198 games, 1,200 hits, 105 home runs, 470 runs batted in, .277 batting average, .342 on-base percentage, .432 slugging percentage

Shane Victorino facing Mariano Rivera (regular season)
0-for-3

Mo Cred

Victorino was 1-for-3 facing Rivera in the 2009 World Series. He singled in Game Two; grounded out for the final out of Game Four; and grounded out for the final out of the clinching Game Six.

Shane Victorino

Year	Date	Result
2006	6/20	Ground out
2009	5/24	Ground out
Postseason	10/29	Single
	11/1	Ground out
	11/4	Ground out
2013	8/18	Ground out

I MADE THE LAST out in the World Series against him in 2009. I remember him coming out [of the bullpen]. We knew what was on the line. It's special to think about getting the opportunity to face the best closer of all time in the biggest moment in the World Series.

Even though we ended up losing, it is special to be able to remember and rekindle those kinds of moments. Like I said, to face him in the biggest game and that's what you play for every year, even though we came up on the losing side, I'll never forget that opportunity.

I knew it was going to be a tough at-bat. We all know what he throws. You know you're going to get the cutter; you're going to get

138

that pitch. I remember it was a good at-bat—ten pitches. Unfortunately, I grounded out to second to end it.

I'm on the way to first base knowing what was on the line and watching them [celebrate]. I left it all on the field. Those kind of moments will be something I can think back on, how I got that opportunity to face him in a World Series.

Vernon Wells
Outfield

Playing Career

Toronto Blue Jays, Los Angeles Angels of Anaheim, and New York Yankees since 1999

Career Statistics

1,731 games, 1,794 hits, 270 home runs, 958 runs batted in, .270 batting average, .319 on-base percentage, .459 slugging percentage

Vernon Wells facing Mariano Rivera (regular season)

6-for-19, 3 extra-base hits, 1 home run, 3 runs batted in, 2 walks, 1 strikeout, .316 batting average, .381 on-base percentage, .632 slugging percentage

Mo Cred

Wells hit the first walk-off home run ever allowed by Rivera in extra innings, on July 20, 2006. He played with the Yankees as Rivera's teammate in 2013.

Vernon Wells

Year	Date	Result
2001	8/30	Walk
2002	4/19	Fly out
	5/20	Ground out
2003	7/11	Ground out
	7/13	Triple
2004	7/22	Ground out
	7/26	Ground out
	8/28	Ground out
2005	4/21	Single
	8/23	Ground out
	9/25	Walk
2006	7/20	Home run (1 RBI)
2007	5/30	Ground out
	7/18	Fly out
	8/6	Strikeout (Swinging)
	9/12	Ground out
2008	4/3	Single
	8/29	Single
2009	8/4	Double (2 RBI)
2010	6/6	Fly out
	9/28	Line out

I HAVE A FAVORITE personal memory. It isn't a good one [for Rivera]. It's my favorite, not his. I'm just one of a handful of guys to ever hit a walk-off home run against him [which I did in 2006]. That's a moment that I'll never forget. I'll always remember jogging around the bases when I hit it.[*]

Those are the kind of memories that will stick with you for a lifetime. I remember everything about it. Personally, it was one of the cooler moments I've ever experienced. Anytime you get a chance to face Mariano it's a memorable experience just because of who he is, what he stands for, and what he's been able to accomplish.

I had my approach going into that at-bat. It was to look for a cutter inside and convince myself to swing at it. I got to a 1-0 count and he threw the pitch I was looking for and I hit it. While the ball was in the air and I was approaching first base it was just a matter of whether it was going to get caught or go out. It landed over the fence and I remember just getting goose bumps, thinking: "I just hit a walk-off home run off the greatest closer of all time!"

Obviously it's a short list of guys who have been able to do that.[**]

I always held him in the highest regard playing against him. You remember watching him jog in at Yankee Stadium, with his music playing, and the fans know that as soon as that song starts playing, they know their closer is coming in, and far more often than not, the game

---

[*]Wells hit Rivera's second pitch over the left field fence in the bottom of the eleventh inning for a walk-off 5-4 victory for the Blue Jays at Rogers Centre, on July 20, 2006.

[**]Rivera has given up five walk-off home runs in his career: to Bill Selby, Bill Mueller, Wells, Marco Scutaro, and Ichiro Suzuki.

is over. It's much better now [as Rivera's teammate] when the music's playing at home—it's not necessarily a bad thing anymore. Now it's a good thing knowing he's coming in to close the door. I think a lot of people are going to miss hearing that music come on once we start getting into ninth innings after this year [2013].

Section Three: Catchers

Sal Fasano

Catcher

Playing Career

Kansas City Royals, Oakland Athletics, Colorado Rockies, Anaheim Angels, Baltimore Orioles, Philadelphia Phillies, New York Yankees, Toronto Blue Jays, Cleveland Indians from 1996 to 2008

Career Statistics

427 games, 245 hits, 47 home runs, 140 runs batted in, .221 batting average, .295 on-base percentage, .382 slugging percentage

Sal Fasano facing Mariano Rivera (regular season)
0-for-4, 2 strikeouts

Mo Cred

The New York Yankees catcher for 28 games in 2006 was behind the plate for 1 of Rivera's 652 career saves.

Sal Fasano

Year	Date	Result
1996	4/22	Fly out
1998	8/9	Strikeout (Swinging)
2000	5/30	Fly out
2006	6/20	Strikeout (Swinging)

OUT IN THE bullpen, we'd talk all the time. What a lot of people don't understand about Mariano is that he was very prepared and he communicated very well. He was a tremendous teammate. He really took an interest. If he knew that you were going to catch him, he would talk to you about what he wanted to do.

It was really fun diving into what his head was like and how he pitches. That's what makes him so unique. He never pitched to home plate. He pitched to the bodyline of the batter. If a left-handed hitter would back up, he wouldn't worry about throwing a strike. He would throw it in the same lane as if the batter was in a conventional position.

Versus lefties he was trying to get closer to the hands and versus righties he was trying to get away from the barrel, away from the hands, more to the extension side. So to a righty he was going more to the other side of the plate. But he could throw it in on them, too. He'd throw it inside and you'd think it was a ball and all of a sudden it moves back to the inside corner and you're frozen.

I've never seen him throw it straight. It's just the natural movement that he has. He could elevate it, he could make it move more, he could make it move less, he could sink it. He could throw to all nine quadrants and expand off the quadrants. He was special. He was an absolute pleasure to catch.

It was a special time in my life. I'll never forget it. It was fun because you just knew he was going to get the outs. I'm telling you, man, it was unbelievable.

Mo Respect

Francisco Cervelli

Cervelli was behind the plate for 34 of Rivera's 652 career saves.

I've faced him in spring training. I think it's better to catch him! I thank God I'm on his side, so I can catch Mariano, because he's not easy to hit.

John Flaherty

Catcher

Playing Career

Boston Red Sox, Detroit Tigers, San Diego Padres, Tampa Bay Rays, New York Yankees from 1992 to 2005

Career Statistics

1,047 games, 849 hits, 80 home runs, 395 runs batted in, .252 batting average, .290 on-base percentage, .377 slugging percentage

John Flaherty facing Mariano Rivera (regular season)

1-for-4, 1 extra-base hit, 1 run batted in, 1 strikeout, .250 batting average, .250 on-base percentage, .500 slugging percentage

Mo Cred

Flaherty was behind the plate for 32 of Rivera's 652 career saves.

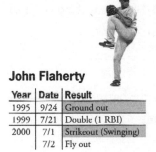

John Flaherty

Year	Date	Result
1995	9/24	Ground out
1999	7/21	Double (1 RBI)
2000	7/1	Strikeout (Swinging)
	7/2	Fly out

WITH MARIANO, IT was never the pitch—it was location. He doesn't shake off. He's very trusting of the catcher and what the catcher is feeling or seeing. That was always gratifying because you felt like when he picked up a save, you had something to do with it. Let's be honest, he can throw the ball wherever he wants and he is probably going to be successful. But from a catcher's standpoint, he makes you feel that you had something to do with it.

You almost have to fight against being overconfident or being too relaxed behind the plate. He lulls you to sleep, because you know the ball is going to be right where your glove is set up. The late life is something you have to be ready for, but I think because of his outstanding control, he was just so easy to catch.

The hitters know what pitch is coming; they just don't know where it's going to be. When a lefty takes a swing and pulls the ball foul, everybody in the ballpark is like, "Oh, he's all over the cutter." Mariano is like, "No, he can't do anything with it, so I'm going to keep [throwing] it."

Most closers I had been around didn't care about anything until the seventh inning, when they got their rhythm going. Mariano pays attention from the first pitch. He cares about the entire club, and who's playing the right way.

Darrin Fletcher

Catcher

Playing Career

Los Angeles Dodgers, Philadelphia Phillies, Montreal Expos, and Toronto Blue Jays from 1989 to 2002

Career Statistics

1,245 games, 1,048 hits, 124 home runs, 583 runs batted in, .269 batting average, .318 on-base percentage, .423 slugging percentage

Darrin Fletcher facing Mariano Rivera (regular season)
0-for-6, 3 strikeouts

Mo Cred

Fletcher struck out as an eighth-inning pinch hitter against Rivera to leave the bases loaded in a game the Yankees won, 3-2, over the Expos at Yankee Stadium on Don Mattingly Day, on August 31, 1997. Rivera earns his 40th save of the season, marking the first of a record nine times in which he will reach 40 or more saves in a season.

TO FACE HIS cut fastball is the toughest assignment in baseball to me. He throws it thigh high, inner half of the plate, where most left-handed hitters like the ball, and then it just keeps following you. You think it's over the inner half of the plate, and it just keeps coming at you. It's the best pitch in baseball.

We have this saying that a pitcher "gets in your kitchen." Rivera's cutter continually gets in your kitchen, and you cannot get it out. He almost kind of lulls you to sleep with his delivery. It gives you a false sense of security, and then the ball is on you and it's exploding.

The best way to approach him, I told myself every year, is to try to make sure the ball is in the outer half of the strike zone, and if it's not, then take it, and hope for a walk.

Darrin Fletcher

Year	Date	Result
1997	8/31	Strikeout (Swinging)
1998	7/18	Fly out
2000	9/13	Strikeout (Swinging)
2001	4/19	Strikeout (Looking)
	9/5	Pop out
2002	7/16	Ground out

Todd Greene

Catcher

Playing Career

Anaheim Angels, Toronto Blue Jays, New York Yankees, Texas Rangers, Colorado Rockies, and San Francisco Giants from 1996 to 2006

Career Statistics

536 games, 397 hits, 71 home runs, 217 runs batted in, .252 batting average, .286 on-base percentage, .444 slugging percentage

Todd Greene facing Mariano Rivera (regular season)
2-for-4, 1 extra-base hit, .500 batting average, .750 on-base percentage, .750 slugging percentage

Mo Cred

Greene spent one season with the Yankees as Rivera's teammate in 2001 and was the catcher for five of Rivera's saves, including career save No. 200.

Todd Greene

Year	Date	Result
1998	8/26	Double
1999	6/18	Foul out
2003	8/7	Fly out
2004	6/9	Single

I CAUGHT MARIANO RIVERA'S 200th save. When Mariano was going into the game, I didn't know it was going to be his 200th save. Afterward, [Yankees' owner] George Steinbrenner sent a bottle of champagne to the clubhouse to congratulate Mo. It was the good stuff—Dom Perignon—George wasn't going to send the cheap stuff. Since Mo didn't drink, he gave that bottle of champagne to me. I took it home and I still have it. I only played with Mo that one year; so for him to share that special moment with me, that was a big deal. The most amazing thing about Mo is that he's a way better person than he is a baseball player. He's a solid individual, a great human being, and someone that I was glad to share a year with.[*]

He might be the most intense competitor I ever played with. He'd rather bite off his finger than blow a save. It wasn't visually noticeable to spectators or even to some of his teammates. When he's on the mound, you look in his eyes, and you know this guy is ready to get your ass out. One of the cool things about being a catcher was that you could look into the pitchers' eyes, and you could see who was scared and who was not, and who was a gamer and who was not. Mo was as intense as anybody I've ever been on the field with.

I remember how well he handled the loss after Game Seven of the 2001 World Series. There were guys who were very upset; but Mo didn't shy away from the reporters, he didn't shy away from the moment. He answered all the questions with grace and dignity. That's probably not a shock to anybody. Sometimes in baseball the villains aren't quite the villains they're made out to be in the media, and the good guys aren't always quite as good as they're made out to

---

[*]Rivera recorded his 200th career save with a six-out performance against the Texas Rangers to protect a 9-7 victory at Yankee Stadium, on August 1, 2001.

be, either. But that's not true with Mo. He's a class individual. To see him have the same manner in accepting defeat as he accepts success was impressive.*

The most surprising [aspect] about that game wasn't the blown save. It was Mariano making a bad throw on the bunt. Mo was the best defensive pitcher I ever played with, and I played with Kenny Rogers, who won [five] Gold Gloves. Mariano was an incredible defender, so for him to throw the ball away was extremely unchar-acteristic. The next play was another bunt—Jay Bell bunted the ball back to him—and he had the wherewithal to throw the ball to third base for the out. You have to give credit on Mo's behalf; he had just thrown the ball away, but then at the very next opportunity he still has the ability to make a great play.

The final out of his 200th save was a two-seamer [to retire Ivan Rodriguez on a ground out to second base]. I probably called for more two-seam fastballs than any other catcher that worked with Mo. He obviously throws a great cutter, but his two-seamer is nasty, too. Early on, he didn't use the two-seamer very much because he didn't need it. I felt it was so good that it was crazy not to use it. I liked to use all the pitches. That was around the time when some teams started to pinch-hit for left-handed batters with their righties. I felt that throwing a two-seamer that comes in on the hands of the righties might elimi-nate some of that pinch-hitting and we would get the match-ups we wanted anyway, which was with the lefties. But Mo threw the pitches he wanted to throw. If he didn't want to throw a [two-seam fastball], he would shake you off and throw a cutter.

----

*Two months removed from the terrorist attacks on the World Trade Center, and just miles away from Ground Zero, Greene caught the ceremonial pitch thrown by President George W. Bush prior to Game Three of the 2001 World Series at Yankee Stadium, on October 30, 2001. It was only the second time a sitting president had thrown out the first pitch in the World Series.

Batting against him, I remember hitting a ball off the right-center field wall off of him in 1998 with the Angels. I could hit a fastball as good as anybody, and Mariano back then was still throwing 95 to 97 miles an hour with that cutter. It's nice to have good numbers against him; I'll take it, though in limited at-bats. I wish I had a lot more at-bats against him.[*]

Jesse Levis
Catcher

Playing Career

Cleveland Indians and Milwaukee Brewers from 1992 to 2001

Career Statistics

319 games, 167 hits, 3 home runs, 60 runs batted in, .255 batting average, .336 on-base percentage, .307 slugging percentage

Jesse Levis facing Mariano Rivera (regular season)

1-for-5, 0 extra-base hits, 1 walk, 1 strikeout, .200 batting average, .333 on-base percentage, .200 slugging percentage

Mo Cred

Levis faced Rivera as a starting pitcher in the minor leagues and as both a starter and reliever in the majors.

I FIRST FACED MARIANO in 1994, when we were minor leaguers in Triple A. He was a starting pitcher for Columbus and I was

---

[*]Greene wins a seven-pitch at-bat against Rivera by doubling off the right-center field wall during a two-run eighth inning in the second game of a doubleheader at Yankee Stadium, on August 26, 1998. Rivera blew the save in the ninth inning but got credit for the 7-6 Yankees win after Derek Jeter's walk-off single.

with Charlotte. He had an electric fastball, with late life. When the ball got about ten feet from the hitter it almost seemed to pick up speed. I think he walked me and struck me out in our Triple A confrontations.[*]

Jesse Levis

Year	Date	Result
1996	7/4	Ground out
	7/6	Single
	7/20	Walk
	9/25	Ground out
1997	6/6	Ground out
	6/8	Strikeout (Swinging)

My first meeting against Mariano as a major leaguer was with the Brewers in Yankee Stadium in 1996. Mariano had just started throwing a nasty cutter. Roy Halladay perfected a cutter early in his career, but back in the mid-to-late 1990s, Mariano was one of the few guys throwing that pitch. His cutter was like no other that I've ever seen. The velocity was 95 miles per hour and just as you start your swing then—oops—the ball moves six or eight inches on your hands.[**]

He pretty much got into your head as a left-handed hitter because if he locates the pitch properly, like he always did, he could saw off your bat. That's why switch hitters have [batted] against him hitting right-handed. I remember [Indians teammate] Carlos Baerga doing that. He may have gone up there right handed because the cutter was so filthy he didn't want to break his fingers on a jam job.[***]

[*]Levis played 111 games for the Charlotte Knights, the Triple A affiliate of the Cleveland Indians' organization, in 1994. He batted .285 with 10 home runs and 59 RBIs.

Rivera started 22 minor league games and posted a 10-2 record at three levels in the Yankees organization in 1994. He was 3-0 at Tampa (Single A), 3-0 at Albany (Double A) and 4-2 at Columbus (Triple A).

[**]Levis grounded out to shortstop on a 3-2 pitch from Rivera in the top of the eighth inning of a Yankees 4-1 win in Yankee Stadium, on July 4, 1996.

[***]Carlos Baerga was the first switch-hitter in major league baseball history to hit home runs from both sides of the plate in the same inning. Baerga accomplished the feat in the seventh inning of a game against the New York Yankees at Cleveland's Municipal Stadium, batting right-handed against Steve Howe and left-handed against Steve Farr, on April 8, 1993. Mark Bellhorn became the second player to do so in 2002, and Kendrys Morales did it in 2012.

I remember getting a pinch-hit single to left field off Mariano. He left a pitch out over the plate and I lined it into left, a very big base hit for me as a pinch hitter.[*] After that single, I didn't get another hit off him. I worked a walk off him one time late in a game. I remember that walk because it was a real tough at-bat. I battled him and fought off pitches. I got to a three-and-two count and he threw a cutter really too close to take. I was fortunate that the umpire called it a ball.[**]

When I was with the Indians in 1999, I got to play with Roberto Alomar, one of the most talented and smartest players I ever played with.[***] He told me to back off the plate and see if Mariano would go back door, to throw the ball toward the outer half of the plate. So I took Robby's advice and made that adjustment. Sure enough, Mariano threw back-door cutters, which are easier to hit on the barrel of the bat. I grounded out, and I didn't face him again after that.

I absolutely loved the challenge of facing the greatest pitchers in the game. Whether it's Roger Clemens, Randy Johnson, or Mariano Rivera, you always hope to give them a great battle. Maybe it wasn't a battle for them, but it sure was for me! Even though they might have gotten me out, it was quite a thrill and something you dream about as a little kid.

---

[*]Levis stroked a pinch-hit line-drive single to left field on a one-and-one count from Rivera in the top of the eighth inning of a Yankees 2-0 win in Yankee Stadium, on July 6, 1996.

[**]Levis drew a walk against Rivera in the bottom of the seventh inning of a Yankees 4-2 win in Milwaukee's Country Stadium, on July 20, 1996.

[***]Roberto Alomar was inducted into the Baseball Hall of Fame in 2011. (See Alomar entry in infielders' section.)

Russell Martin

Catcher

Playing Career

Los Angeles Dodgers, New York Yankees, and Pittsburgh Pirates since 2006

Career Statistics

1,052 games, 925 hits, 108 home runs, 473 runs batted in, .255 batting average, .349 on-base percentage, .396 slugging percentage

Russell Martin facing Mariano Rivera (regular season)
0-for-1, 1 strikeout

Mo Cred

Martin spent two seasons with the Yankees as Rivera's teammate in 2011 and 2012 and was the catcher for 37 of Rivera's 652 saves, including the record-setting 602nd save.

CATCHING MARIANO FOR that [record-setting 602nd] save was definitely a very special day for me. Especially to get the last out on a strikeout like that—on a perfect pitch—we're probably going to be watching that replay for a very long time.*

---

*Minnesota's Chris Parmelee took a fastball for strike three to end the game and wrap up the record-setting 602nd save in the Yankees' 6-4 win over the Twins at Yankee Stadium, on September 19, 2011. Rivera embraced catcher Martin and was met by the rest of his teammates in front of the mound. After some prodding from Jorge Posada, Rivera stayed on the field for a few minutes to soak in his accomplishment. He stood on the mound and tipped his cap as cheers rained down from the Bronx crowd.

"For the first time in my career, I'm on the mound alone, there is no one behind me," said Rivera. "I can't describe that feeling. It was priceless. I didn't know it could be like that. It was a feeling like that when we won the World Series. I'll give you that, that emotion."

Russell Martin

Year	Date	Result
2010	6/27	Strikeout (Looking)

That many saves is incredible. He deserves it. He's one of the hardest-working guys I've ever seen and he's been doing it at a high level for a long time. When you see a guy that works that hard and is that prepared, you expect him to go out there and do what he's supposed to do. Mo does it consistently every time he goes out.

It's funny, because on his 600th save I didn't even realize it, until everyone started hugging him and giving him high fives. He probably wishes I didn't throw out [Seattle's Ichiro Suzuki trying to steal second base], so he could get a punch out. We got the win, first and foremost, and he got the 600th save, which is a nice round number.[*]

His focus level is amazing. He never really comes out of his game. He never loses focus. He keeps his composure at all times. That's what amazes me the most about him. How he can stay composed and make pitches, pitch after pitch after pitch. Because he's a closer, it's always a tight situation, it's always pressure filled, but it's really easy to catch him because of his command.

My first time catching him was in spring training [in 2011]. We never did a bullpen [session], so the first time catching him was during a game situation, even though it was spring training. He's awesome the way he can hit his spots [on] both sides of the plate. He has pinpoint control. You don't move your glove much at all. It was a pleasure catching him.

He has good life on the cutter. It has very late movement. Once the hitter starts to swing, that's when it starts moving. That's the best cutter I've ever caught. Normally, you see some sort of spin on the ball. With his, you don't see the spin, there's no sidespin. It just cuts. I don't know how he does it.

---

[*]Rivera joined Trevor Hoffman as the only closers to earn 600 saves, pitching a scoreless ninth inning to preserve the Yankees' 3-2 win over the Mariners at Seattle's Safeco Field, on September 14, 2011. The final out was recorded when Martin threw out Ichiro attempting to steal second base.

He has command on both sides of the plate. He starts it in off the plate against the righty, and it ends up on the corner. It feels like you've got to swing at a ball that is going to hit your front knee and the next thing you know, it's on the corner. For a lefty, it's a challenge to keep the ball fair. When he's on and hitting his spots, you're not going to do much damage against him.

It's better being back behind the plate than being in the [batter's] box against him. But I got a hit off him in the [2008] All-Star Game.*

Chad Moeller
Catcher

Playing Career

Minnesota Twins, Arizona Diamondbacks, Milwaukee Brewers, Cincinnati Reds, Los Angeles Dodgers, New York Yankees, and Baltimore Orioles from 2000 to 2010

Career Statistics

501 games, 315 hits, 29 home runs, 132 runs batted in, .226 batting average, .388 on-base percentage, .352 slugging percentage

---

*Martin singled to right field facing Rivera during an eight-pitch at-bat in the top of the tenth inning of the 2008 All-Star Game, played at Yankee Stadium, on July 15, 2008. The American League defeated the National League, 4-3, in fifteen innings.

In his only regular season at-bat facing Rivera, Martin struck out looking on a three-two pitch in the bottom of the tenth inning of a Yankees' 8-6 victory at Dodger Stadium, on June 27, 2010.

Chad Moeller facing Mariano Rivera (regular season)
1-for-2, 0 extra-base hits, .500 batting average, .500 on-base percentage,
.500 slugging percentage

Mo Cred

Moeller, a back-up catcher for the Yankees in 2008, was behind the plate
for 5 of Rivera's 652 career saves.

Chad Moeller

Year	Date	Result
2000	7/30	Single
2009	5/20	Line out

EASIEST GUY I'VE ever caught. Plain and simple, the easiest guy I've ever caught. You know where the ball's going to be every time. And it's just amazing that everybody knows what's coming, and nobody's going to square it up. He's thrown the same pitch over and over and over, and nobody's done anything with it yet.

Facing him you're just picking a side [of home plate]. Not the pitch, you're just picking a side. He has a two-seam fastball, which he started using for right-handers a little bit, just when I think he really wanted to embarrass them.[*]

But he could always lock the right-handers up because he'd throw the ball right at them, and they'd jump out of the way and it was strike three. It'd come right in the front door.

---

[*]Moeller faced Rivera twice, ten years apart, both times in a non-save situation. He singled in his first at-bat as a member of the Twins in a 7-4 Yankees' win in Minnesota's Metrodome on July 30, 2000. He lined out in his second at-bat a member of the Baltimore Orioles in an 11-4 Yankees' win at home, on May 20, 2009.

Gustavo Molina

Catcher

Playing Career

Chicago White Sox, Baltimore Orioles, New York Mets, Boston Red Sox, and New York Yankees from 2007 to 2011

Career Statistics

26 games, 6 hits, 0 home runs, 1 run batted in, 2 runs, .128 batting average, .160 on-base percentage, .170 slugging percentage

Mo Cred

Molina, a back-up Yankees catcher in 2011, was behind the plate for 1 of Rivera's 652 career saves. Molina caught twelve pitches in the ninth inning of a 5-2 win over the Texas Rangers, on April 16, 2011. It was Rivera's 575th save.

I FEEL BLESSED [FOR] the chance to catch him. I've caught a lot of good pitchers, but he's the top one. He always said, "Give me a good target, a low target or a high target, and I'll hit it."*

He dominates the whole plate—in and out, up and down—with one pitch. He throws one pitch, a cutter. It's unbelievable. The batters know what's coming and they still can't hit it. It's impressive on both sides—catching him and facing him. Speed, power, and control on both sides of the plate.

The most amazing stuff I've ever caught. He's something special. You will never see [the likes of him] again. He's a machine.

[When the injury occurred] you knew he felt bad for his team and the organization about what happened. It's great to see he came back and is pitching so well.

---

*Molina appeared in three games and played a total of nineteen innings for the Yankees in 2011. He had six plate appearances and recorded one hit, a double.

Salvador Perez

Year	Date	Result
2011	8/15	Ground out
	8/16	Strikeout (Swinging)
2013	5/11	Double
	5/12	Double play

Mo Respect

Salvador Perez

The young Kansas City Royals catcher, who is 1-for-4 facing Rivera, on catching Rivera's final All-Star Game appearance at Citi Field in New York, on July 16, 2013.

It was unbelievable. To see him coming through the bullpen like that and catching him, it was the best thing. I will never forget it in my life.

I was a little nervous, for sure. I went out to talk to him, and he told me: "Just give a target down and away. If I shake you off, I will go inside."

I said: "Okay, that's easy."

When the inning was over, I told him, "Good job, you are the best pitcher in the league. I am so proud to catch you in your last All-Star Game. This means a lot to me."

Mo Respect

Wil Nieves

Nieves was behind the plate for one of Rivera's 652 career saves.

He loves eating at Benihana. He would always call me and say: "Wil, let's go to Benihana."

It's always nice to have him around, to soak up whatever you can from him. He's just a great pitcher, and people obviously know him as a player. But he's a better person than a player.

A.J. Pierzynski

Catcher

Playing Career

Minnesota Twins, San Francisco Giants, Texas Rangers, and Boston Red Sox since 1998

Career Statistics

1,763 games, 1,782 hits, 172 home runs, 800 runs batted in, .283 batting average, .322 on-base percentage, .428 slugging percentage

A.J. Pierzynski facing Mariano Rivera (regular season)

1-for-16, 1 extra-base hit, 1 walk, 1 hit by pitch, 3 strikeouts, .063 batting average, .167 on-base percentage, .125 slugging percentage

Mo Cred

Pierzynski's .063 batting average is the lowest of any player with a hit against Rivera. He gave Rivera a battle during a ten-pitch at-bat on April 27, 2011.

TO GET TO ten pitches with Mariano, I mean, it's the end of the game; it isn't *Money Ball,* where you want to get his pitch count up! There's no such thing as a moral victory in baseball.*

The first time I faced Mariano Rivera was at Yankee Stadium in 2001. That was a long time ago. I was with the Twins then. I got a hit [off him] my first at-bat. He threw me a cutter and I [hit] it over the third baseman's head for a double down the left-field line. At that

---

*The Yankees defeated the White Sox, 3-1, at Yankee Stadium, on April 27, 2011. Rivera earned the save by pitching a perfect ninth inning, though he needed twenty-three pitches to nail it down. Pierzynski fouled off four consecutive three-and-two pitches before grounding out weakly to the first baseman unassisted to end the game. It was Rivera's 567th career save.

A.J. Pierzynski

Year	Date	Result
2001	5/10	Double
2002	5/10	Strikeout (Swinging)
	5/11	Ground out
	5/17	Strikeout (Swinging)
	5/19	Walk (Hit by pitch)
2003 (Postseason)	10/2	Line out
2006	7/14	Fly out
	8/8	Fielder's choice
	8/9	Line out
2007	5/16	Ground out
	6/5	Ground out
	6/7	Strikeout (Swinging)
2008	4/23	Ground out
	9/15	Ground out
2009	8/2	Walk
2011	4/27	Ground out
	8/1	Ground out
2013	6/25	Fly out
	7/25	Fielder's choice

point I was one-for-one against him. I thought I own this guy. I haven't gotten a hit since. Now I'm 1 for 14. He's made up the difference.[*]

I remember one time facing Mariano in Yankee Stadium when [Ken] Griffey was on our team. Griff was giving me grief because I was saying, "Oh, great, I'm going to break a bat again."

He said, "Have confidence."

So I told him, "I'm so confident I'm going to use your bat."

I took his bat, and I'm up there in his stance, and I hit the ball three inches in front of home plate. [Yankees catcher Jorge] Posada picked up the ball and threw me out for the last out of the game. I came back to the dugout holding a piece of [Griffey's] bat, and I told him, "There's your confidence, Griff!"[**]

You're at a disadvantage because he never makes a mistake and his ball moves so late. You know what pitch is coming, but it doesn't matter, you still can't hit it. You have two choices. You can either hit the ball out front and then you hook it foul, or you can let [the ball] get deep and then it breaks your bat, or you hit a weak ground ball. You're stuck in between. You can't take a pitch, because it seems he never

---

[*]The Twins defeated the Yankees, 5-4, in ten innings at Yankee Stadium, on May 10, 2001. Pierzynski ignited the winning rally with a one-out double, and moved to third base on Christian Guzman's single. Even though Rivera retired the last two batters on a strike out and a bouncer to first, Pierzynski scored the winning run on a passed ball by Yankees' catcher Joe Oliver.

[**]The Yankees beat the White Sox, 4-2, at Yankees Stadium, on September 15, 2008, giving Rivera thirty-six saves on the season. Pierzynski swung at a one-and-two pitch and hit a weak dribbler that the catcher handled for the game's final out. It was Rivera's 479th career save.

throws a ball, he always puts it in the perfect spot. You're fighting an uphill battle because he's so good.

I was catching him in the All-Star Game in 2002 and I was laughing because the National League batters had never faced him before. They didn't know what to expect. You can watch him on television and wonder, "How do people *not* hit that?" But until you step into the [batter's] box you don't realize how hard he is to hit, and how much [his ball] moves. At that All-Star Game, I asked him to show me how he holds his cutter. He showed me the grip and I try to replicate it when [I fool around and] I throw my bullpen sessions. I can't throw it like he does. Then again, nobody can.*

Why am I doing this interview? Because he's Mariano Rivera, and everyone is one-for-fourteen off the guy! Whenever I see him I just laugh, and he laughs back. In a way, it's fun facing him, because you know the history and you know what he's done in his career. But you also know you're going to lose one bat, he'll break at least one, so when you go up to the plate to face Mariano, you take your least popular bat, your least favorite bat. He owes Louisville Slugger a ton of money! I figure, with all those bats I've sacrificed over my career, I owe it to him to give him some praise.

Jorge Posada

Catcher

Playing Career

New York Yankees from 1995 to 2011

---

*Pierzynski caught Rivera in the ninth inning of the 2002 All-Star Game, played at Miller Park in Milwaukee, Wisconsin, on July 9. That game ended in a controversial 7-7 tie after eleven innings when both teams had used all available pitchers.

Career Statistics

1,829 games, 1,664 hits, 275 home runs, 1,065 runs batted in, .273 batting average, .374 on-base percentage, .474 slugging percentage

Mo Cred

Posada was behind the plate for 368 of Rivera's 652 career saves, and teamed with Rivera to win four World Series championships in 1998, 1999, 2000, and 2009.

WE DON'T GET to the playoffs, we don't win championships, we don't do a lot of the things that we were able to do without this guy. Mo's special. It's just not about what he brings to the field, he's a special man. He's a quiet leader, but a very legit leader in the clubhouse. There will never be anybody like Mariano Rivera. There's nobody that's going to come close to what he's been able to do.

The best thing about catching him is I never had to bat against him. It's amazing that he's been able to do it for so long with one pitch, which he executes over and over again. I know him so well. He stands there on the mound, and I just give a sign for location—either in or away—and he goes ahead and throws it. You're calling the pitch, so you know what's coming. You're prepared for it. The pitch breaks either this way or that way.

Everybody talks about his cutter but [where] he puts a cutter is what makes him so effective. One of those things about Mariano, he has great control, that cutter will not go away. I can't put him into words. People don't understand how good he has been. He's a perfect example of committing to what you do. There's nobody better.

The first time I met him, it had to be in the Instructional League, in 1991. He was going through rehab. He had had elbow surgery and he was just tossing [a ball] here and there. Mariano is a freak of nature. His heart is humongous. So I knew Mariano was going to be 100 percent [recovered from his knee injury of 2012]. I expected Mariano to come back and be the old Mariano.

164

Nothing he does surprises me. I think he can pitch three, four more years. It's up to him. I'm pretty sure that he can still do it. But his family wants him home. That's the toughest thing. As Yankee fans, we want him here because we need him here.

Curtain Call

Jorge Posada urged Mariano Rivera to get back on the mound to soak in the Yankee Stadium crowd's cheers after Rivera surpassed Trevor Hoffman with his record-setting 602nd career save by closing out a 6-4 win over Minnesota on September 19, 2011.

[The idea] just came in my head. I said, "Stay on the mound a little longer."

It was his moment, so we needed him to stay on the mound. I was super excited. This was an important moment. Nobody, ever, is going to get even close to this. It's amazing we were watching [him set records] right in front of us.

Asked to describe that moment, Rivera said: "Oh, my God. For the first time in my career, I'm on the mound alone. There's no one behind me, no one in front of me. I can't describe that feeling because it was priceless."

Mo Respect

Jorge Posada

Posada released this statement praising Rivera on the day Rivera held a press conference to announce his retirement, on March 9, 2013.

There is only one Mariano Rivera. There won't be another person who will come along and do what he did. No one does it like him. It was an honor to catch him and play alongside him for as long as I did. He made my job as a catcher so much easier. Mariano is a special person and obviously a special player.

I'm so happy he is going out on his terms. Now every time he steps into a ballpark this year, teams and fans can celebrate and appreciate what he has meant to this great game we play.

Austin Romine

Catcher

Playing Career

New York Yankees since 2011

Career Statistics

69 games, 31 hits, 1 home run, 10 runs batted in, .201 batting average, .248 on-base percentage, .279 slugging percentage

Mo Cred

Romine has been behind the plate for 12 of Rivera's 652 career saves.

I REMEMBER THE FIRST time I caught him; I was making my major league debut. I caught his 599th career save. I remember not even knowing where I was and just trying not to mess it up for him.*

Since this was my debut, I was kind glad it was just over. I was glad I didn't mess anything up. I remember he told me, "Great job," and patted me on the chest. I think he knew that I was a little worked up being my first time and he made me feel real comfortable.

I went out to talk to him when he first came into the game and he was like, "Just go. Relax and have fun. We're going to get through this."

He didn't have to say anything. He could have just come in there and said, "Go back there and go catch," but he made me feel comfortable and calm. That's who he is and what he does to the people around him.

---

*Romine, who entered in the seventh inning, was making his first appearance in a major league game, catching Rivera, who was making his 1,036th appearance. Rivera worked the ninth as the Yankees beat the Angels, 6-5, in Anaheim, on September 11, 2011. Rivera picked up his 40th save of the season—his eighth season of 40 saves—and the 599th of his career.

Terry Steinbach

Catcher

Playing Career

Oakland Athletics and Minnesota Twins from 1986 to 1999

Career Statistics

1,546 games, 1,453 hits, 162 home runs, 745 runs batted in, .271 batting average, .326 on-base percentage, .420 slugging percentage

Terry Steinbach facing Mariano Rivera (regular season)

1-for-13, 0 extra-base hits, 0 RBIs, 4 strikeouts, .077 batting average, .077 on-base percentage, .077 slugging percentage

Mo Cred

Steinbach was the catcher for the formidable Oakland Athletics teams that won three consecutive American League pennants (1988–90) and the 1989 World Series. A three-time All-Star, Steinbach was the Most Valuable Player of the 1988 game. He is currently the bench coach for the Minnesota Twins.

Terry Steinbach

Year	Date	Result
1995	5/28	Strikeout (Swinging)
	5/28	Fly out
	5/28	Fly out
	6/6	Strikeout (Looking)
	6/6	Ground out
	9/1	Strikeout (Swinging)
	9/1	Ground out
1996	5/21	Strikeout (Looking)
	5/31	Line out
	6/2	Single
	8/23	Pop out
	9/2	Fly out
1997	8/9	Pop out

WHY ARE YOU talking to me? You should be talking to guys who've hit off him and had success. [Laughs.] I remember him early in his career as a starter and middle reliever. My approach [when facing Rivera] was not too successful. I tried to be aggressive early in the count, because maybe, in his mind, he's trying to throw a get-me-over pitch to get ahead in the count. If he gets two strikes on you, because he has such good command, and he can locate his pitches so consistently and throw the ball where he wants to, he's

167

almost unhittable. To be quite frank, I did not like to get into any two-strike counts with him because I think more often than not, he's going to come out ahead.[*]

I distinctly remember seeing the cutter for the first time. I was playing with the Twins and we went to Tampa to play [the Yankees in 1997 in] a spring training game. When Mariano came into the game, Scotty Ullger, who now is the Twins' first base coach but at the time was our hitting coach, he gives us the scouting report and says: "We know him from early in his career when he was a starter and middle relief guy."

And now, all of sudden, Mariano starts throwing the cutter and [the pitch] is darting in and out, and we come back to the bench and say, "What is he throwing?"

He came up with a cutter and that pitch catapulted him to the closer role. So I was there for the introduction of the cutter and the beginning of this phenomenal career that's he had.

What makes him so difficult to hit is his location. Rivera is so precise with his pitches. Even though you know the cutter is coming, he has tremendous command of that pitch. He can throw it away from the righties and he can run it in on the lefties. His control is phenomenal and you have to give Mariano credit mentally, too, because his pitch selection is also very good. He does mix in four-seam fastballs every now and then, even though the cutter is his bread and butter [pitch]. He can also front door the cutter to the righties. Against a right-handed hitter, like I was, he liked to throw the cutter away and have me go out

---

[*]Rivera earned his first major league win against the Oakland Athletics, on May 28, 1995. Making his second major league appearance as a starting pitcher, Rivera scattered seven hits over five innings in a 4-1 Yankees victory. Steinbach struck out with the bases loaded and two outs to end the first inning threat; flew out to center in the third inning, and flew out to deep right field in the sixth. Steinbach faced Rivera again on June 6 of that year. He struck out looking in the second inning and grounded out in the third. Steinbach faced Rivera for the first time as a relief pitcher on September 1, 1995. He struck out swinging in the sixth inning and grounded out to shortstop in the eighth inning.

there and chase it. But every once in a while he would throw a front-door cutter, [which means] he throws the ball at the hitter and allows it to break over the inside part of the plate. And when he mixes in a straight four-seamer, wow, it really makes it difficult for the hitter to put the ball in play.

Now that I'm the bench coach, I don't think I'll give our players any advice [before they face Rivera]. I'm one-for-thirteen against him, so I don't think I'm the guy they should be asking. I think they might be better off on their own.[*]

Mo Respect

Chris Stewart

The New York Yankees former catcher was behind the plate for 28 of Rivera's 652 career saves.

Being back there and having the experience with him, knowing that I'll be able to tell my kids and my grandkids I caught one of the best pitchers—if not the best—of all time, it's a truly humbling moment for me. It's a blessing that I've been cherishing for the entire season.

I'll go out there and second guess him every now and then, but he's been doing this forever, so I don't know if it's me second guessing myself or what. He knows what he's doing out there, and I let him do his thing, and obviously most of the time it works out pretty well.

---

[*]Steinbach's only hit off Rivera was a line drive single to left field in the bottom of the eighth inning of a Yankees' 11-4 win over the Athletics in Oakland, on June 2, 1996.

Kelly Stinnett

Catcher

Playing Career

New York Mets, Milwaukee Brewers, Arizona Diamondbacks, Cincinnati Reds, Philadelphia Phillies, Kansas City Royals, New York Yankees, St. Louis Cardinals from 1994 to 2007

Career Statistics

734 games, 476 hits, 65 home runs, 230 runs batted in, .234 batting average, .313 on-base percentage, .379 slugging percentage

Mo Cred

Stinnett, a Yankees back-up catcher in 2006, was behind the plate for 2 of Rivera's 652 career saves.

CATCHING MARIANO WAS awesome. It's fun to be able to put down one finger and know you could sit in a rocking chair behind home plate and the pitcher is going to be able to locate to both sides of the plate and hit your glove. I never saw him miss bad, the ball is always right there.

He has a good idea of what he wants to do, and executes to the hilt. He might throw a shorter cutter early in the count to get ahead, but with two strikes, he can make the pitch cut even more. The first few times catching him in spring training and in the bullpen sessions I noticed he had a heck of a sinker, too. He never threw it in a game because he didn't want to get beat by it.

The biggest factor about Mo coming into the game is the mindset that the game is over. Every single ballplayer who sees him walk onto the field knows he goes out there and does his job. He's going to get three outs, the game is over, it's all said and done. If you're on his team then you go celebrate. After catching a save, my adrenaline was pumping; I was more excited than he was.

I can't remember any difficult outings; with him, it's usually one, two, three. I do remember a game in Detroit early that season. Curtis Granderson came to the plate, and Mariano's first pitch was a cutter inside for a called strike. I noticed Granderson move his feet an inch or two away from the plate. The next pitch is a foul ball off his knuckles. Same thing, I see he scoots back another two or three inches off the plate. Mariano notices, too. Next pitch I call for is a cutter away, Mariano hits the glove, strike three looking. I watched many a lefty hitter back off the plate, only to have Mariano throw to the other side and catch the corner. He can do that any time he wants to.[*]

I never faced him in a regular season game, but I faced him twice in spring training games when I was with the Reds from 2001 to 2003. That was during Mariano's heyday, though it seems every year is a heyday for him. When you face a pitcher like Mariano Rivera, you do remember your at-bats against him. I don't care if it's on a back field at a B game in spring training, you remember.

The first time I faced him was in Tampa and I struck out. You see the ball coming, and you think you can hit it, so you start to swing at the ball in a certain spot. Then the ball disappears. By the time your bat head gets to the spot, the ball is gone. It's either below your bat head or at the end of your bat head.

The second time I faced Mariano, in Sarasota, now you know what pitch is coming—the cutter—and as a right-handed batter he takes away your power by making you hit the ball the other way. I hit a soft fly ball to right field. Game over.

It's so tough to hit his cutter because you can't prepare for it. You can't practice hitting that pitch. There's not a pitching machine in the world, or a batting practice pitcher anywhere, who can simulate that pitch. That's why Mariano is so successful.

---

[*]Rivera earned the victory when the Yankees scored five runs in the eleventh inning to beat the Tigers, 11-6, at Comerica Park, on May 30, 2006. Granderson struck out on three pitches and was the second out of the bottom of the eleventh.

Mo Respect

Tom Wilson

Wilson caught Rivera in the Yankees' minor league system in 1994 and 1995, and played in the major leagues with four organizations. After his retirement, he became a scout for the Yankees.

Tom Wilson

Year	Date	Result
2002	5/20	Ground out
	7/16	Fly out
2003	7/13	Strikeout (Swinging)

I don't care if he wasn't viewed as a prospect outside [the organization], if you played with him you knew he was special. He never got rattled. The game came to him and he dealt with it.

A bad inning or a bad game, you had no idea. The expression on his face never changed. He was a pro then like he is a pro now. Nothing has changed. He was and is totally unflappable. You never saw a glimpse of fear or nervousness in his eyes. No situation overcame him; he controlled situations.

Gregg Zaun

Catcher

Playing Career

Baltimore Orioles, Florida Marlins, Texas Rangers, Kansas City Royals, Houston Astros, Colorado Rockies, Toronto Blue Jays, Tampa Bay Rays, and Milwaukee Brewers from 1995 to 2010

Career Statistics

1,232 games, 878 hits, 88 home runs, 446 runs batted in, .252 batting average, .344 on-base percentage, .388 slugging percentage

Gregg Zaun facing Mariano Rivera (regular season)

2-for-16, 1 extra-base hit, 1 run batted in, 1 walk, 4 strikeouts, .125 batting average, .176 on-base percentage, .188 slugging percentage

Mo Cred

The first time Zaun ever faced Rivera he drove in an unearned run with a force out in the Yankees 13-10 win over the Orioles at Camden Yards, on April 30, 1996.

Gregg Zaun

Year	Date	Result
1996	4/30	Ground out (1 RBI)
	6/28	Strikeout (Swinging)
	7/13	Foul out
2000	8/1	Ground out
	8/3	Ground out
2003	6/10	Ground out
2004	7/26	Double
	8/26	Ground out
	10/2	Ground out
2005	9/16	Single
	9/25	Walk
2006	4/19	Fly out
	4/30	Pop out
	9/30	Strikeout (Swinging)
2007	9/12	Strikeout (Swinging)
2008	9/23	Strikeout (Looking)
2009	5/10	Foul out

I DIDN'T REALLY GET an opportunity to face him too often early in my career, because as a backup catcher, if the game was on the line, I wasn't playing. I faced him seventeen times in sixteen years. I wasn't in the game at those key moments, and mercifully so. All he did was frustrate me. I was 2-for-my-lifetime against Mo. I got him for a single and a double.

The double [in 2004] was a ball I hit down the left-field line. It was a forty-two hopper. A-Rod was playing me way off the third base line. Mo threw me a back-door cutter, and I snaked it in between A-Rod and the third base bag. The base hit [in 2005] came as a direct result of [Jason] Giambi playing first base. I hit a ground ball, and as soon as I hit it, he ran to first base. Had he taken two steps to his right, he would have been able to make an easy backhand play. But I think he assumed [second baseman Robinson] Cano was going to get it. So I feel I was really 1-for-16. I remember fouling two balls off my shin and destroying my shin during that at-bat. It was a very painful at-bat.*

Both of my hits against him were in the Rogers Centre [in Toronto] with the Blue Jays. I never got a hit against him in Yankee Stadium. I hit quite a few balls into the third deck, and off the facing of the third deck, but well foul. I couldn't keep the ball fair against Mo. The only times I ever barreled him up were balls that went foul. I had some good battles with him, but I never came out on the winning end.

After I got a couple of hits against him, then he started throwing me that back-door cutter. Whenever he threw me a back-door cutter—something other than the typical pound-me-inside-on-my-knuckles-pitch—I'd laugh or giggle or holler at him during a game.

There were a couple of times when I looked out at him, and I said, "C'mon, really Mo? You can run that pitch to both sides of the plate? You're that good? You're going to rub salt in the wound? You get me out with ease anyway! Do you really have to rub my nose in it by throwing a pitch on the other side of the plate?"

I never really had much of an approach against him. Some switch-hitters thought you should bat right-handed against him. I had that theory, too, but I was too chicken to go up there right-handed. I hadn't seen a right-on-right breaking ball since Little League. When I thought about going up there against Mariano right-handed, with

---

*Zaun hit a ground ball single to right field on the ninth pitch of the at-bat against Rivera with two outs in the bottom of the ninth inning of a game the Yankees won 11-10, at Rogers Centre in Toronto, on September 16, 2005. In the win, Rivera earned his 376th career save and his 40th save of the season. It was the sixth time Rivera had saved 40 games in a season. He would accomplish that feat nine times in his career, a record he shares with Trevor Hoffman. No one else has more than four seasons reaching the 40-saves plateau.

his 95-miles-an-hour cutter with a little bit of wrinkle, there was no chance I wanted any part of that.

My pride kept telling me, one of these days, I'm going to get him, I'm going to square him up and keep it fair. I'll finally figure out how to hit him, and it's going to make all this agony that I've gone through all these years, somehow, all worth it. That's the way it went for most of my career. Guys who owned me early on, I figured out how to hit them. If I faced Mariano enough times, I thought, sooner or later, I'm going to figure it out, or he's going to make a mistake.

Nothing I tried worked. He was breaking all my bats. It got to the point at the end of my career I was ordering special bats just for him. I ordered half a dozen 32-inch bats. I normally used a 34-inch bat, but [Roberto] Alomar told me to get a shorter bat, so the barrel would be closer to my hands because that's where all the balls were ending up. Mariano was always pounding me in on my knuckles. I figured a shorter bat would help me to be able to get to that inside pitch a little better. Unfortunately, after I ordered those 32-inch bats, I went to the National League with the [Milwaukee] Brewers and I didn't get a chance to face Mariano again. Those six 32-inch bats never got used.

Guys would not take their good wood up to bat against him. They wouldn't. I've seen guys have a favorite bat, one they'd been rolling with for a week and half, and when they'd come up against Mariano, these guys would take garbage batting practice wood up there, because they knew they had no chance. He had people beat before they even stepped in the box.

You knew the at-bat against him was going to be extremely difficult. He's so good at protecting leads because you rarely saw him give up multiple hits in an inning, and he doesn't walk anybody. That's why a lot of guys tried to take him deep, to hit a home run against him, because they knew you couldn't string hits together against him very often. That played into his hands, too, because guys would get big with their swing, trying to hit it out of the ballpark, and that's exactly the polar opposite of what you want to do against him. Your swing needs to get shorter against him.

I asked Bill Mueller, who hit Mo really good, what's the secret? Why do you hit him so much better than anybody else? What's your approach?

He said, "I swing to where the ball is going to be, not to where it is."

I thought to myself, "That makes perfect sense, but it's totally counterintuitive."

Why would a baseball player ever think to swing where the ball is going to be? You're always taught to swing where the ball is. But that's a lesson I learned way too late, obviously, because it didn't work. Nothing worked.

I love the fact that when he closes the ballgame there's no fist pumping, there's no bow and arrow marksmanship. He simply shakes the catcher's hand, turns around, and slaps high fives with his teammates. To me, he's the ultimate professional. I wish more players of this generation would react to being successful like he does. He's a classy guy. I would probably soil myself if I ever saw him demonstrate outwardly like Fernando Rodney or [Jose] Valverde after a save. Mariano's got 600 saves and he acts like, "Yup, been there, done that, let's go home."

Saves By Catcher

Jorge Posada	368
Joe Girardi	73
Russell Martin	37
Francisco Cervelli	34
John Flaherty	32
Jose Molina	31
Chris Stewart	28
Austin Romine	12
Ivan Rodriguez	7
Todd Greene	5
Chad Moeller	5
Joe Oliver	4
Alberto Castillo	3
Jim Leyritz	2
Kelly Stinnett	2
Chris Turner	2
Kevin Cash	1
Sal Fasano	1
Mike Figga	1
J.R. Murphy	1
Gustavo Molina	1
Wil Nieves	1

Credit: Elias Sports Bureau

Section Four:
Designated Hitters

Jack Cust

Designated hitter and Outfield

Playing Career

Arizona Diamondbacks, Colorado Rockies, Baltimore Orioles, San Diego Padres, Oakland Athletics, and Seattle Mariners from 2001 to 2011

Career Statistics

670 games, 510 hits, 105 home runs, 323 runs batted in, .242 batting average, .374 on-base percentage, .439 slugging percentage

Jack Cust facing Mariano Rivera (regular season)

2-for-6, 2 extra-base hits, 1 home run, 1 double, 1 run batted in, 2 strikeouts, .333 batting average, .333 on-base percentage, 1.000 slugging percentage

Mo Cred

Cust hit a home run off Rivera on August 15, 2003.

Jack Cust

Year	Date	Result
2003	8/14	Pop out
	8/15	Home run (1 RBI)
2007	6/29	Strikeout (Swinging)
2008	7/19	Strikeout (Looking)
2010	7/5	Fly out
2011	5/28	Double

I'LL NEVER FORGET the home run. It was one of my first home runs in the major leagues, so it was fresh. I was a young player facing a pitcher who I've watched destroy hitters for years. Facing Mariano was surreal. Living in Flemington, New Jersey, I grew up being a Yankees fan. Now, here I was, batting against Mariano Rivera and seeing Bernie Williams in center field and Derek Jeter playing shortstop; it was crazy.

Hitting a home run off the greatest closer of all-time is still one of the best experiences I've had in baseball.*

The night before the home run, I faced Rivera as a pinch hitter. I didn't get a hit—he jammed me with a cutter and I popped up—but I got an at-bat against Mariano, and got to see how his pitches moved. You can watch a pitcher on tape, but until you face him, it's a totally different animal. The next night, when I got an at-bat against him, he threw me a back-door cutter and I hit it out to the opposite field. I was lucky that he tried to back door me instead of going with his bread and butter—the cutter inside to the left-handed hitter.

[John] Flaherty was catching. I always wondered if [Jorge] Posada was catching would I have hit the homer? Hitting home runs to the opposite field is what I did best when I was hitting the ball for power, so it was playing to my strength to let me extend my arms. When Posada was catching, Mariano threw the cutter inside all the time to lefties. Every pitch was in, in, in, until he jammed you or struck you out. Until the home run, he'd never thrown me an outside pitch. The home run was the first time [Rivera] ever threw me a pitch away. It was a good pitch on the outside corner. I saw the ball start further away from me, so I thought I had a chance to get good wood on it. I got the barrel on it and it ended up going out.

When I hit the home run [the Orioles] were three runs down, and since it was a solo shot, it wasn't a big deal. Later in my career, I hit a double off of Mariano that started a game-winning rally in Seattle. He threw me a back-door cutter and I hit a line drive down the left-field line for a double. Then Adam Kennedy won the game with a

---

*Cust led off the bottom of the ninth inning against Rivera with the Orioles trailing 6-3 at Baltimore's Camden Yards, on August 15, 2003. With the count one-and-one, Cust lofted Rivera's third offering over the left-center field wall for a home run to make it 6-4. Baltimore put the tying runs in scoring position with two outs when Rivera retired Jay Gibbons—who was 3-for-23 in his career facing Rivera—to record his 25th save of the season and the 268th of his career.

walk-off hit; it was a little blooper like the hit Luis Gonzalez got for Arizona in the [2001] World Series.*

[Another] great experience was when Mariano came in specifically to face me in Yankee Stadium. I went to the old stadium a lot, so I knew the crowd in a full stadium was loud. I was with Oakland and Mariano came in to face me with runners in scoring position and two outs in the eighth inning. I got the whole Yankee Stadium experience; it was definitely cool. I had a lot of family and friends in the stadium. I felt confident because I'd hit the home run off him. I don't know if he knew that, but I knew I did, so even though he's the best in the game, I had confidence in myself. I had a good, long at-bat, seeing six or seven pitches. The count was three-and-two. He threw a cut fastball up over the plate that just spun. It backed up; it never had any cutting action. But it was an effective pitch up in the zone and I swung through it. He got me there, and he got me plenty of other times, too.**

What he does is amazing. He makes it look like the easiest job in the world, but it's not. I feel like he could [close] for another ten years. He can probably throw a ninety-miles-per-hour cutter for the rest of his life. He keeps himself in great shape. I saw him once before I reached the big leagues. One off-season, me and my buddies went out to dinner and Mariano was eating in the same restaurant. I didn't talk to him, but that was the closest I've ever been to him, besides when he was 60 feet away trying to get me out. He looks older than he is. And he's not as tall as I thought; you watch him on television, and he has such a big presence, I guess that makes him seem taller.

---

*Kennedy blooped a single to shallow center field off Rivera in the twelfth inning, lifting the Mariners to a 5-4 victory over the Yankees at Seattle's Safeco Field, on May 28, 2011. With one out, Justin Smoak singled and Cust doubled sharply to left field, advancing the potential winning run to third base. Rivera intentionally walked Franklin Gutierrez to load the bases. Kennedy, who was 1-for-12 in his career against Rivera, then looped a soft single into shallow center field, scoring pinch runner Luis Rodriguez with the winning run.

**Rivera entered the game to face Cust and protect a 2-1 lead with two runners on base and two outs in the eighth inning. The game was played before 52,622 fans in Yankee Stadium, on June 29, 2007. Cust struck out swinging on the seventh pitch of the at-bat. Rivera pitched a scoreless ninth inning for his 424th career save.

Mo Respect

Eric Hinske

Hinske was 3-for-13 with 5 strikeouts facing Rivera. He played with Rivera on the Yankees' 2009 World Series championship team.

Eric Hinske

Year	Date	Result
2002	4/9	Strikeout (Swinging)
2004	7/22	Strikeout (Looking)
	7/26	Strikeout (Swinging)
	9/21	Single
2005	4/21	Single
	8/23	Fly out
	9/25	Single
2006	4/30	Ground out
	8/20	Strikeout (Swinging)
2007	6/1	Ground out
	8/29	Ground out
	9/16	Fielder's choice
2008	7/9	Strikeout (Looking)

He's broken many Eric Hinske bats in my day. I got a couple of hits off him but usually they're jam shots over the shortstop's head or something, trying to stay inside the ball. I think it's better to be a right-handed batter against him. At least the ball is going away from you.

He's a great person, a great teammate, a religious man. He's just an all-around good human being. He's left his mark on the game, on and off the field.

Kevin Maas

Designated hitter and First base

Playing Career

New York Yankees and Minnesota Twins from 1990 to 1995

Career Statistics

406 games, 287 hits, 65 home runs, 169 runs batted in, .230 batting average, .329 on-base percentage, .422 slugging percentage

Mo Cred

As a Yankees rookie in 1990, Maas set a major league record for the fewest at-bats (72) needed to hit ten home runs.

IFACED MARIANO ONCE, on a backfield at the Yankees' minor league complex, in Tampa, Florida, in the summer of 1995. I had played for the Minnesota Twins during the first part of that year, but then I had a severe hamstring injury, and wound up getting released. The Yankees offered to bring me back to big league camp in the spring of '96, but they wanted me to play out the remainder of '95 in Triple A. Before I was assigned to the Triple A team in Columbus, I spent a week or two rehabbing my leg in Tampa, and working to get my swing back. Mariano was down there at the same time.*

I had already spent four and a half years in the big leagues and Mo was just breaking in. He had a few rough starts with the Yankees and he got sent back down to Columbus. Before going to Columbus, he went down to Tampa to play in some rookie league games. Those were intra-squad games, to get us some at-bats, and to get Mo some innings to pitch. That's where I faced him.

I remember Mo being this guy that everybody was talking about as the future of the staff, the future Yankee who had great stuff, a great fastball. He threw really hard back then, and I was excited to face him even though we probably had ten or fifteen fans there. I knew that the Yankees were obviously looking at me in a different light, having come back to the organization, and Mo was on his way up. The Yankees had released me in the spring of '94. A year and a half later I was back, so every at-bat I felt I had something to prove to the Yankees, to show them they made a mistake. I wanted to earn a shot again. I still had something to prove.

---

*Rivera began the 1995 season in Columbus. The Yankees called him up on May 16 to replace the injured starter Jimmy Key. Rivera made his major league debut against the California Angels on May 23, and allowed five earned runs in three innings in a 10-0 loss. After struggling through three more starts, he was demoted to Columbus on June 11. On July 4, he made his first start back in the major leagues, and pitched eight scoreless innings against the Chicago White Sox, striking out 11 batters and allowing just two hits.

I looked up my statistics [during that time in rookie ball] and I was 4-for-9, and I know one of those four hits was against Mo. I remember getting one good at-bat against him. I could see the good life on his fastball and the good command that he had early on, and thinking, I better get the bat head out in front. Sure enough, he didn't have his cutter back then, I was looking for a fastball in and he threw me a fastball in. I remember hitting a laser to right field. I hit an absolute rocket because he threw me what I was looking for. I was guessing, and I got the right pitch. Maybe at that point in his career he wasn't as smart as I was.

I remember thinking if only I had gotten the ball up in the air it would have gone over the administration building. I remember thinking, "Okay that meant something." Because I knew everyone was so high on Mo, and I was able to turn around one of his fastballs and hit a rocket to right field for a hit. The buzz was there about Mo back then, and that's why it meant something to me, why it stands out for me. That was the only time I ever faced Mo.

Edgar Martinez

Designated hitter

Playing Career

Seattle Mariners from 1987 to 2004

Career Statistics

2,055 games, 2,247 hits, 309 home runs, 1,261 runs batted in, .312 batting average, .418 on-base percentage, .515 slugging percentage

Edgar Martinez facing Mariano Rivera (regular season)

10-for-16, 5 extra-base hits, 2 home runs, 6 runs batted in, 3 walks, 4 strikeouts, 1 hit by pitch, .625 batting average, .700 on-base percentage, 1.188 slugging percentage

Mo Cred

Rivera named Martinez as the toughest batter he ever faced. No hitter has had the sustained success that Martinez had with a minimum of twenty career plate appearances: a .625 batting average with two home runs and six runs batted in.

Edgar Martinez

Year	Date	Result
1995	6/11	Home run (3 RBI)
	6/11	Single
	8/25	Walk
	8/25	Home run (1 RBI)
	9/5	Strikeout (Looking)
	9/5	Double
	9/5	Single (1 RBI)
	10/4	Single
1996	5/25	Double
	8/18	Double
1997	8/23	Intentional walk
1999	3/5	Reached on error
	8/28	Walk (hit by pitch)
2000	8/5	Single (1 RBI)
	8/30	Single
	10/17	Ground out
2001	10/17	Ground out
2003	4/30	Strikeout (Looking)
	5/1	Ground out
	5/7	Strikeout (Looking)
	8/8	Strikeout (Swinging)
2004	5/15	Intentional walk
	8/14	Single

IT'S HARD TO tell why [I had success against Rivera]. For some reason, I never felt like I was doing great against him. I think it's because you always felt that it was going to be a tough battle, a difficult at-bat. Against some other pitchers, if you do well, you feel comfortable at the plate, but with Mariano, it was never a comfortable at-bat. A lot of the hits were not hard hit; I was able to find some holes.*

At the beginning of his career, as a starter, he threw hard. He was trying to beat you, to dominate you, by throwing fastballs, but it was straight and over the plate. I felt confident that I would make solid contact. I didn't try to do too much. As a short reliever he developed the cutter, and he perfected that pitch. For me, being a contact hitter, I always look [for pitches] middle-away and I liked to

---

*Martinez was 9-for-11 facing Rivera at one point. He reached base in fourteen of his first fifteen plate appearances (two homers, three doubles, five singles, two walks, one hit-by-pitch, one reached on error, one strikeout). But Rivera turned the tables and retired Martinez in six of the last seven at-bats.

use the whole field. Most of his pitches went middle-away, and he was good at keeping the ball down and away. On those pitches, I hit the ball to the right side of the field. As a reliever he was more of a pitcher, using location. He had great command. He was very effective low and away, but he also knew when to throw a pitch high in the zone. I think he was successful because he knew the hitters' swings; he knew where you had a hole [in your swing], and he could throw to that area.

I think what makes him great is his command and his location; knowing where to throw the pitch. A good example is when I faced him in the 2000 American League Championship Series. I made the last out of the game. He got me out with a sinker inside. I never remember him throwing me a sinker before. That was the first time I ever saw a sinker from him. He knew when to change his plan, when to go with something completely new, something different that you're not expecting. The location of the pitch is important. If he missed by just two inches it would have been a different outcome. I would have hit the ball solid. But he got inside and I hit a ground ball to shortstop. I remember that pitch and I remember that swing and I felt that if [the ball] was only two inches more toward the barrel I would have hit that ball hard.*

There is something about him, in the way he competes. You could tell he was very well prepared. He had everything a great pitcher needs to succeed: movement on the ball, command of his pitches, and a presence on the mound. He's not going to make many mistakes. It was always a challenge to face Mariano, especially in close games. You have to admire his ability to handle pressure when the game is on the line. It seems like he wanted to be in that difficult situation. When he's on the mound he has a presence. His demeanor is very professional. Even with his success, his body language is very normal and unassuming. You don't notice anything he does that tells you, I don't like this guy; I want

---

*Martinez was the potential game-tying run when he made the final out of the 2000 American League Championship Series. The Yankees defeated the Mariners, 9-7, in Game Six, to capture their third straight American League pennant.

to beat this guy. Sometimes I think if the Yankees didn't have Mariano, maybe the Mariners win a World Series.*

I never heard that Mariano thought I was the toughest batter for him. That is a great compliment. We always had a mutual respect. He's the best reliever I ever faced. Not only is he an amazing pitcher, he is a great person. I congratulate him on an amazing career. It was an honor to play with him in the All-Star games and it was a great experience competing against him.

Mo Says

At the press conference announcing his retirement, Rivera was asked to name the toughest batter he ever faced.

The toughest—and thank God he retired—Edgar Martinez. Oh my God. I think every pitcher will say that, because this man was tough. Great man, though—respected the game, did what he had to do for his team. That's what you appreciate about players, when a player comes and does what is right for the game of baseball, for his team and teammates.

David Ortiz

Designated hitter

Playing Career

Minnesota Twins and Boston Red Sox since 1997

Career Statistics

1,969 games, 2,023 hits, 431 home runs, 1,429 runs batted in, .287 batting average, .381 on-base percentage, .549 slugging percentage

---

*The Yankees also defeated the Mariners in the 2001 American League Championship Series in five games, though the Mariners had won an American League–record 116 games that season.

David Ortiz facing Mariano Rivera (regular season)

11-for-32, 3 extra-base hits, 1 home run, 4 runs batted in, 2 walks, 4 strikeouts, .344 batting average, .382 on-base percentage, .500 slugging percentage

Mo Cred

Ortiz has more hits facing Rivera in the regular season, 11, than any other batter.

David Ortiz

Year	Date	Result
2000	7/28	Single (2 RBI)
	9/1	Single
	9/3	Fly out
2002	5/19	Line out
2003	5/27	Single
	8/30	Single
	9/7	Fielder's choice
Post-season	10/11	Foul out
	10/14	Single
	10/16	Double
2004	4/24	Fly out
	4/24	Strikeout (Swinging)
	7/1	Single
Post-season	10/13	Strikeout (Swinging)
	10/17	Strikeout (Swinging)
	10/17	Pop out
2005	4/6	Ground out (1 RBI)
	7/14	Strikeout (Swinging)
	7/16	Pop out
	9/9	Fly out
	9/11	Walk
2006	5/23	Pop out
	8/18	Home run (1 RBI)
	8/20	Double
	8/20	Fly out
2007	6/3	Line out
	9/16	Pop out
2008	7/25	Fly out
	9/28	Reached on error
2009	4/24	Strikeout (Swinging)
	8/7	Single
	8/9	Walk
2011	5/16	Foul out
	8/5	Ground out
	8/30	Double
2013	5/31	Single
	7/20	Foul out
	8/18	Single
	9/5	Line out
	9/8	Strikeout (Looking)

HE'S A GUY [who] is going to be irreplaceable. Everybody right now in the league [tries] to throw cutters, pretty much every pitcher [has] a cutter right now, but [it's] not like Mariano's. Not even close. There's one second before it's on your hands. And he's the only one that I have ever faced [like that].*

He's special. What can I tell you? He's the type of guy that basically says, "What doesn't kill you, makes you stronger."

When you talk to Mariano, it doesn't even feel like you are talking to a guy that is going to the Hall of Fame [on the] first ballot. He's so humble

---

*In two postseason series facing Rivera, Ortiz was 2-for-6 with two strikeouts.

and so respectful and funny. He says things that sound funny, things you aren't expecting him to say. He never would look [down] at anyone over his shoulder.

I was sitting right next to him during the [2013] All-Star Game and I pulled out my camera and said: "This is a once-in-a-lifetime thing, let's take a whole bunch of photos."

I did take lots of photos with him. I didn't ask for his autograph at [the] All-Star [Game] as I was giving him his space, but I will. Actually, I do have an autographed jersey of his framed in my house in my basement. I got it a couple of years ago and asked him myself for it. But I got to get a new one now!

Luke Scott

Designated hitter and Outfield

Playing Career

Houston Astros, Baltimore Orioles, and Tampa Bay Rays since 2005

Career Statistics

889 games, 725 hits, 135 home runs, 436 runs batted in, .258 batting average, .340 on-base percentage, .481 slugging percentage

Luke Scott facing Mariano Rivera (regular season)
2-for-16, 1 extra-base hit, 1 home run, 1 run batted in, 1 walk, 1 strikeout, .125 batting average, .176 on-base percentage, .313 slugging percentage

Mo Cred
Scott hit a game-tying home run off Rivera on September 19, 2010; it was the sixty-second homer Rivera has allowed.

Luke Scott

Year	Date	Result
2008	4/20	Ground out
	5/22	Ground out
	5/27	Pop out
	5/28	Reached on error
	8/22	Line out
	9/20	Pop out
	9/21	Ground out
2009	4/9	Ground out
	9/1	Double play
2010	4/29	Fly out
	6/1	Single
	6/3	Strikeout (Swinging)
	9/19	Home run (1 RBI)
2011	4/24	Fly out
	5/18	Pop out
2012	4/6	Intentional walk
2013	7/28	Ground out

YEAH, ABSOLUTELY, THAT was one of the biggest [hits] of my career, if not the biggest. Considering the situation, the best closer I think that's ever taken the mound, it's just another experience that I'll never forget. I'm thankful for the opportunity and the way things worked out. It was a lot of fun against a real good [pitcher].*

He's not going to try to fool you. It's real simple. He's got one pitch. His success is based on the quality of his stuff. He's got a late-moving cutter, but it's also his movement, and his location. He's got very good control.

I've got [sixteen] at-bats against Mariano Rivera. In all those at-bats, I haven't been counting how many hits I have; I've been counting how many balls have actually been [fully] on the plate in the strike zone, instead of being on the corner or just off. I've seen maybe three pitches where the whole ball has crossed the white of the plate, which is pretty impressive. Everything is on the black. Either the ball is running off the plate, or it's off the plate running toward the black.

To me, he's been that good, and I'll go as far as to say to other people, he's been that good. As a lefty he's going to try to run that cutter in on your hands, to speed up your swing. And when you start laying off of it, that's when he'll go to the back-door cutter.

---

*Scott was 1-for-12 with a single against Rivera before hitting a game-tying home run in the bottom of the ninth inning at Camden Yards in Baltimore, on September 19, 2010. Scott eventually scored the game-winning run in the eleventh inning when he raced home from second on Ty Wigginton's hit for a 4-3 win.

Mike Sweeney

Designated hitter and First base

Playing Career

Kansas City Royals, Oakland Athletics, Seattle Mariners, and Philadelphia Phillies from 1995 to 2010

Career Statistics

1,454 games, 1,540 hits, 215 home runs, 909 runs batted in, .297 batting average, .366 on-base percentage, .486 slugging percentage

Mike Sweeney facing Mariano Rivera (regular season)
4-for-14, 1 extra-base hit, 3 RBIs, 2 walks, 0 strikeouts, .286 batting average, .389 on-base percentage, .357 slugging percentage

Mo Cred

A five-time All-Star, Sweeney finished second in the American League batting race with a .340 average in 2002, and set a Royals franchise record for runs batted in with 144 in 2000.

WHEN YOU'RE AT Yankee Stadium and Mariano Rivera is coming in the game, it feels like a horror movie. It's like the horror movie, *Friday the 13th*, when you hear the music and you know Jason is coming, as the viewer, you're scared to death, because you know what's going to happen. That's the feeling you get when you see No. 42 coming through the bullpen gate and you hear "Enter Sandman" blasting [through the speakers] at Yankee Stadium. Just like in the horror movie, you know the end result, you know what's going to happen, and more times than not, Mariano will finish the game and get the save.

The one memorable at-bat against Mariano Rivera that really stands out to me is in 2009. I was a member of the Seattle Mariners and Felix Hernandez was pitching and had given up one run. We go into the bottom of the ninth down 1-0. After Felix had pitched the ninth, he

Mike Sweeney

Year	Date	Result
1996	8/2	Single (1 RBI)
	8/5	Walk
1997	5/2	Line out
	8/14	Line out
1998	8/18	Sacrifice fly (1 RBI)
1999	8/19	Line out
	9/8	Ground out
2000	4/14	Foul out
	9/4	Line out
2001	4/5	Ground out
2002	8/15	Pop out
2003	8/20	Single (1 RBI)
2004	4/30	Walk
2005	8/26	Single
2006	4/11	Walk (Hit by pitch)
2007	9/7	Ground out
2009	6/30	Ground out
	9/18	Double

comes in the dugout and untucks his shirt, he knows the game is over, and he can't do any more but sit on the bench and watch our at-bats [against Rivera]. One out. Two outs. All of a sudden, [Mariners' manager] Don Wakamatsu says, "Sweeney, you're up."

I say, "What? Thanks for the warning."

I had a bat in my hand, I ran to the on-deck circle and got loose, and the first pitch I saw [from Rivera] I hit a ball to the right-center-field gap that was a ground-rule double. I crushed it. And as I came off the field for a pinch runner, Ichiro [Suzuki] came up and hit the first pitch he saw for a walk-off home run, a walk-off two-run home run. I'll never forget it because when you get two outs against Mariano Rivera and there's nobody on base, it's almost a forgone conclusion that the game's over. I was up [at bat] and I was excited about having a chance to be the hero and be in that game situation against the greatest closer in history. So I promptly hit a double and then Ichiro hits the walk-off home run and I remember Felix Hernandez was in awe, because he thought the game was over. He jumped into my arms and he said: "Sweeney I can't believe it, I can't believe it, we got it, we got it, we got the win."*

Against Mariano Rivera, with his cutter going away from a right-handed hitter, my mentality was to try to hit the inside part of the baseball. If you stay inside the ball, you have a better chance to square it up. I would block out the left-field side of the field and [try to hit the ball] from the center fielder over to the right fielder and drive the

---

*Michael Saunders pinch-ran for Sweeney and scored ahead of Ichiro in a 3-2 Mariners win at Safeco Field, on September 18, 2009. Until this point, Rivera had converted forty of his forty-one save chances that season, including thirty-six in a row.

ball in that gap. When a left-handed hitter bats against Mariano, that cutter will break a bat seven out of ten times. He breaks bat after bat after bat. I remember [Kansas City Royals teammate] Johnny Damon breaking three bats in one at-bat against Mariano Rivera at Yankee Stadium. He broke two bats on foul balls that were [pitches] in on his fists, and then the third [broken bat occurred when] he grounded out to first base. Ironically, right-handed hitters have a better chance of success against him than left-handers do. Mariano Rivera defies statistics; he defies logic.

I don't think I ever struck out against him. That's because of my desire when I walked into that batter's box to put the barrel of the bat on the baseball. When you're facing a pitcher like Mariano Rivera your senses are heightened, your adrenaline is pushed, and your mind is driven to be something better than you are at normal times, because you're facing the best. So whenever I stepped in the box against No. 42 it was my desire to be great because I was facing the greatest. Mariano Rivera, even though he's the greatest closer in major league history, is a one-pitch pitcher. He throws a cutter. What makes him so effective is his ability to locate that pitch. He's as precise as a heart surgeon. He's on the corners, at the knees, and then he raises your eye level. When you face Mariano Rivera you cannot ever expect a pitch to be thrown down the middle of the plate; it just doesn't happen.

I was blessed to play in five All-Star games. One of my greatest All-Star Game memories—one of my greatest memories in baseball, period—was when Mariano and I were in Detroit in 2005. I remember after the [player] introductions sitting on the bench in the first inning in the dugout at Comerica Park [in Detroit], and I look over and sitting next to me is Mariano Rivera. He asked me how I'm doing, and we stared having a conversation. We're talking about our faith, our family, what drives us in life, and the next thing I know, I look up and it's already the fourth inning. Mo and I were two of twenty-five guys that were chosen to be on the American League All-Star team and we're in the All-Star Game and we're totally oblivious. We were talking about what really matters in life, and we were in the moment, talking for about forty minutes. I couldn't believe it. So I said, "I better go to the cage and get warmed-up."

He said, "I better go to the bullpen and get loose."

That was probably the greatest moment of my baseball career. We didn't talk about how to throw a cutter, or what it's like to be a Yankee. We talked about what really matters: faith and family and what we have in common. It was awesome. I'm happy to bring life to the wonderful man that he is.*

---

*The American League All-Stars defeated the National League All-Stars, 7-5. Sweeney struck out swinging in a pinch-hitting appearance against Philadelphia pitcher Brad Lidge. Rivera faced one batter and earned the save, striking out Houston's Morgan Ensberg to end the game.

Section Five: Pitchers

Jonathan Albaladejo

Relief pitcher

Playing Career

Washington Nationals, New York Yankees, and Arizona Diamond-backs from 2007 to 2012

Career Statistics

66 games, 6 wins, 3 losses, 4.34 earned run average, 76 innings, 77 hits allowed, 32 walks, 56 strikeouts

Mo Cred

Albaladejo spent three seasons in the bullpen with Rivera while playing for the Yankees in 2008, '09, and '10.

THE MOST IMPORTANT thing I learned from Mariano is the mental part of the game. His mental strength is amazing. He wins the battle before he throws a pitch. You can see the confidence on his face every time he steps on the mound. He knows he's going to get the hitter out, and the hitter knows it, too.

He's always relaxed. Nothing ever gets to him. Or at least he doesn't show it. His expression stays the same. I saw him get mad only once. It happened so quick you noticed it only if you were looking at him at that particular moment. [It happened] right after he threw a pitch that got hit and a run scored. By the time he got the ball again, he was the same guy as before. I try to stay relaxed, but sometimes the game gets to me more than I would like.

My years in the bullpen [with Mariano] was a wonderful time. When you're a Yankee, they let you know on day one that the goal is to win games. Everybody in the bullpen was pulling for each other, because everybody wants to win. That's your job. We were a tight group. There was no feeling of, "I want your spot; you want mine."

Everybody in the bullpen pretty much sits in the same place every day. We all sit together, we all talk. There's a bench [in the bullpen] and Mariano sat at the end. He was the last one to show up, he comes by the sixth inning, and that was the only spot open. It wasn't like everyone was trying to sit next to him.

He really didn't have a routine. The phone rings, he'd grab a heavy ball to stretch for a minute, then he'd start warming up. He throws two balls and he's ready to go. It's impressive.

When he comes out [of the bullpen] in Yankee Stadium, the game stops for a moment. Everybody goes crazy. The first time I ever heard [the crowd cheering for him] it gave me chills. I think about it now and I get chills. It was awesome.

We sat across from each other [in the Yankees locker room]. He would sit quietly at his locker, really polite; always has a smile on his face. Any chance he gets to talk to the younger Latin players he will help them out. Talking about the game, what you can do to improve, sharing his experiences.

He's always trying to help everybody. He finds a way to speak to you and tries to help you in any way he can. I learned a lot from him—not only about baseball, about life. I appreciate all he did for me. He's a wonderful guy and treats everybody with respect, and everybody respects him.

Bronson Arroyo

Pitcher

Playing Career

Pittsburgh Pirates, Boston Red Sox, and Cincinnati Reds since 2000

Career Statistics

391 games, 138 wins, 127 losses, 1 save, 4.19 earned run average, 2,278 innings, 2,321 hits, 623 walks, 1,479 strikeouts

Mo Cred

Arroyo competed against Rivera's Yankees as a member of the Red Sox in the 2003 and 2004 American League Championship Series.

YOU ALWAYS SEE guys who want to have a bunch of facial hair and they want to look mean and have people think that they're a little off or a little crazy and they don't have command of their hundred-mile-an-hour fastball, they try to use that intimidation to beat guys.

The thing about Mariano is he didn't have to use any of those weapons. He didn't have to use any intimidation at all. He didn't have to use a brash attitude on the mound. He went out there cool, calm, and collected for all these years and dominated at that position without having to use that as an edge at all.

Mo Respect

Dellin Betances

Betances was Rivera's teammate in the Yankees' bullpen from 2011 to 2013.

Being a hometown New Yorker, I grew up watching the Yankees, and Mariano was always one of those guys you watched and are like, Man, I wish I could meet that guy.

Now becoming teammates with him is an honor for me. It's an honor to be around him and be in the bullpen with him.

[Meeting Rivera] was nerve-racking, I guess. At first, I was like, Oh man, I can't believe I'm standing next to Mariano. But he's a real humble guy, a nice guy, and he tries to teach you as much stuff as he can. He loves working with the younger guys.

I don't know what's so great about [his cutter]. It just doesn't make any sense. To watch it on TV, it doesn't look any better than half the other guys in the league throwing their cutter. Yet he continues to make it work and it's not like he's only done it when he throws 95 miles an hour. He's still doing it at 91, 92, and he still gets guys out. It's mind-boggling.

Joba Chamberlain

Pitcher

Playing Career

New York Yankees and Detroit Tigers since 2007

Career Statistics

260 games, 23 wins, 14 losses, 5 saves, 3.85 earned run average, 444 innings, 433 hits, 182 walks, 446 strikeouts

Mo Cred

Chamberlain was Rivera's teammate with the Yankees from 2007 to 2013 and was a member of the 2009 World Series championship team.

HE'S ALWAYS PLAYING jokes on everybody [by] throwing gum at people and doing stuff like that. Everybody sees the baseball side of things, but they don't get to spend the time in [the bullpen] with him and joke [around]. I [enjoy] watching him play jokes on people and throw gum. He's really good at throwing gum, too. Shocker, I know, but yeah, he always finds a way to keep guys loose.

[The funniest joke was] probably in spring training when he threw a rosin bag at our bullpen coach that hit him on the head and it exploded. Why did he do it? I don't know. He was just being Mo, I guess. It wasn't a mean thing. It was funny, actually. He was just tossing it and it happened to hit him and explode. It was pretty fun. It was pretty cool. Not something you see every day. Obviously, my kid is going to know who he is. So he's going to know the baseball side, that's irrelevant. I think the life side is more fun than the baseball side.

He's always there to talk to about certain situations, certain counts. He always keeps it fun in the bullpen. I think it's a good way to keep us relaxed but also keep us in the game when we start talking about at-bats and certain situations. The way he keeps things fun is he's always laughing and joking. People have no idea [there is] this side of him. If they could only see half the stuff I can't talk about! But that's the fun part for us, seeing the human side of Mariano, because when he pitches he's really not human. So it's fun for us to see that side of him.

David Cone

Pitcher

Playing Career

Kansas City Royals, New York Mets, Toronto Blue Jays, New York Yankees, Boston Red Sox from 1986 to 2003

Career Statistics

450 games, 194 wins, 126 losses, 3.46 earned run average, 2,898 innings, 2,504 hits, 1,137 walks, 2,668 strikeouts

Mo Cred

Cone was Rivera's teammate with the Yankees from 1995 to 2000. He was a member of four World Series championship teams.

TO ME, WHAT sets him apart is being able to repeat what's already perfect mechanics. It's what you would teach a Little Leaguer, frame by frame. Mariano's arm slot is the same every pitch. No one else does that. He gets lots of arm extension. I call him Inspector Gadget because it's like his arm has an extra extension that pops out of his shoulder. There is also that great wrist action; his wrist is like a blur at the end of the pitch.

There have been so many great memories. Every time I see [former Atlanta Braves pitchers Tom] Glavine or [Greg] Maddux or [John] Smoltz, I say: "You could have four or five rings if you had Mariano Rivera."

We joke about it, but when you think about it, it's probably true. When I think of Mo, I think, "Wow I've got four World Series rings on the same team with him, and every time I see him I want to say, thank you." That's how strongly I feel about him, how good he's been in the clutch.

It was a comforting feeling when Mariano went to the bullpen in the fifth inning when we had a lead or it was a close game. That's when you'd see his game face. It's different for a closer because things have to fall right for Mariano to do his job. You've got to have the lead, and it's got to be a close enough game. So he had a different look on his face when the game was close and it looked like he was going to get into the game.

I don't think there's ever been a pitcher, especially a closer, that's been so calm on the mound. You get spoiled with how efficient he is. It's boom, boom, boom, game over. There's no walking the bases loaded, no tightrope walks. There's never been a closer like him—ever.

Dennis Eckersley

Pitcher

Playing Career

Cleveland Indians, Boston Red Sox, Chicago Cubs, Oakland Athletics, and St. Louis Cardinals from 1975 to 1998

Career Statistics

1,071 games, 197 wins, 171 losses, 390 saves, 3.50 earned run average, 3,285 innings, 3,076 hits, 738 walks, 2,401 strikeouts

Mo Cred

Eckersley was elected to the Hall of Fame in 2004. He was the American League's Most Valuable Player and Cy Young Award winner in 1992. He and John Smoltz are the only pitchers in major league baseball history with a 20-win season and a 50-save season in their career.

MARIANO RIVERA HAS just been absolutely automatic ever since he took over closing games [in 1997]. He's the greatest closer who ever lived. He is going to go out on top. He is just too great.

He has such impeccable control. People talk about Mariano having this one pitch, this phenomenal cutter. It looks like a fastball until it gets ninety percent of the way there, and then, at the last fraction, it moves from right to left. And it's so hard for the hitters to pick up. And they know it's coming. That's the crazy thing. He has such great control with it. He puts it right where he wants to, and he has such a beautiful delivery. He's just so automatic. The motion looks effortless. It is just that one step and [the ball] is next to his ear. And the repeating [of that motion] is what is incredible.

I was totally different. We couldn't be further [apart] the way we went about it. He's very much like the iceman, you know, unemotional. For the long run, that's probably what you want, is someone

205

to be less affected by it because I think emotionally it would wear you down after a while; it wore me down.

It's incredible [what he's done in the postseason]. If you add up all of his postseasons, it's almost two years' worth of pitching. And his earned run average is phenomenal, because this is where the money is. That's what sets him apart from everybody else. You know, I did it in Oakland. And the atmosphere in Oakland, it doesn't even come close to matching the expectations and the pressure that goes along with pitching for the New York Yankees.

I sat down with him about two years ago for [a television interview on] TBS, and I talked about the few failures that he's had. He has this inner peace. He's a very spiritual guy. I walked away from the interview wanting to have what he has, beyond pitching. It's this inner peace about him that must go into the success that he's had over this long course of time.

He is a unique guy in every way. First of all, he is gifted. It is beyond all that. He is one of a kind. Not everybody is humble and graceful, to be that type of a player. The thing I like about him more than that is the aura when you are around him. He seems so peaceful and centered. The aura doesn't change. The velocity is down only a tick, and the consistency is still there.

Most Postseason Saves*

Mariano Rivera	42
Brad Lidge	18
Dennis Eckersley	15
Jason Isringhausen	11
Robb Nen	11

*Since saves became an official statistic in 1969

Tom Gordon

Pitcher

Playing Career

Kansas City Royals, Boston Red Sox, Chicago Cubs, Houston Astros, Chicago White Sox, New York Yankees, Philadelphia Phillies, and Arizona Diamondbacks from 1988 to 2009

Career Statistics

890 games, 138 wins, 126 losses, 158 saves, 3.96 earned run average, 2,108 innings, 1,889 hits, 977 walks, 1,928 strikeouts

Mo Cred

Gordon spent two seasons in the bullpen with Rivera while playing for the Yankees in 2004 and 2005.

MARIANO IS ONE of the greatest ambassadors that could ever live and be a part of professional sports, so not just baseball itself. What Mariano represents is professionalism, leadership, and character—and all those great things that come with a great man. I was really blessed to be a part of that Yankees organization for the 2004 and '05 seasons and have him as a guy to look up to.*

I was even older, an older player, having been around the game three or four years more, but Mariano was someone that you can look up to, get advice from, and learn the game from, even as you continue to get into the latter years of your career. For me, to be in the same clubhouse with Mariano, I idolized him as a player, he's one of my idols today, along with Hank Aaron, Johnny Bench, and the greatest iconic baseball players in our time. Like I said, Mariano is an ambassador, a total

---

*In two seasons with the Yankees, Gordon was 14-8 with 6 saves and a 2.38 earned run average.

professional, in every possible way for major league baseball, and even for young kids of our future.

A lot of guys come up [to bat] thinking that Mariano doesn't change speeds on that cutter, but he does. What's been most effective is that Mariano not only changes speeds, he's pinpoint with his control on that pitch. That's what gets hitters looking to other areas, and then, bam, they're beat. He's defined the great pitch in the game, and he's been the best in the entire game of baseball at ever possessing a pitch that doesn't need to be worked with too much, doesn't need to be tinkered with, doesn't need to be over analyzed, but at the same time, he's gotten it down to a science. He does that by his pinpoint control.

His control every single night on that pitch has been phenomenal. I've never seen a guy that goes to the bullpen and he throws a change-up, he'll throw a four-seam fastball, he can show you three major league pitches, but he only works with one. What I was able to learn from that is that Mariano has the same exact mechanics every single day. He worked as hard he can work at becoming one of the best in the game at recognizing his mechanics. He also was able to go out consistently and repeat his arm slot on that pitch, every single day. For a guy to pitch four or five times a week, that's a really remarkable thing to do. I got a

---

Mo Respect

Rich "Goose" Gossage

The mustachioed fire baller earned 124 victories and 310 saves during his Hall of Fame career from 1972 to 1994.

It's a huge psychological advantage when you've got a guy like Mariano and a great setup corps, to know that it's a six-inning ballgame. You've got the lead, and it's over.

He's the consummate professional. He acts the way guys should act. Kids should take a page out of his book on how to act on the mound, not acting like fools jumping up and down, showing hitters up.

chance to be in a position to close, but I needed all three of my pitches. For him, he was able to change speeds often, but also mix in that 94 to 95 miles an hour cutter. He learned that pitch down to a science.

Jason Grimsley
Relief pitcher

Playing Career

Philadelphia Phillies, Cleveland Indians, Anaheim Angels, New York Yankees, Kansas City Royals, Baltimore Orioles, and Arizona Diamondbacks from 1989 to 2006

Career Statistics

552 games, 42 wins, 58 losses, 4 saves, 4.77 earned run average, 936 innings, 954 hits, 498 walks, 622 strikeouts

Mo Cred

Grimsley spent two seasons in the bullpen with Rivera while playing for the Yankees and together they helped the team win two World Series titles in 1999 and 2000.

WHEN HE GOT to the ballpark it was almost like he was on a stopwatch. He went about his business in the same manner every day. I learned a lot from watching his routine. He had success with his routine, so he repeated it. He made his day repeatable. This wasn't a superstition. This wasn't that he had to tie his shoe a certain way or wear his hat a certain way, or put on a left sock first. This was a consistency with which you approach your job.

He was consistent in the way he worked in the gym, how he did his cardio workout, his throwing program, when he came out to the bullpen, how he warmed up to get ready for a game. It was the same every time. If you experience success doing it one way, repeat it, because it relaxes your mind.

Mariano looked like he was on autopilot the whole time. Some of us in the bullpen called him "The Ghoul" because nothing affected what he did. It didn't matter if it was a spring training game or the seventh game of the World Series. Mo had the same approach, the same look, the same demeanor, and the same style. That's what made him great. The gravity of the game didn't change Mariano the way it does change some people. I don't think he got better in the big situation, he just didn't change the way he approached his job in those big spots.

My lasting memory of Mo was his consistency in the way he treated everybody the same way, whether [the player had] been there for ten years or if it was his first day [with the Yankees]. I think that played a big part in what made him great. He's not only consistent on the mound, but he's consistent in his approach as a human being. He treats everybody with the same class and respect that he expects to be treated

Mo Respect

David Huff

The left-handed pitcher joined the Yankees in the middle of the 2013 season.

There is one play I've seen in person that sticks out for me. I never realized how athletic he was until he was facing Luis Valbuena against us [Cleveland Indians] in 2010. Valbuena hit an inside cutter that broke his bat. The barrel was spinning back up the middle at Mariano and so was the ball. He jumped over the barrel, landed, quickly dropped down and threw the ball to first. I was wowed. He is a really good player. Him winning the World Series [five times] and dominating with one pitch, it's unbelievable.

with. You don't often see that from a player of his caliber—from the best pitcher to ever put on a baseball uniform.

Mariano's greatness was expected, so there was never anything surprising about it. Mariano on his worst day was still amazing. Halfway through the season you look up and he's got twenty-five or thirty saves. He was as close to automatic and a sure thing as this game has ever seen.

Phil Hughes
Pitcher

Playing Career

New York Yankees and Minnesota Twins since 2007

Career Statistics

182 games, 56 wins, 50 losses, 3 saves, 4.54 earned run average, 780 innings, 787 hits, 245 walks, 656 strikeouts

Mo Cred

Hughes was Rivera's teammate with the Yankees from 2007 to 2013.

BEING DOWN IN the bullpen with him in 2009 was really an eye-opener. As a starter, you rely on him to come in for the ninth inning and stuff like that, but you don't really get a feel for what it's all about until you're down there [in the bullpen with him]. Those playoff situations where you're leaning on him to not only get you four outs, but sometimes six or seven [and still] his demeanor out there never changed.

If we're in a situation where he's going to have to come in and save the game, you can see [something] click. That fire that you see in his eyes when he starts to do his routine and stretching and all that, you definitely notice when he kind of clicks, and he's ready to go. When he knew he was going to have to throw two, maybe three innings at times, he always answered the bell.

One moment that stands out I think is the last out of the 2009 World Series. It's sort of cliché, but just to see his reaction after already having four championships, the way he's jumping around like a little kid. You can tell at his age, it never gets old, and I'm sure that's the thing he'll miss the most—competing on the field, and those moments of celebration. It's something you don't often get in the real world.

Mo Respect

Jason Isringhausen

Isringhausen earned 300 career saves while pitching for five teams from 1995 to 2012.

I think there should be a lot more attention given to what Mariano has accomplished. There's only going to be two guys with 600 saves, and after Rivera, there won't be anyone more. It will never happen again.

Shawn Kelley

Relief pitcher

Playing Career

Seattle Mariners and New York Yankees since 2009

Career Statistics

177 games, 14 wins, 11 losses, 3.77 earned run average, 181 innings, 168 hits, 62 walks, 193 strikeouts

Mo Cred

Kelley joined the Yankees in the bullpen as Rivera's teammate in 2013.

COMING FROM ANOTHER organization, you always hear about him being this "great guy, great teammate, an unbelievable person." You heard everything about him, and when you meet him, he doesn't disappoint you or let you down.

You meet him and are like, "Wow!" You almost think no one could live up to those expectations. Nobody could be that good, or that unflawed, that people can say that. But when you meet him, he's the real deal, he's the full package, and he's what everyone thinks he is.

One of the things that really showed his character to me was how he takes thirty to forty minutes out of his day during batting practice on the road to stop and sign autographs for guys. He goes down the line and signs for all the guys. He's not asked to do that. But the fact that he does that, and he deals with the people sticking stuff and throwing stuff at him, and he just sits there and signs for like thirty to forty minutes, is impressive. You don't see that.

As much as everyone would like to do it, it's kind of a hassle. You have to get ready for a game. At that time, when batting practice is ending, you have to eat. He says, "I can take thirty minutes out of my schedule and give back to the fans."

Mo Respect

Pedro Martinez

The three-time Cy Young Award winner pitched for the archrival Boston Red Sox for seven years from 1998 to 2004.

I love Mariano. If I have to actually get in a line and wait for an hour to get Mariano's autograph, which I thank God I don't have to do, but if I had to, he would be the guy I would do it for.

Believe it or not, Mariano took me in his truck and drove me around New York to go house shopping [when I signed with the Mets prior to the 2005 season]. He's the one who introduced me to the area where he lived and that's where I bought my house.

Not everyone has the luxury to have Mariano as your driver and take you around and then take you to his house to share time with his family. Me and Mariano share the same agent, that made it easier. But at the same time, it's a mutual respect that we have for each other, and love.

Al Leiter

Pitcher

Playing Career

New York Yankees, Toronto Blue Jays, Florida Marlins, and New York Mets from 1987 to 2005

Career Statistics

419 games, 162 wins, 132 losses, 2 saves, 3.80 earned run average, 2,391 innings, 2,152 hits, 1,163 walks, 1,974 strikeouts

Mo Cred

Rivera saved a victory for Leiter in Game 4 of the 2005 American League Division Series against the Los Angeles Angels; it was Leiter's final major league appearance.

MARIANO IS UNBELIEVABLY consistent. If you look at Maria-no's delivery and compare it from 1995 to today, it's exactly the same motion. You can look at video and overlay his delivery from his rookie season to now—and we're talking nineteen years later—and it looks almost identical. His release point, and the flight of the ball, is the same. Repeating your delivery over and over again is really hard to do, because pitching is such an unusual motion. Things happen to your back, your leg, your finish, it's not ever supposed to be the same, but for Mariano, it still is.

Joe Nathan
Relief pitcher

Playing Career

San Francisco Giants, Minnesota Twins, Texas Rangers, and Detroit Tigers since 1999

Career Statistics

714 games, 57 wins, 30 losses, 2.76 earned run average, 341 saves, 858 innings, 625 hits, 311 walks, 912 strikeouts

Mo Cred

Nathan became major league baseball's active saves leader following Rivera's retirement.

IGREW UP IN the New York area as a Mets fans. I never went to Yankee Stadium and experienced Mariano's entrance as a fan. I've only seen it competing against him. It's always cool to see him come out of the bullpen in New York because the fans stick around. At a lot of other stadiums the people take off early, they leave before the ninth inning, but in New York that's not the case. In New York, you want to see this guy pitch; you want to hear the song when he comes in.

As a player on the opposing team, I don't want to hear the song because that means we're losing, it's late in the game, and Mariano is coming in for the save. I think it's crazy that Mariano [makes his entrance to] a Metallica song. I'm not sure if "Enter Sandman" is a song he picked, or if somebody helped him, but however it came about, it works great.*

I watch the way Mariano goes about his business, the way he handles himself in tough situations. I pay attention to the way he conducts himself. I watch how poised he is. He doesn't jump around after a save. He just shakes hands and gets off the field and comes back to do it again tomorrow. I've always thought he was a good role model for players in the major leagues and for young kids coming up from the minor leagues. He respects his opponents, and doesn't show anybody up. I try to emulate him. He's the type of guy that I look up to. I enjoy getting a chance to talk to Mariano when we're at All-Star Games and when we go into town to face the Yankees.**

Everyone says the postseason is when he's at his best. His great performances stand out more in the postseason because everyone's paying closer attention. He doesn't treat situations any differently by making them bigger or smaller, whether it's a pick-up game in his backyard or the seventh game of the World Series. He's not going to get too excited. He's just going to get outs. Watching him in the postseason is just like watching Mariano as usual. He's the same guy doing his job whether it's the regular season or the postseason.***

What Mariano has accomplished is amazing. He has over 600 saves. That's a ridiculous total. I started closing when I was about thirty years

---

*Rivera did not pick "Enter Sandman" as his entrance song. The Yankee Stadium scoreboard production crew began playing the song in the summer of 1999, having witnessed in the previous year's World Series how enthusiastically San Diego fans reacted to closer Trevor Hoffman entering games accompanied by AC/DC's "Hells Bells." Nathan's entrance song is "Stand Up and Shout" by Steel Dragon, a fictional band from the Mark Wahlberg film *Rock Star*.

**Nathan has been selected to the American League All-Star team six times.

***Nathan's Minnesota teams lost twice to Rivera's Yankees in the postseason, in the American League Division Series in 2004 and 2009.

Joe Hands it to Mo

Texas Rangers' closer Joe Nathan earned his first career All-Star Game save in 2013, arguably the greatest moment of the six-time All-Star's career. Nathan immediately found Rivera and handed him the game ball, knowing that while he might have technically been the closer, the game belonged to Rivera, who was named the Most Valuable Player.

To be able to hand the ball over to him that I saved with him in the bullpen was pretty cool. It's no secret how much I look up to him, so to be able to do that for him was awesome.

It's a thrill and an honor just to get the chance to talk to him. I sat down and had a 20-, 30-minute conversation and just picked his brain. We all learn from each other and we can all probably take something from each [other].

This game is all about adjustments and trying to make yourself better. And even Mariano, I'm sure, is doing what he needs to do to have the edge when he goes out there.

old, so the only way I'm going to reach 600 saves is if I get the opportunity to close games when I'm fifty! His longevity, his endurance, his durability are at an incredibly high level. Getting my 300th save was amazing. But I'm still competing in the middle of my career, so I don't focus on saves. What matters most is trying to secure wins for my team. When I hang up my spikes, then we'll see how many saves I got. When people asked me what getting 300 meant, I said, "It's one save closer to 400."

I'm not going to [approach] the saves total of Mariano Rivera, but if I can be in the same sentence with him, that will be quite an accomplishment.*

---

*Nathan notched his 300th career save by closing out a 5-4 victory over the Tampa Bay Rays on April 8, 2013. The final out came on a controversial three-and-two curve ball that was called strike three by umpire Marty Foster, who later admitted the pitch was not a strike. Only five closers in baseball history have amassed 400 saves in their career: Mariano Rivera (652), Trevor Hoffman (601), Lee Smith (478), John Franco (424), and Billy Wagner (422).

Denny Neagle

Pitcher

Playing Career

Minnesota Twins, Pittsburgh Pirates, Atlanta Braves, Cincinnati Reds, New York Yankees, and Colorado Rockies from 1991 to 2004

Career Statistics

392 games, 124 wins, 92 losses, 3 saves, 4.24 earned run average, 1,890 innings, 1,887 hits, 594 walks, 1,415 strikeouts

Mo Cred

Neagle was Rivera's teammate on the Yankees' 2000 World Series championship team.

I WAS ALSO ON the other side with Atlanta in the 1996 World Series when John Wetteland was the closer for the Yankees and Mariano was setting up for him. I can tell you without a doubt that our hitters were actually looking forward to facing the closer, rather than the guy who was the set-up man. It's rare for a team to feel that way. I remember our hitters saying, "Thank God, Wetteland is coming in, at least we've got a chance now."

By no means is that a knock against John Wetteland, he had a great career, too. But because Mariano had such amazing stuff, you knew what kind of talent he was even before he was closing.

The young Mariano Rivera could throw pretty hard. The radar gun might read 94 or 95 miles per hour. Although hitters knew he was throwing hard, 95 [m.p.h.] actually feels like 99 [m.p.h.] against him. Some pitchers are maximum effort. They're all arms and legs coming at you. Rob Dibble [of the Reds] and Mitch Williams [of the Phillies] come to mind, guys who rear back and give it everything they have. Mariano's motion is so smooth and the mechanics of his delivery so effortless, the ball seems to get on top of you in a heartbeat. Guys I played with [in Atlanta] like Ryan Klesko and Javier Lopez couldn't believe how quickly the pitch got on them. They would come back to the dugout saying, "God, I thought I was right on that pitch and before I knew it, it was by me."

He was so effortless it didn't seem like he was throwing that hard.

Being on the same team with him was special; he was a joy to watch. One thing about Mariano that jumps out is how he carries himself on a day-to-day basis. Mariano personifies what being a professional is all about. When I joined the Yankees he already had the resume, and he had the credentials to back it up. Some players let their egos get in the way, they feel they're above the game, and they act like they're above the fans. Not Mariano Rivera. Look up the word "professional" and you'll see Mariano's picture; if he's not the face of what it means to be a professional, he's certainly one of the faces of it.

Every once in a while, a person comes along in a sport that you can't help but take notice of. Even his fellow competitors and teammates take notice of how they work: what they do to prepare, how they throw, when they throw. I consider myself a big fan of the game, as well as a competitor playing the game, and there are a select few players that I would stop whatever I was doing to watch them go about their business. I had the pleasure of playing with Greg Maddux for three years in Atlanta; he was one of those guys. To watch the way he carried himself, prepared for games, studied hitters, it was amazing, even the littlest things were important to watch because you can't help but learn from a guy like that.

It's the same thing with Mariano. I watched how he prepared, how he took care of his body, and the way he carried himself. He has the same routine every day and he goes out to the bullpen at a certain point in the game. I can't remember his exact routine, but I do know he would go to the bullpen a lot earlier than other closers. That's another personality trait of Mariano's that goes to show you what kind of person and what kind of teammate he is. He wanted to show his fellow relievers that he wasn't above them. He also went to the bullpen early to be able to help out another reliever. He wanted to be there to help in any way he could.

One game that sticks out in my head was my fourth or fifth start for the Yankees. We were in Kansas City, and I remember it was a hard-fought game. I pitched really well, but we were losing 1-0. Then in the top of the ninth inning we were fortunate to put together a big rally, but the Royals fought back to make a game of it. Then Mariano came in to save it. It wasn't anything in particular that he did. It wasn't a wow moment; he didn't strike out the side or anything like that. But I remember sitting on the bench with a comforting feeling that I was going to get the win for the team.*

In years past, playing on teams with different closers, even good ones like Mark Wohlers in Atlanta, as good as they were, there's something about Mariano that is a very comforting factor. As a starting pitcher you pace the ninth inning until you get that W. It's baseball and crazy things can happen, but when Mariano walked on the mound it was lights out, game over, chalk this up as a W for the team. Even before the third out was called, you liked your chances to win because Mariano was in the game.

I thank God I didn't ever have to bat against him, because otherwise I would have had some splinters in my hands.

---

*Neagle and the Yankees defeated the Royals, 7-3, at Kauffman Stadium, on September 7, 2000. Neagle had allowed only four hits and one run through eight innings, yet trailed 1-0. The Yankees' offense exploded for seven runs in the top of the ninth, but the Royals staged a comeback of their own. The Yankees survived poor relief pitching and eventually needed Rivera to retire Carlos Beltran for the final out with the potential tying run on deck. It was Rivera's 162nd career save.

Jeff Nelson
Relief pitcher

Playing Career

Seattle Mariners, New York Yankees, Texas Rangers, and Chicago White Sox from 1992 to 2006

Career Statistics

798 games, 48 wins, 45 losses, 33 saves, 3.41 earned run average, 784 innings, 633 hits, 428 walks, 829 strikeouts

Mo Cred

Nelson spent six seasons in the bullpen with Rivera while playing for the Yankees and together they helped the team win four World Series titles in 1996, 1998, 1999, and 2000.

▌REMEMBER HIM IN 1995, his rookie year, when I was with Seattle. Our hitters couldn't touch him. I remember some of our hitters probably thanking [Yankees' manager] Buck Showalter that he didn't pitch Mariano in some key situations [in the American League Division Series].*

He's got such a smooth wind-up and an easy delivery. The ball gets on you fast and that makes it hard for a batter to pick up his cutter. As a rookie, he was throwing harder than he is now. Back then he could hit 96 [miles per hour]. He would pound left-handed hitters inside, pitch right-handed hitters away, and then also climb the ladder. A fastball up in the zone looks good to a hitter, but with

---

*Trailing the Yankees two games to none in the best-of-five division series in 1995, the Mariners roared back to win three straight games to advance to the A.L. Championship Series. Inexplicably, Rivera pitched a total of just two innings in relief in the final three games.

Mariano, the ball gets on you so quickly that he gets a lot of swings and misses. Add that to his cutter, which is so hard to pick up, and that's what makes him so dominant to face. If the Yankees had the lead and he came in the game, you could tell the other team is thinking: "Oh no, Mo's coming in and it's over."

My job was to pitch the seventh or eighth inning, and to get my outs, because I knew if I did my job, Mariano was coming in to pitch the ninth inning. My goal was to leave Mariano with three outs; I didn't want him coming in in the eighth inning—[Yankees' manager] Joe Torre didn't want him coming in in the eighth. I wanted to get those outs in the eighth and let Mo pitch the ninth.

Even though he's pitching one inning, he is by far the most dominant pitcher I've ever seen. Players all around the league know that if it's the ninth inning and the Yankees have the lead, [the game] is over. Opposing managers cringe when they see him running out from behind the outfield wall.

It was his routine to come out to the bullpen in the seventh inning to get ready for the ninth. He's quiet. The only time he lets loose is when it's a blowout, when the game gets out of hand, and he knows he's not getting into the game; then he'll relax a bit, he'll smile and joke around. On those nights he would come out [to the bullpen] to participate in a gag or a joke and then he'd go back to the dugout.

You don't know by looking at him if he's done a great job or bad job, he stays the same all the time. He forgets about his past outing, whether it's good or bad. If it's bad, and he gave up the game, the next night he wants the ball again. He's got a short memory, and that's the key to being a great reliever.

Andy Pettitte

Pitcher

Playing Career

New York Yankees and Houston Astros from 1995 to 2013

Career Statistics

531 games, 256 wins, 153 losses, 3.85 earned run average, 3,316 innings, 3,448 hits, 1,031 walks, 2,448 strikeouts

Mo Cred

Rivera has saved a win for Pettitte 72 times in their careers—the most of any starter-closer duo in baseball history.

WE WERE KIND of up-and-coming starters in the organization. I know in '95 he broke in the rotation. I was in the rotation and he came up during the middle of the year, made a few starts. Then they turned him into a reliever. Just to see him coming up, pitching with me in that '95 rotation. Then to see him now, turned into a reliever and what he's been able to do, it's amazing to see, that's for sure.

Man, there are so many favorite times that I think about. Game Seven against Boston in 2003 was a special moment. He kind of rose above everything, just like, "I got another inning in me." He probably could have pitched as many innings as we needed him to, if Booney [Aaron Boone] wouldn't have hit that home run.

We just have a special relationship. I don't know how to explain it. Obviously, when you spent as much time together after as many years as we've been together, you just kind of grow a little closer to one another than you would with other teammates. He's always been there for me.

Obviously I feel real secure and good about things whenever you see that guy comes running in from the bullpen in the ninth inning.

For someone that has done the things Mo has done in this game and been as great as he has, it's special for me watching him this year knowing this is going to be his last year. After this, he won't be closing any games for us, so I'll savor it as much as I can.

It's exciting for me to know he's going to get the opportunity to do the things he's been looking forward to doing with his family. But also it's sad, knowing he's not going to be going back out there taking the mound at Yankee Stadium in the ninth inning and closing games out for the Yankees after this year. It's been a blessing for me to be able to say I've played with him, and obviously, if he's happy, I'm happy.

Most Win/Save Combinations, All-Time*	
Andy Pettitte and Mariano Rivera (New York Yankees)	72
Bob Welch and Dennis Eckersley (Oakland Athletics)	57
Mike Mussina and Mariano Rivera (New York Yankees)	49
Dave Stewart and Dennis Eckersley (Oakland Athletics)	43
Jimmy Key and Tom Henke (Toronto Blue Jays)	37
Kevin Tapani and Rick Aguilera (Minnesota Twins)	37
*Since saves became an official statistic in 1969	
Courtesy of the Elias Sports Bureau	

J.J. Putz

Relief pitcher

Playing Career

Seattle Mariners, New York Mets, Chicago White Sox, and Arizona Diamondbacks since 2003

Career Statistics

554 games, 36 wins, 32 losses, 189 saves, 2.99 earned run average, 553 innings, 452 hits, 178 walks, 585 strikeouts

Mo Cred

Putz beat out Rivera to win the Rolaids Relief Man award in 2007 as the American League's top relief pitcher.

I **HAD AN OPPORTUNITY** to talk with [Mariano] in 2006, the first year I was closing. He spent about forty minutes with me talking behind home plate at three o'clock in the afternoon before batting practice. It was just an honor to be on the field with him, but also to be able to talk to him and kind of pick his brain was pretty special. [It's] something I'll never forget.

He's amazing. It's hard enough pitching late in the game with an arsenal of pitches. But to be able to go out there and be as dominant as he is—he's undoubtedly the most dominant late-game reliever ever to play the game—and the fact that he did it with one pitch, makes it that much more remarkable.

In my opinion, he's not just the best reliever of all time; I think he's the best pitcher—period—of all time. Just the dominance he's had for almost two decades, on the stage that he's done it on, all the postseason records he holds, it's mind-boggling.

Nobody wants to remember a guy like Mo getting carted off [the field] on a John Deere tractor. He's been one of the biggest attractions in this game, and the fact that he came out [after his 2012 knee injury] and said he's not going out like that really made me smile.

David Robertson

Relief pitcher

Playing Career

New York Yankees since 2008

Career Statistics

339 games, 21 wins, 14 losses, 8 saves, 2.76 earned run average, 329 innings, 267 hits, 143 walks, 428 strikeouts

Mo Cred

Robertson, who has spent time in the bullpen as Rivera's teammate with the Yankees since 2008, is considered by most baseball experts to be Rivera's heir apparent.

TRY NOT TO think about [the pressure of taking over for Rivera as the closer]. If I get the opportunity to close ball games, I'm going to try to do the same thing I've been doing in the eighth inning. You have to get three guys out; you've got to keep the momentum on your side and not make a lot of mistakes.

If I get the opportunity [as the next Yankees' closer] hopefully I can do well, but as of now, I'm not worried about it. We got the best guy there is right now at the back of bullpen. If we can get a lead I am very confident we can keep the lead and win the ball game. Mariano is good—he's really good. Every time I watch him pitch, I think, gosh, he never seems to make mistakes. He's just amazing. He's always on top of his game. He's one of a kind. He's not worried about the end [of his career]. He's enjoying his last year and having fun winning ball games.

Most impressive about Mariano is his confidence, his consistency, and his mound presence. It doesn't matter who's in the [batter's] box, he knows he's going to make pitch after pitch after pitch. Either you're going to get lucky and get a hit, or he's going to get you out. He throws one pitch. He'll throw a sinker every now and then, but he lives and dies by that cutter. People know it's coming and he still gets them out. It's unbelievable. I think hitters get themselves out because by the time guys get in the [batter's] box they're already thinking about how that cutter is going to eat them up.

When he takes the mound you don't ever see him flustered or mad because he gave up a hit. He battles his way out of situations. You never see his facial features change. Nothing bothers him. When he had that blown save against the Mets, the next day, in the clubhouse, he was laughing and joking and carrying on like nothing happened. It's a reliever's life. You can have bad games, two or three in a row, but you've got put yourself together for the next game. It's like hitting; if you get in a slump, you have to dig your way out of it.*

Mo Respect

CC Sabathia

The indomitable Yankees' ace was Rivera's teammate on the Yankees from 2009 to 2013, and was a member of the 2009 World Series championship team.

He's been one of the best players in Major League Baseball for a long time, and to do it all with the Yankees is unbelievable.

Every day is the same for him, whether we win or lose, good or bad, you can never tell. He's always the same. That's something special in baseball, and he has that.

He's been consistent in every way. He comes in and does his work. He's focused. That's the word that comes to mind.

Just being able to be on his team for the last five seasons and have the feeling that when he comes in the game, it's pretty much over, has been awesome.

---

*Rivera's blown save on May 28, 2013 against the Mets at Citi Field was the first time in 1,072 career games that he'd blown a save without retiring a batter. Ironically, Rivera had thrown out the ceremonial first pitch, and then took the loss on his final pitch.

I thought what was done for him at the [2013] All-Star Game was amazing. It was great how he took the field by himself, and got a standing ovation from the crowd, and from players on both teams. I got chills watching it on television. And to get the Most Valuable Player award, too, he's just so deserving of all the respect he gets. He's such a nice guy. He's the same guy every day. When you meet Mariano Rivera you know you're meeting someone special. He's one of the best people I've ever known in my life.

Curt Schilling

Pitcher

Playing Career

Baltimore Orioles, Houston Astros, Philadelphia Phillies, Arizona Diamondbacks, and Boston Red Sox from 1988 to 2007

Career Statistics

569 games, 216 wins, 146 losses, 22 saves, 3.46 earned run average, 3,261 innings, 2,998 hits, 711 walks, 3,116 strikeouts

Mo Cred

Schilling and the Diamondbacks defeated Rivera's Yankees in the 2001 World Series and Schilling did it again in the 2004 American League Championship Series as a member of the Red Sox.

MARIANO IS AN incredibly intelligent guy. He's always had unbelievable command, and he's somebody who has studied his craft.

He's a knuckleballer without a knuckleball. The knuckleball is a fluke, it's a freak pitch; there have only been four or five guys who have mastered the pitch. A lot of guys can throw a cutter—and a lot of guys throw really good cutters. But until the last five years of his career, people said his career was built on that one pitch, but it gets back to what I believe every pitcher must have to be a truly good pitcher—command. There's a difference between control and command. Control is the ability to throw strikes. Command is the ability to throw a strike where you want to. Mariano commands his cutter to both sides of the plate.

It was never just a cutter; it's not just one pitch. What a lot of people don't understand is that his cutter is six pitches: To a left-handed batter he can throw it down and in, at the belt and in, and at the chest and in; and to a right-handed batter he throws it down and away, down and in, and at the belt and in. In theory it's one pitch, but he has such command of it, that actually it's like six pitches.

John Smoltz

Pitcher

Playing Career

Atlanta Braves, Boston Red Sox, and St. Louis Cardinals from 1988 to 2009

Career Statistics

723 games, 213 wins, 155 losses, 154 saves, 3.33 earned run average, 3,473 innings, 3,074 hits, 1,010 walks 3,084 strikeouts

Mo Cred

Smoltz's Braves lost to Rivera's Yankees in the World Series in 1996 and 1999.

WE FACED MARIANO in the World Series in 1996, when he was the set-up man for the Yankees and they had a really good closer in John Wetteland. Mariano was so dominant that when he went out of the game, you thought, "Now we have a chance—and Wetteland, a good closer, was coming in the game!" Even then, you could see the future; very few times can you see the future in a player's progression when he goes from set-up man to closer. He was closing games when we faced the Yankees again in the 1999 [World] Series and you could see what a great job he did when he got in that position.

He's made general managers have nightmares in the sense that if you put Mariano on any team he'd still be the greatest closer to ever pitch. I don't know if his impact would be as devastating on another team, because the Yankees were always in the postseason. It's the chicken and the egg argument. Your team has to have the lead to get to him, and when you do get to him, the game is over. He's the most consistently dominant closer in that role of any guy I've ever seen. The Yankees had other outstanding players, but he single-handedly was responsible for why the Yankees won those four out of five world championships. He's an automatic first-time Hall of Famer. To have the statistics that he has is one thing, but to do it in the clutch, to get better in the postseason, is remarkable.

Mariano has changed the way the role of the closer is viewed. People today still think of the closer as a specialized role. It's different from years ago when relievers went three innings to get a save. Baseball isn't played against time, there's no clock ticking, but the clock ticking in everyone's mind is that if we don't have the lead in the sixth inning, we better get it now, or by the seventh, because Mariano could come in and pitch two innings. He is such a great weapon to have, because your strategy changes if you're the opposing manager, and the starting pitcher on your team feels better knowing that even if you get in trouble, there's Mariano behind you to back you up. There's such a psychological disadvantage [for an opponent] when Mariano comes in the game. You could say he had what Tiger [Woods] had for a long time when he stepped on the golf course, an advantage before he even threw a pitch.

He's genetically able to do things unlike any other pitcher. If he could teach the cutter to somebody else I don't think they could duplicate it. Everyone thinks pitching and bowling is the same where you have these mechanics down pat and you can repeat it. He has an ability to repeat his mechanics so smoothly, to make it look as easy as he does, it seems like he can throw forever.

Mike Stanton

Relief pitcher

Playing Career

Atlanta Braves, Boston Red Sox, Texas Rangers, New York Yankees, New York Mets, Washington Nationals, San Francisco Giants, and Cincinnati Reds from 1989 to 2007

Career Statistics

1,178 games, 68 wins, 63 losses, 84 saves, 3.92 earned run average, 1,114 innings, 1,086 hits, 420 walks, 895 strikeouts

Mo Cred

Stanton spent seven seasons in the bullpen with Rivera while playing for the Yankees, and together they helped the team win three World Series titles in 1998, 1999, and 2000.

WITHOUT MARIANO, [the Yankees] might have won a World Series or two, but we don't win all of them. When you have a guy like Mariano at the end of the game, especially in the postseason, who you know is a slam dunk to close out the game—he's got 42 career postseason saves—when you have that guy at the end of a ballgame it makes your team that much better. You know that if you're winning late in the game there's a pretty good chance you're going to win at the end. When that door opens and No. 42 comes galloping out of the bullpen, running like a gazelle because he's such a great athlete, it's like one out for your team right there. You can see guys in the other dugout put their heads down, because they know they're going to be lucky to just square a ball up, much less get a run.

You look back at one of the few blown saves he had in the postseason—that was the Luis Gonzalez blooper over second base to lose Game Seven of the 2001 World Series—you see nothing is squared up on the guy. It's unbelievable. It's not really one pitch. He's got a fastball that cuts and he'll let up on it and turn it over, but it's still all the same velocity. For big league hitters not to be able to put the head of the bat on the ball consistently, when all you're doing is throwing with one velocity, it doesn't matter how good those pitchers are, it's absolutely incredible. He's been a freak of nature his whole career.

What you look at when you talk about the greatest closer ever is how he goes about his business. There have been a lot of great closers, but for most of them, it's always an adventure because they walk batters and always have guys on base. Not Mariano. I'd love to know the numbers, but it seems a large percentage of his saves come three up and three down. There's no drama whatsoever. Hands down, there's not even a question, he's the greatest closer of all time. Dennis Eckersley was very good for several years, but what Mariano's done, the way Mariano's gone about it, the way he's carried himself over the years, the mystique of doing it on the biggest stage in sports, year in and year out, with ice water running through his veins, I don't think there's an argument.

Mariano being the closer made my job easier. The job of a relief pitcher is to get someone else out of trouble. If I get in trouble, the next guy down the line, it's his job to get me out of trouble. And if it's a ball game the Yankees really have to have, there's a good chance Mariano's going to pitch more than one inning, so you just have to get a couple of outs.

What's uncanny is how effective he is pitching to the first batter he faces. I want to know the batting average against him when facing the first batter; it can't be higher than a .200 average. To repeat his mechanics, to put the ball where he wants to, it's a blatant refusal to ever lose.

Most Games Pitched, All Time

Jesse Orosco	1,252
Mike Stanton	1,178
John Franco	1,119
Mariano Rivera	**1,115**
Dennis Eckersley	1,071
Hoyt Wilhelm	1,070
Dan Plesac	1,064
Mike Timlin	1,058
Kent Tekulve	1,050
Trevor Hoffman	1,035

Tanyon Sturtze

Pitcher

Playing Career

Chicago Cubs, Texas Rangers, Chicago White Sox, Tampa Bay Rays, Toronto Blue Jays, New York Yankees, and Los Angeles Dodgers from 1995 to 2008

Career Statistics

272 games, 40 wins, 44 losses, 3 saves, 5.19 earned run average, 797 innings, 886 hits, 333 walks, 480 strikeouts

Mo Cred

Sturtze spent three seasons in the bullpen with Rivera playing for the Yankees in 2004, 2005, and 2006.

THE BIGGEST THRILL was being able to play catch with Mariano every day, and learning from him how to be a reliever. When I came to New York I was a starter and I really had no idea how to pitch out of the bullpen. He was a tremendous help to me in making the transition from a starting pitcher to a relief pitcher.

We were throwing partners for all the years that I was with the Yankees. I jumped [at the chance] because I wanted to be next to him. To play catch with Mariano is not like playing catch with anyone else. If you don't hit him in the chest he got upset. It wasn't playing catch to play catch—it was playing catch to work. That's what he taught me. When you get to the field it's time to work.

He makes having a simple catch into a game of concentration. It's amazing to watch him play catch. You put your glove at a certain spot on your body—at your left shoulder or on your right hip—and he can throw the cutter right to that spot. Of course he threw cutters. I don't think Mariano can throw a ball straight anymore, everything is a cutter and everything is right in the spot he wants to hit. He's a perfectionist. It's impressive to watch his work ethic and the way he goes about each day at the ballpark. That's why he's the greatest of all time.

Of course he was the captain of the bullpen. To go out every single night and do what he does on the mound is very impressive. Sometimes people take for granted how great he really is. It's not that easy to get three outs in the ninth inning. So many times he got out of a difficult situation that you didn't think was possible. He would make your jaw drop twice a month. It certainly made our job as relievers a lot easier knowing that if we made a mess he was coming in behind us and he'd clean it up. If we put him in a bad position with men on base with nobody out, he'd shatter three bats and get out of it. He was like Houdini—he'd always find a way to escape.

He helped me become a better person and a better reliever. Everything that he tells you has a meaning behind it. Mo is one of those guys that radiate positivity. To be around somebody who is like that, it rubs off on you. You won't find a better person, or a more positive person. He truly treats everybody the same, whether you have one day in the big leagues or twenty years in the big leagues, it doesn't matter to Mariano.

Rick Sutcliffe

Pitcher

Playing Career

Los Angeles Dodgers, Cleveland Indians, Chicago Cubs, Baltimore Orioles, St. Louis Cardinals from 1978 to 1994

Career Statistics

457 games, 171 wins, 139 losses, 6 saves, 4.08 earned run average, 2,697 innings, 2,662 hits, 1,081 walks, 1,679 strikeouts

Mo Cred

Sutcliffe was the 1979 Rookie of the Year and the 1984 National League Cy Young Award winner.

IT WAS AN emotional farewell to Mariano at Yankee Stadium. It's as close as we'll ever get to perfect in the game of baseball. Mariano started tearing up. We were crying with him. It was great emotion, great theater. I thought what they did at the All-Star Game would never be topped, when he came in by himself in the eighth inning, and everyone in the world stood up and applauded, but this was even better.*

I salute the Yankees for thinking of it, and [Derek] Jeter and [Andy] Pettitte for going out to the mound. It was perfection. At the All-Star Game at Citi Field, the ovation Mariano got from the fans when it was just him out there on the mound, and also from his peers on both sides of the field, tells you there's never been anybody—player, pitcher, reliever, starter—like Mariano Rivera before.

Mariano thrived playing in New York. There's no other organization in baseball that has had twenty consecutive winning seasons. That sustained success gave Mariano the opportunity to save all those games. We know Trevor Hoffman also has 600 career saves, but the separation of Mariano Rivera and any other closer is what he's done in the postseason, and no other organization has been there as many times as the Yankees.

No pitcher has such an impact on the opposing team by just warming up. As a manager you know you only have twenty-four outs to get the lead, because if you're behind going into the ninth inning you're going to lose that ballgame. The one statistic that jumps out at me, and there's so many of them with Mariano Rivera, is he pitched in 96 postseason games, and every one of them was with the game on the line, and he only had one loss, in the 2001 World Series against Arizona. I spoke to [Yankees' manager] Joe Girardi and Joe told me the bullpen of the New York Yankees has been the biggest key to their success

---

*Rivera made his final Yankee Stadium appearance in the team's home finale, a 4-0 loss to Tampa Bay, on September 26, 2013. Rivera recorded two outs in the eighth inning and two outs in the ninth, but what will be remembered is the normally calm pitcher crying uncontrollably on the mound while embracing Pettitte and Jeter, who had been sent out by manager Girardi to make the pitching change to signal the end of Rivera's career.

in championship games. Looking back on it, they've always had that closer in Mariano Rivera to go out there and nail down those World Series victories.

Joe was saying there's no doubt in his mind that Mariano could be effective for two or three more years. But he's lost that desire to prepare to play. The desire to play is always going to be there. It's the preparation that Mariano Rivera put into everything, not only physically, as you look at him the body is still the same, but the mental part of it. We know that he had the legendary cutter, but he did the research, he did the homework, to find out where to place that cutter to stay away from opposing hitters' power. He always talked about staying away from slugging percentage. He not only had the ability to throw that pitch but to locate it, and know where to locate it.

Heartfelt Hugs

I didn't expect for him to be quite so emotional. He broke down and just gave me a bear hug, and I just bear-hugged him back. He was really crying. He was weeping. I could feel him crying on me.

—Andy Pettitte

We've been through everything together. I'm just happy he was able to go out like this. What the fans did for him this whole homestand was awesome. I'm grateful I've been his teammate for parts of 21 years.

—Derek Jeter

After the eighth inning, I knew I was going back for the last time. It was a totally different feeling. I had all the flashbacks from the minor leagues to the big leagues all the way to this moment. It was a little hard. I was able to compose myself and come back out.

They both came to get me out and I was thankful they came out. I needed them there and they were there. I was bombarded with emotions and feelings that I couldn't describe. Everything hit at that time. I knew that that was the last time, period. I never felt something like that before.

—Mariano Rivera

When I think of Mariano Rivera I think about Greg Maddux. He was the greatest starting pitcher of my time, Mariano being the greatest closer. It's not natural ability, as much as both of those guys were smarter than the other people they went up against. When I think of Mariano Rivera, we always talk about his cutter, but it's the intelligence that he has to prepare, to stay away of where the hitter can do the most damage. He throws it to both sides of the plate, and he would elevate it to finish people off. So that's where the encyclopedic mindset comes into play, separating him from other people that have equal ability.

Mo Respect

Justin Verlander

The Detroit Tigers' ace gave Mariano Rivera a warm hug as Rivera walked off the mound following his final All-Star Game appearance at Citi Field in New York, on July 16, 2013.

I didn't tell Mariano anything. It was just an embrace. I wanted to show my respect for his career and what he's done. I just wanted to give him the respect that he deserved.

I didn't plan to be the first one out there. It just sort of happened that way. I was standing by the dugout railing and I was the first one he came to. For him to come over and give me a hug, what an experience, that's something I'll always remember.

It's kind of surreal for me. I had tears in my eyes. It was so special. I'll never forget it. I have so much respect for him as a person and as a player, and that's the experience I'll never forget. That is a moment, absolutely, one hundred percent. Being his teammate for the day is something I'm going to tell my kids about.

Ron Villone

Relief pitcher

Playing Career

Seattle Mariners, San Diego Padres, Milwaukee Brewers, Cleveland Indians, Cincinnati Reds, Colorado Rockies, Houston Astros, Pittsburgh Pirates, Florida Marlins, New York Yankees, St. Louis Cardinals, and Washington Nationals from 1995 to 2009

Career Statistics

717 games, 61 wins, 65 losses, 8 saves, 4.73 earned run average, 1,168 innings, 1,115 hits, 637 walks, 925 strikeouts

Mo Cred

Villone spent two seasons in the bullpen with Rivera while playing for the Yankees in 2006 and 2007.

YOU KNEW WHEN Mariano Rivera arrived in the bullpen—especially at home—because everyone in the crowd near the bullpen got loud. If you didn't know he was in the bullpen, you sure felt his presence by the rumble in Yankee Stadium. When he walks into the bullpen he's there to get ready to take care of business.

Mariano is the consummate professional. He knows how to go about his business, and how to take care of business. He understands the task at hand every single day. He doesn't change; he doesn't veer from the course of success. He had a routine. Anybody who's successful has a routine. Baseball players are creatures of habit. Mariano was good at his routine, which was to get to the bullpen at the same time every day, and to do the same things to get ready before the game.

Believe me, he *is* intense. You don't weigh his intensity by looking at the emotion in his face; you measure his intensity by what's between his ears. He's a mild-mannered man. He has an inner strength and an ability to hold everything together, even in the most pressure-packed situation in sports. He's that way on a daily basis, whether it's the first game of the season or the last game of the World Series. You can't teach it. He has the innate ability to take pressure and put it in his pocket. If you need to describe the term "closer," he describes it better than anybody ever has. He's the singular meaning of domination.

He's all about finding a way to get better. It's not one thing—it's everything. He's all in. He's a team player and he understands what it takes to win. He not only leads by example, he leads with that nice, soft, very confident voice of his, that seems to be saying, "I know how to win, so you should listen to me."

He doesn't tell you what you have to do; he shares the information that works for him. Experience is the best teacher. He'll tell you what he's thinking. For him to do that shows he's not holding anything back, and that's the reason so many people around him are successful.

I enjoyed being around him every day. He was always willing to share information to help me get better. You're trying to find ways to win, and he'll help you with your preparation for the game by talking to you about how to get the hitters out so we can strand the [base] runners. He's very aware of how his bullpen mates are feeling and relates well to us. It's almost as if he had eyes in the back of his head. He knew how much you'd been throwing, and if you were tired, he'd suggest you take it easy that day during your [pre-game] throwing routine.

Mariano is confident, but I don't think anybody in baseball ever gets comfortable, because if you do, somebody's able to beat you. He's always confident, always in control; he has unbelievable poise on and off the field. I remember one game in Detroit when he pitched three innings. Before the game, [manager] Joe Torre was walking around the clubhouse talking to us—he was always asking us questions, he was a great communicator—because Joe thought he might need to extend the bullpen a little bit that night [because the scheduled starting pitcher Aaron Small was coming back from a hamstring injury].

Mariano said, "I'm ready."

He was always ready; he didn't blink. You never saw Mariano sweat, he never lost confidence, and he never wavered. Nothing ever shocked him, and he was never surprised. During the outfield pre-game [warm-ups] and in the bullpen you had the feeling that something was going to happen that night. Sure enough, it was a tight game and Mariano went in and pitched three innings for the win.*

Mo Respect

Adam Warren

Warren was Rivera's teammate in the bullpen in 2012 and 2013.

He pulls me aside every now and then, if I have a rough game, and gives me some advice [on] how to pitch, sometimes how to approach the mental aspect of the game. He has helped me pitch at this level by taking me under his wing a little bit and shown me the way. To be able to be teammates and talk and pick his brain is pretty amazing.

John Wetteland

Relief pitcher

Playing Career

Los Angeles Dodgers, Montreal Expos, New York Yankees, and Texas Rangers from 1989 to 2000

---

*Rivera pitched the ninth, tenth, and eleventh innings of an 11-6 win at Detroit, on May 30, 2006. It was the first time Rivera went three innings in a regular-season game since September 6, 1996—a span of nearly ten years.

Career Statistics

48 wins, 45 losses, 330 saves, 2.98 earned run average, 765 innings, 616 hits, 252 walks, 804 strikeouts

Mo Cred

Wetteland was the Yankees' closer in 1995 and 1996, and his four saves in the 1996 World Series earned him the series Most Valuable Player award.

THE 1996 TEAM was a very special team. We were a real close-knit group. We came to the park expecting to win every day, and went about our business in that fashion. I get reminded of 1996 a lot. It was obviously a highlight moment of my career just being involved with that club, being a part of that [World Series championship]. It's hard to think about that team without thinking about every single person on that team, and how they contributed.*

I had two good set-up men going into that year in [Bob] Wickman and Jeff Nelson. Mo wasn't a set-up man when he came into the pen. He was just a long guy, a spot starter. He was a kid, but he was a special kid. He grew into the role of set-up man. The other guys had been doing the job for years. You know how it works. You start pitching good, and you start getting better roles. It didn't take long until Mo was setting up.

Usually a closer has one great set-up man, now I had three. Obviously he was a luxury. You look at the game for the last twenty years, and the evolution has been how to shorten the game from the back end. We made the game six innings. I think it was Tony La Russa who said: "It's a six inning ball game when you play the Yankees."

Obviously Mo made my job easier, and everybody else's, too. That's the thing about a bullpen, if we understand we're a unit, and we're handing the ball off to each other, it makes us all better. Now Mo imparts that [philosophy] to his pen.

---

*The Yankees defeated the Atlanta Braves in six games to win the 1996 World Series. The Yankees were champions for the first time since 1978, and the triumph started a run of four Yankees titles in five years.

I was with Mariano has long as I needed to be with Mariano, and he'll tell you the same thing. The Yankees needed Mariano then, and when I became expendable, it was the perfect storm. It was a shrewd business move. That man was ready to step in, I could get a job somewhere else; everyone won. But I find it remarkable how he succeeded in his first year closing. Remember, you're talking about a young kid who was rubbing elbows with veteran [bullpen] guys for about half a year and seeing how it's done. We would play catch every day and work on things, but it's still just half a year [before] he's closing for the Yankees.*

When I departed after being the [World Series] MVP, that's got to be a really tough spot for the next guy. I know that position of closing for the Yankees, it's tough enough, and then you throw that on there, too. Once you saw Mariano come through that, those are the kinds of things that mark closers. To see him handle that kind of a situation in his career, the way he did, you knew he going to be just fine. Now, it's twenty years later, and he's achieved all those numbers, who could call that? But you knew he was going to be just fine. Mariano had a great arm. You knew he was going to be something special at the back end of ball games. I don't think we set out thinking he would save 600 games. I saw him after he got his 600th save, and I hugged him, and I told him, "Now go out and get another 600."

When I first saw him pitch, he was a starter, and he was hittable. He had a fastball, slider, and change-up, with good command, but there wasn't a lot of separation [in the velocity between] the slider and the fastball. The fastball had explosiveness to it, but he really lacked a second pitch that was good enough to offset the fastball. So I saw him get hit around quite a bit. You can have a good major league career if you have command of three pitches, even two, if you have command of

---

*Wetteland saved each of the Yankees' victories in the 1996 World Series, earning the Series Most Valuable Player honors. His seven postseason saves that year are also a record. With Rivera waiting in the wings, the Yankees chose not to offer Wetteland a new contract, and he signed as a free agent with the Texas Rangers in November 1996.

them. But you're going to get hit a little bit. There needs to be a separator. And when the cutter arrived on the scene, it was the separator. Major league hitters will tell you, "I swear I was on that pitch, and the next thing I know, I'm holding talcum powder."

If you look back, in retrospect, it becomes clear why we're [talking about Mariano Rivera] so many years later. I've never seen anybody pay so much attention to detail when they're young. I remember when he came into the bullpen in '96 we had a good corps of [veteran] guys there. He was like a little kid, he never said a word, he just sat there, watching, and taking in everything he could. He sat there quietly, but he was listening to what was being said when we talked about hitters; nothing escaped him—nothing.

That's absolutely what he was all about. I think that may have been the catalyst as to why he always seems to stay one step ahead of the game and the way hitters approach him. He knows there's pitching involved, not just throwing, and he evolved to use different ammunition. He's a very intelligent, wise man. He knew how to make some correct assessments along the way. So when you look back, from where he started, and the process of how Mariano Rivera was not a scared kid, but a wide-eyed kid, who becomes far and away the greatest closer that ever lived, you can kind of see it.

The thing that blows my mind is how his body holds up. We all take care of our body, but there are a special few that are blessed with the ability to keep going. That's something that's very special that I can't explain. I love Mariano to death. There's a lot of history there, a lot of great moments shared. Quite honestly, as I'm thinking about it, we spent time talking about baseball, but a lot of time talking about life, where we are as human beings, talking about the way things are. What I love most about Mo is he's got such a humble spirit about him. That carries you a long way as a closer. Things can bite you, so you need to stay on an even keel.

Section Six: Management

Mike Borzello

Borzello was the New York Yankees bullpen catcher from 1996 to 2007.

IN 1996, MARIANO became the set-up guy and John Wetteland, our closer, started talking to him every day. Wetteland knew Mariano would take over for him the following year. That's something that got lost—how important Wetteland was to him. The closer doesn't usually take the next closer under his wing. Wetteland did, and Mariano did [the same] with every reliever that came through.

Mariano became their mentor. He schooled the relievers one by one. He would sit with each one separately at times and do what Wetteland did for him to make sure they had a better chance at success. I always marveled at that dynamic. If someone had a tough outing, I saw him talk to them about how to let tough situations go. I always thought that was impressive. Wetteland triggered it, but Mo had the intelligence to absorb it and take it to another level with all the guys through the years.

So many guys get distracted about other things, especially off the field: money, their own personal achievements. I never saw that in Mo. He was always focused on the team, on what do you need me to do? In twelve years with him I never heard him mention anything about his contract, his number of saves, his earned run average, or any personal achievement.

I'd say: "We've got to get to 40 saves."

He'd say: "How many do I have now?"

He really didn't know.

I don't think he ever threw a ball that bounced in my twelve years of catching him in the bullpen. He would pitch up and down and in and out, but never in the ground. It's the most amazing thing. He wasn't trying to strike you out. He was looking to get you out in one or two pitches by shattering your bat.

Mo Respect

Bruce Bochy

Bochy, manager of the National League All-Star team at the 2013 Major League Baseball All-Star Game at Citi Field, on July 16, 2013, on the tribute to Rivera:

For him to get honored like that was a very special moment, which he richly deserves. It was moving. I can't say I know him, but I've heard enough about him to know that he's such a class person and a great ambassador to the game. Our players showed their respect and appreciation for all he's accomplished in his career and the person that he is, so it was a really neat deal, a neat moment.

Brian Butterfield
Coach

Butterfield has been a major league coach with the New York Yankees, Arizona Diamondbacks, Toronto Blue Jays, and Boston Red Sox since 1994.

Mo Cred

Butterfield was Rivera's manager with the Fort Lauderdale Yankees of the High A Florida State League in 1992.

I KNOW I GRADED him favorably—I think all of us did—because of the athleticism, the willingness to work, the type of individual [he is]. I've not seen anybody like this [in three decades] around the game. I think anybody would have a hard time projecting what he's become. He's the greatest of all time—and it isn't even close.

He was a very athletic guy. He had a fastball right around 91, 92. Then he started getting stronger. He was a tremendous kid, very respectful, a hard worker, and one of the fastest kids in the organization. Always looking to get better. He was a wonderful kid to be around—soft-spoken, funny.*

He's always had a very good delivery. You had a feeling he could repeat his pitches because good athlete and good delivery usually equals a guy who can repeat his pitches. He did not [have a breaking ball]. And he did not have the cutter. He might have had a little tiny one— just with a little cut off of his natural fastball—but I don't know when he started developing *The Cutter*.

I was the first base coach for the Yankees [in 1995] when [Rivera was promoted] to the major leagues. As a coach, that was the first time I'd seen him [pitch] in a long time. The jump in velocity stood out—he was a bigger, stronger athlete. When we had him, he was just a young kid.

He's a great role model for any of those young pitchers who come up: Just keep your eyes open and watch that guy.

Bill Evers

Evers was the minor league manager of the Yankees' Triple-A Columbus Clippers.

Mo Cred

Evers, who has over 1,200 career victories as a minor league manager, was Rivera's manager with the Columbus Clippers in 1995.

---

*Rivera had a 5-3 record for the Yankees at Fort Lauderdale in 1992. He allowed 15 earned runs in 59 innings pitched—for a 2.28 earned run average—and only 45 runners reached base against him. He allowed 40 hits and 5 walks while striking out 42 batters.

WITHOUT A DOUBT Mariano is one of the greatest players I've ever managed. I had the opportunity to manage Mariano, [Derek] Jeter, and [Jorge] Posada at Columbus in 1995, so I'm a very fortunate individual.*

At that time in his career Mariano was a starting pitcher and was trying to learn a breaking ball as well as a change-up. It was coming along so-so, and the last game he pitched before he went to the big leagues, he threw a no-hitter, and after that game, the next day, I got to tell him he was going to the big leagues. That was exciting. Naturally, he was elated to be going to the big leagues. He couldn't say enough good things about how happy he was, how all his hard work was paying off, and he was looking forward to the challenge.

I never thought he'd become a reliever. I thought he would be a good starting pitcher because his ability to locate the fastball was getting better and better throughout the course of his starts, and his secondary pitches were making progress. His fastball was very explosive to both sides of the plate. At that time, he didn't have the precise command that he has now, but he was able to locate his fastball well to both sides of the plate.

The biggest reason why he hadn't been to the big leagues sooner was his [lack of] velocity. When he was pitching for me his velocity had decreased. Instead of throwing 95 he's throwing in the high 80s. It turns out that he wasn't throwing the fastball as hard as we thought because the [radar] gun readings were wrong. Then [Yankees executive] Gene Michael came to town [with his own radar gun] and saw Mariano pitch the no-hitter. Michael saw what the gun readings were, and that convinced him [of Rivera's velocity]. The next day Mariano was called to the big leagues. History may have been different had

---

*Rivera had a 2-2 record for the Yankees at Columbus in 1995. He allowed 7 earned runs in 30 innings pitched—for a 2.10 earned run average—and only 28 runners reached base against him. He allowed 25 hits and 3 walks while striking out 30 batters.

Michael not been there that day. Thank goodness for all concerned that he was there and Mariano got that opportunity because he is going to be a Hall of Famer.*

My best memory was being able to give him the ball every fifth day and watch him perform his craft and observe a man that went about his job in the right manner. Mariano was the kind of guy that goes out and does his work. He was a quiet role model. He didn't say a whole lot, and he was very unassuming. He did most of his leading by example. You never had to worry about Mariano coming to the field and not doing his work, or not giving his maximum effort for that day. He is what any manager wants on his club; if you had twenty-five Mariano Riveras life would be very easy for the manager.

He went out and performed as best he could day in and day out, and best of all, he was a great competitor, whether he had his best stuff or he didn't. One of his best attributes is his mental toughness and his inner drive. Most guys, when things don't go their way, you would see them throwing gloves or you could actually see the frustration on their face. But Mariano has great inner self-discipline and the ability and mental toughness to not let anybody know things are getting under his skin, and that is a quality that has made him who he is.

I was the bench coach for the Tampa Bay Rays in 2006 and 2007. He's very special for the simple fact that he has not forgotten; he's a very grateful individual. Any time I would see him he would make it a point to always come by, shake my hand, give me a hug, ask how my family was doing, and we would talk for five or ten minutes, or for however long he had before he had to go do what he had to do. He is

---

*Rivera was credited with an official no-hitter against the Rochester Red Wings, even though the game was shortened to five innings by rain, on June 26, 1995. Rivera struck out six and walked one. He had been up with the Yankees earlier that season, but was 1-2 with a 10.20 earned run average and was sent back down to Columbus for more instruction. He returned to the Yankees and finished his first major league season with a 5-3 record and a 5.51 earned run average.

a genuine individual who really cares and he showed his gratitude by always making it a point to come by and say hello.

Terry Francona

Manager and First base

Playing Career

Montreal Expos, Chicago Cubs, Milwaukee Brewers, Cleveland Indians, and Cincinnati Reds from 1981 to 1990

Managing Career

Philadelphia Phillies (1997–2000), Boston Red Sox (2004–2011), and Cleveland Indians (since 2013)

Mo Cred

Francona won World Series titles with the Red Sox in 2004 and '07.

WE HAD A few guys who had a little bit of success against Mo. There weren't too many, but certain guys. We probably had as much success against him as anybody—now we probably faced him more than anybody, too, but it's no day at the beach. I didn't like when we heard that song, "Enter Sandman." That was not a good feeling.

There's a reason he's done what he's done for so long. You know that cutter is coming and you still can't hit it—or you hit it and it doesn't go very far. It bores in on lefties and cuts away from righties. There's no rotation and he throws hard. And he's been so unbelievably durable. That's what's almost as amazing as anything. Relievers have a couple of good years and then there's a down year. He's done it forever and continues to get better.

It's hard to compare closers over the generations because guys back so many years ago would pitch three innings to get a save. But in the modern era, I don't know if there's anybody that can touch him. He's just quiet class.

Joe Girardi
Manager and Catcher

Mo Cred

Girardi was a member of four World Series championship teams as a Yankees player and manager (1996, '98, '99, 2009).

I'VE HAD THE good fortune of catching and coaching and managing him and it's a treat. I've loved being a part of it.

I was traded here [to the Yankees] in '96, and I saw him for the first time in spring training. I remember asking myself, "Who is this guy with great stuff?"

Little did I know what an impact he'd have on the '96 season and, really, on the next seventeen seasons.

As a catcher, when he burst on the scene in '96, it was fun being back there to watch him dominate hitters. His location was so good that you could ask for a pitch on the inside, outside, up, down and he could throw it there. He's been as dominant as anyone I've ever caught. Seeing him do it so many years later is hard to fathom.*

---

*Girardi caught Rivera's first career save, an 8-5 victory over the Angels in Anaheim, on May 17, 1996. Girardi was 2-for-4 in the game, including a fifth-inning single to drive home Derek Jeter with the go-ahead run and give the Yankees a lead they would not relinquish.

When I caught him, he didn't throw a sinker. It was more just the cutter and his control was so great. Hitters really couldn't pick it up. They knew it was coming, but the movement was so late and so sharp that they couldn't adjust to it.

I remember left-handed hitters saying that because of the late, sharp movement the only place they could hit it hard was over the first base dugout. You couldn't keep it fair.

I love it when he comes into the game. You just feel like it's over. This is the guy who I believe is the best closer that's ever been in the game. He's certainly made my job a lot easier.

His accomplishment getting the most saves is incredible. I don't know if we'll ever see anyone like him again—that's how remarkable this accomplishment is. I don't know if we'll ever see another Mariano Rivera. I really don't believe we will.

All-Star Game Moment

I thought it was a great All-Star Game tribute to Mo, and the way the players handled it was extremely special. You could see he was choked up by it. Sometimes, it's hard to control your emotions, but I think it meant a ton to Mo.

—Joe Girardi

Mo Respect

Mike Harkey

Harkey has been the Yankees' bullpen coach since 2008.

The best moment was when he got the last out of the World Series in 2009. He really never gets too high and never gets too low. So, that being said, the World Series games are always going to be the most memorable because that's where you're going to see him the most jubilant. And that's because it's all over and he has time to celebrate and take it all in. Any other time has just been another day at work, which sets him apart from a lot of the closers out there. There's not much emotion out there, there's not much fanfare; it's just him doing his job.

Jim Leyland

Manager

Leyland managed the American League team in the 2013 Major League Baseball All-Star Game at Citi Field, on July 16, 2013.

How did you prepare the players for that tribute to Rivera?

I said to the players before the game, "I'm not a motivational speaker but my motivation for tonight is to work our fannies off and bring in the greatest closer of all time."

Why did you decide to bring Rivera into the game in the eighth inning, and not wait for the ninth?

I did lie—for one inning—for obvious reasons. I think you all understand that if something freaky would have happened to the lead, if [the National League] scores some runs and takes the lead, there possibly wouldn't have been the ninth, so that's why I did it.

What do you remember most about the game?

The night was full of emotion. To be honest with you, that was one of the toughest games I ever had to manage because you have all these different scenarios that might happen. Even though we won the game, and a lot of guys did a very, very good job, not to slight anybody else, but really, the show was really about trying to manipulate so we got Mariano [in the game] at the right time.

Was Mariano appreciative of your plan?

Mariano and I have a great relationship. We're friends, believe it or not. We don't hang out together, but we're friends.

Any special moment you'd care to share about your relationship?

Earlier this year, when he was in Detroit for the last time, I presented him with a picture of him throwing a pitch at Tiger Stadium and Comerica Park. He said something then that will stick with me forever, but I won't tell you what that was.*

Bill Livesey

Livesey was the New York Yankees' Scouting Director and Vice President of Player Development from 1991 to 1996.

IN OUR MINOR league system we tried to build in high standards and we watched the kids like a hawk, to see who can live up to those high standards. We also like to win so we can see who steps up their game, to see who has a history of answering the bell. Every test we could give Mariano at the minor league level he passed with flying colors. I don't know if anybody projected him to be in the Hall of Fame, but we knew he was a special kid, somebody who was part of our core group. We had spent a lot of time trying to determine who was part of our core group.

Scouts joke that if we could take kids and open them up, we would know what's going on inside and we would make fewer mistakes! That's why we had high standards for our minor leaguers, so kids could separate themselves as much as possible. The more demands you put on them, the fewer surprises you have later on. The Yankees had a history of trading young talent, but during this time, we decided as an organization that we were going to keep the core group together at all costs, and trade away other guys. It was very clear very early on that Mariano

---

*The Tigers were the first team in the regular season to pay tribute to Rivera on his farewell tour, before the series finale on Sunday, April 7, 2013. Leyland presented Rivera with framed photographs of him pitching at Tiger Stadium and Comerica Park, with dirt from the mounds at both parks. Rivera then joked to the crowd that he is old enough to have pitched in both places.

was a big part of that core group. We were fortunate to have our people identify Rivera, Bernie Williams, Derek Jeter, Jorge Posada, and Andy Pettitte. Those guys were a big part of a few championship teams.*

The first time I saw Mariano was during pitchers' fielding practice his first summer in the Gulf Coast League [in 1990]. His athleticism stood out immediately. That really caught my eye, because sometimes, young kids are gangly and on the way to becoming good, but Mariano was a real athletic specimen from the get-go. He could move his feet easily and he repeated athletic skills time and time again. He was a recent convert to pitching when we got our hands on him. In his amateur days I think he was a shortstop, and to this day, he can go out and play center field and chase the ball down with anybody.

He had a setback, an arm injury, but putting that aside, he developed quickly [as a pitcher due to] his athleticism and outstanding arm. He had tremendous arm speed. He threw 95 to 96 [miles per hour], but most of all, he threw strikes; he was always under control. He could repeat pitches and he had the ability to consistently throw strikes from the very first day. Once a kid establishes that he can throw strikes and do what is required of him in the lower levels, he gets a chance to move up, and Mariano certainly did.

His minor league record as a starting pitcher is pretty darn good. He projected as someone special, as someone well above average. He had a good repertoire of pitches: a plus-plus fastball, a solid change-up, a slider, and a curve ball. He was the full package. With Mariano, whatever you saw from him as a pitcher, he had even better inner qualities as a person. He had a great work ethic, and he's very low to no maintenance. He had an inner confidence that drove him, and he had humility. He was an outstanding kid to be around.

We all knew he was a top prospect, and I was excited when he got the call up to the big leagues. I had a satellite dish and was watching

---

*The Yankees appeared in the World Series seven times between 1996 and 2009, and won five championships, in 1996, 1998, 1999, 2000, and 2009.

his first [major league] start. For whatever reason, he didn't have an impressive performance, but I knew we weren't seeing the real Mariano. People didn't get a true picture of who Mariano was when he got called up that first time. After the game, I took part in a conference call to discuss what [other scouts] had seen from Mariano, and how this compared to what we've seen from him in the past. I tried to make the point that what we saw that night wasn't classic Mariano.*

He was sent back to the minor leagues, and he pitched like a guy with something to prove. He made very sure [the decision makers] knew that first game wasn't the real him. Most top prospects only experience successes, but sometimes you need to see how somebody reacts to a little bit of adversity, as that shows another side of you. Mariano knew that some people were questioning him a little bit now, and he went back to the minor leagues with a vengeance. He proved that first big league outing was just a blip on the road, and he was not going to be denied. That was a defining moment for him. Later that year the Yankees brought him back and Buck [manager Buck Showalter] put him in the bullpen. Nobody ever questioned Mariano again.

The bullpen turned out to be an ideal role for him, because he doesn't have an ounce of panic. Part of his success is that he's extremely bright and can make adjustments. The ability to make adjustments is one of the things we watch in the minor leagues, because when you get to the big leagues, your career will be determined by the adjustments you're able to make. Mariano made adjustments; whether they [were] social, cultural, or baseball related. He had to get acclimated to a new country, a new language, and then he shifted his role to the bullpen, he added the cutter, and the rest is history.

It's hard to describe his accomplishments, because he doesn't have average expectations for himself. People that know Mariano know how

---

*Rivera made his first major league appearance against the Angels in Anaheim, on May 23, 1995, and it didn't go well. Rivera started the game but lasted just three innings as he was knocked around for five runs and eight hits in a 10-0 loss.

much he cares. He hasn't changed a bit after all these years. He's the same person, only now with a lot more medals. He always had that confidence, but with an equal dose of humility.

Mitch Lukevics

Lukevics was the New York Yankees' Director of Minor League Operations from 1989 to 1995.

FIRST SAW HIM when he was this skinny right-hander in the Gulf Coast League. He was long and lanky, with a lightning-quick arm. From day one, he had the ability to throw a baseball in a thimble. It was most remarkable for a young kid to have such uncanny ability, that's what stood out about him. This young guy came to the Yankees with real good *now* stuff, as you can see by his Gulf Coast League statistics. You look at his hits-to-innings ratio, the walks-to-strikeouts—it's phenomenal. Our Panama scout Carl "Chico" Heron, who passed away, did a great job signing this bright raw resource.*

You have to give Mariano credit. Here was a young man coming to the United States from Panama who learned our language and learned our culture while trying to make his way in professional baseball. It's not easy to do. In those days organizations didn't do as much as they do today. They had players come on over, and hoped they'd fit in; they might give some English lessons. Nowadays all teams have some sort of culture assimilation program, with language training, much more

---

*Rivera had a 5-1 record for the Yankees in the Gulf Coast League in 1990. He allowed one earned run in 52 innings pitched—for a 0.17 earned run average—and only 24 runners reached base against him. He allowed 17 hits and 7 walks while striking out 58 batters.

than what Mariano had. But he was around a lot of good character players—Derek Jeter, Jorge Posada, Andy Pettitte, and Bernie Williams were the head of the class without question—and I think being around those good character players helped him get acclimated to the United States at such a young age.

He had elbow surgery and he came through it with flying colors. I remember he was reluctant to go on a rehab assignment because he was young and married, and he didn't want to leave his wife.

We said, "Mariano, your career will benefit down the road by doing this; it can only help your journey of getting to the big leagues, and catapult your career."

He didn't want to go. Only when we convinced him the rehab would benefit his family did he agree to go. We needed him to stay on course. I'm glad he did.*

Mo Respect

Joe Maddon

Maddon has been manager of the division rival Tampa Bay Rays since 2006.

He's the best ever at what he does. It will be a long time before you get somebody better than that, I think.

The way he was able to be so consistent, unbelievably consistent, and the hotter the game, the better he was. It's just incredible what he's done, and in such a simple manner. That's the part that's really so impressive. The guys would always yell from the bench, in a joking way, "He's tipping his pitches!"

So here's a guy that everybody knew what pitch was coming all the time and you still couldn't do anything with it. It's unbelievable how he was nails. He nailed it.

---

*Rivera underwent surgery in August 1992 to repair ligament damage to his right elbow. He successfully rehabilitated his elbow in early 1993 and resumed pitching that season.

Bob Melvin

Manager and Catcher

Playing Career

Detroit Tigers, San Francisco Giants, Baltimore Orioles, Kansas City Royals, Boston Red Sox, New York Yankees, and Chicago White Sox from 1985 to 1994

Managing Career

Seattle Mariners (2003–2004), Arizona Diamondbacks (2005–2009) and Oakland Athletics (since 2011); two-time Manager of the Year (2007, 2012)

Mo Cred

Melvin caught Rivera in 1994 and 1995 as a member of New York's Triple-A Columbus Clippers affiliate.

CAUGHT HIM LATE in my career—and early in his—in Columbus. He didn't have a cutter then. When I caught him in Columbus, he was throwing a four-seam fastball. He had great late life on his fastball, and he liked to pitch up in the zone. It was tough to stay on top of it. Later on, it turned into a little bit of a cutter. The decision to go with the cutter was a good move for him.

I've seen [him progress] from day one until now. He's had an unbelievable career. And not only that, he's as good a person as he is a player. He's meant so much to the game, and to that organization. We're seeing him at the top [of his game]. It's rare that a guy goes out on top like this, and that is the case with him.

I wish him the best in his career afterward. I'd love to be able to say we see him again at some point in time.

Mark Newman

Newman has served the New York Yankees as Coordinator of Minor League Instruction from 1989 to 1996; Vice President, Player Development and Scouting from 1996 to 2000; Vice President, Baseball Operations since 2000.

Are you satisfied by how Rivera's career turned out?

WHEN WE SIGNED Mariano in 1990, I don't remember anyone saying: "This guy is going to be a major leaguer."

He was a very good athlete and he could throw it over the plate, but nobody wrote out the Mariano development plan that said he would someday throw 98 miles per hour, have the finest control on the face of the planet, would learn a cutter and, oh by the way, that's all he's going to throw.

Did Rivera have that laser-like focus as a young player?

Pete Rose and Jack Nicklaus are the greatest concentrators I've ever seen, and I'd put Mo right in that group. I bet no pitcher in history has thrown more pitches from the same arm slot without deviation than Mariano Rivera.

What was it about Rivera that made scouts believe he'd be a good relief pitcher?

Back then [getting relegated to the bullpen] meant we didn't think you were a prospect. But what you saw from the beginning was the same composure, the same mound demeanor. Nothing gets to him. I don't know if Mo felt greater pressure in the ninth inning of a World Series game, or when he was a young guy rehabbing his elbow after surgery [in 1992] so he didn't have to go back to Panama and be a fisherman.

Was surgery the reason the Yankees left Rivera unprotected in the 1992 expansion draft?

A great moment in Yankees history! But Mariano wasn't even in the discussion then. He wasn't a consideration. We were just worried about losing three big leaguers in Brad Ausmus, Carl Everett, and Charlie Hayes in that draft.

Juan Nieves

Pitching Coach

Playing Career
Milwaukee Brewers from 1986 to 1988

Mo Cred

Nieves, the current Boston Red Sox pitching coach, was a minor league pitching instructor for the Yankees from 1992 to 1996.

I SAW MARIANO FOR the first time in minor league spring training in 1992. You knew he had a presence about him right away. He had the serenity of a pitcher. His dedication and routine—he was very calm, yet a gladiator on the mound. The records speak for everything. But you could tell—the presence, the demeanor—it was coming. It was a matter of time.

He was mostly a straight fastball guy, threw some change ups, really solid delivery, was able to throw strikes all the time. Just a great delivery, [but because of the lack of secondary pitches] he projected more as a reliever.

I hope people watched him a lot, because there's only one of those guys. He's in a league of his own. We're speaking about the best of the best.

Herb Raybourn

Raybourn is a former New York Yankees scout and Director of Latin American Operations who signed Rivera to an amateur free agent contract, which included a signing bonus of $3,500, on February 17, 1990.

HE WAS A great find. I was fortunate. The good Lord was with me. I was there [in Panama] the year before and I passed on him. He was a shortstop then. He showed good range, and I saw that he could run, he had a good arm, and he had good hands. But I didn't think he'd be able to hit that well in the big leagues, as far as the long ball.

As a scout, you're signing players to get to the big leagues, not Double A or Triple A. The fielding was very good. I gave him good marks in his fielding and throwing. But his hitting was questionable. I couldn't project him playing in the big leagues as a shortstop, so I just gave up on him.

I went back [to Panama] a year later and we got him. I got a call from a young player who was the regular catcher for Rivera. He said, "Mr. Raybourn, I have a player for you. His name is Mariano Rivera."

I said: "The Mariano Rivera I knew was a shortstop."

He told me that he was a pitcher now. We went for a workout behind his house [in Puerto Caimito]. It didn't even have a mound. It was just a slope.

I took a scout with me who hadn't seen Mariano. He brought along a radar gun. The radar gun wasn't really being lit up. Mariano was throwing 84, 86 [miles per hour]. He wouldn't have been signed in the States. In the States, if you see a boy throw like him, you skip past. He threw nine pitches. I saw enough at nine pitches.

What I liked about Mariano was the fluidness of his arm. He had one of those nice loose arms. Plus, his ball had a lot of movement. You could picture him pitching in the majors, being a starter or a reliever.

Why didn't any of the other scouts sign him before I got back to Panama? There was no competition. There was nobody else when I came along. I couldn't offer $50,000 to a guy who hasn't gotten one offer. Nobody had given him even a hint of an offer. You had to go with what the market calls for. Nobody else liked him.

His father [also named Mariano] is a wonderful person. He's a very reserved man. He worked hard [to make a living as a fisherman in Panama]. And the mother [Delia], whenever I would stop by and see them, she fixes a fish soup for me. The only really physical work Mariano was doing was the fishing. But all that fishing, and pulling on lines—even though he was weighing about 160 pounds, his arms had a little bit of definition. I could picture him pitching in the big leagues with that arm. The looseness was the thing that really impressed me.

Hoyt Wilhelm [the late Hall of Fame pitcher who was a Yankees minor league pitching coach in 1990] would use Rivera whenever he could. Hoyt loved his arm. Three days before the end of the season, Hoyt says: "Herb, do you think we could use Mariano to start a game?"

I asked Hoyt when he last pitched.

He said: "Yesterday."

"He's only going to have two days of rest," I said.

Scout's Honor

Former Yankees scout Herb Raybourn filed this report assessing Mariano Rivera shortly before he signed the pitcher who would become the greatest closer the game as ever known.

Physical Description: Tall. Lean. Broad shoulders. Long arms. Big hands. Long, strong legs. Good pitching body. No glasses. No injuries.

Abilities: Loose, live arm. Fastball has sinking action. Fastball ranges between 84 and 87. Good athlete. Can also play the infield and outfield. Can also hit.

Weaknesses: Needs work with mechanics. Lacks strength.

Summary: Has potential to become an above-average pitcher.

Hoyt said: "Let's throw him in there! His arm bounces back. He'll be able to pitch. He's going home as soon as he finishes the game—and he's got all winter to rest up."

Well you know what? He pitched a seven-inning, no-hit, no-run game.

I really couldn't project him too far out, but I knew he was going to do well. I thought he could go pretty far, put it that way.

Mo Respect

Larry Rothschild

Rothschild was Rivera's pitching coach from 2011 through 2013.

It's an honor [to coach him]. Any time you're around the guy that is probably the best in the game—and maybe the best ever—at what he's doing, no matter how much you've seen and what you've done, it's an honor to be around, especially when you see the way he's carried himself.

Glenn Sherlock
Manager and Coach

New York Yankees and Arizona Diamondbacks

Sherlock managed and coached in the Yankees' organization from 1989 to 1995. He is currently bullpen coach for the Diamondbacks.

Mo Cred

Sherlock was Rivera's manager for the Yankees' rookie league team in Tampa in the Gulf Coast League in 1990.

HE WAS VERY quiet. He didn't speak a lot of English. He was a very nice kid that went about his business in a professional manner. He was very intelligent, very classy, very respectful, and very determined. He had great aptitude.

Obviously we didn't know at that time that he was going to be maybe the greatest relief pitcher of all time. I don't know if anybody is that smart. What we did see was that he had a very good work ethic and he did a lot of the little things very well, like the bunt defenses and the pitchers fielding practice. He put a lot of effort into [his work]. He was an extremely good athlete.

Hoyt Wilhelm [the Hall of Fame pitcher] was our pitching coach and he used to play a game with the pitchers so they could have some fun. He'd let them bat and shag [fly balls] and Mariano could really hit and he could really play the outfield. He was clearly one of the best athletes we had on the team. He was just a great athlete.

He was close to qualifying for the ERA [earned run average] title that year, but he needed [five] more innings because he had mostly been pitching as a reliever. We had a doubleheader on the last day of the season, so we talked to Mitch Lukevics, the farm director at the time, about starting Mariano in one of the games. We got an okay and Mariano pitched a seven-inning no-hitter, which was pretty amazing.

Mo Respect

Mike Scioscia

Scioscia has managed the Los Angeles Angels of Anaheim since 2000.

I mean this in a good way, but he's a freak. You don't see people dominate the way he has for so long. Of any relief pitcher in modern-day baseball, no one has had more of an impact on their club than Mariano has with the Yankees.

Joe Torre

Manager

Torre was the Yankees' manager for twelve seasons from 1996 to 2007. The Yankees made the postseason each year of his tenure, and won ten American League East division titles, six A.L. pennants, and four World Series championships.

I WOULDN'T BE WEARING World Series rings without him. What he's done in a high-pressurized role for a high-pressurized organization in the City of New York, it's not easy to do. Trust me.

I felt privileged to manage him. He certainly kept me there as a set-up man that first year. He's the best I've ever been around. Not only the ability to pitch and perform under pressure, but the calm he puts over the clubhouse. He was very important for us.

We found going in to the 1996 season that he was always very quiet. We didn't know where he fit [in our bullpen rotation], and all of a sudden, he became the seventh and eighth inning guy. He's an intimidating guy even though he doesn't huff and puff out there on the mound. He has that velvet hammer, where he's just very smooth, very easy, and then all of a sudden, things explode.

We turned him into a closer in 1997. Oakland came into New York early in the year, and beat Mo in the ninth. It's never a good sign when your new closer is really down in the dumps. I remember saying: "This may happen a few more times, Mo, but you're our closer and you're going to have to live with it."*

---

*In the ninth game of the 1997 season, his first as the closer, Rivera was called into the game against the Athletics in the top of the ninth inning to protect a 1-0 lead at Yankee Stadium, on April 11, 1997. Rivera had all of seven career saves at this point. Oakland slugger Mark McGwire promptly hit Rivera's first pitch over the fence for a game-tying home run. Rivera surrendered two more hits before securing the third out of the ninth, and the Yankees went on to lose, 3-1, in twelve innings.

It took him a little time, but he got that swagger.

He never blames anybody. We saw that early on, which always bodes well for teammates. He's such a responsible person, and he's got such elegance, and a great deal of class. I signed a picture of his the other day of him and former teammates, and underneath my autograph I wrote: "Nobody did it better."

And that's not only on the field, that's off the field. What he did as a closer on the field is just a fraction of what he does off the field. He's a special human being. I know last year [2012] he was torn [over whether or not to retire after the season], but once he got hurt, there was no way he was going to go out like that. I'm very happy for him.

Mo and Joe

Joe Torre, speaking at a ceremony to honor Mariano Rivera at Houston's Minute Maid Park on the final day of the 2013 season:

I started managing the Yankees in 1996 and I was there for twelve years. Trust me, you don't get a chance to manage for George Steinbrenner for twelve years unless you have somebody like Mo coming out of the bullpen.

In addition to all of Mariano's accomplishments, the thing that I most appreciated was the fact that when somebody came into our clubhouse, a player [traded over] from another ball club or [called up] from the minor leagues, and looked like he was out of place somewhat, Mariano would be that guy that would go over and put his arm around him.

What he does that doesn't happen on the field was so important to our success because I think we tend to forget that this game of baseball is played by people and these players certainly were made to feel welcome by Mo.

Mariano Rivera Career Stats

Regular Season

Year	W	L	ERA	G	SV	IP	H	ER	BB	SO
1995	5	3	5.51	19	0	67	71	41	30	51
1996	8	3	2.09	61	5	107	73	25	34	130
1997	6	4	1.88	66	43	71	65	15	20	68
1998	3	0	1.91	54	36	61	48	13	17	36
1999	4	3	1.83	66	45	69	43	14	18	52
2000	7	4	2.85	66	36	75	58	24	25	58
2001	4	6	2.34	71	50	80	61	21	12	83
2002	1	4	2.74	45	28	46	35	14	11	41
2003	5	2	1.66	64	40	70	61	13	10	63
2004	4	2	1.94	74	53	78	65	17	20	66
2005	7	4	1.38	71	43	78	50	12	18	80
2006	5	5	1.80	63	34	75	61	15	11	55
2007	3	4	3.15	67	30	71	68	25	12	74
2008	6	5	1.40	64	39	70	41	11	6	77
2009	3	3	1.76	66	44	66	48	13	12	72
2010	3	3	1.80	61	33	60	39	12	11	45
2011	1	2	1.91	64	44	61	47	13	8	60
2012	1	1	2.16	9	5	8	6	2	2	8
2013	6	2	2.11	64	44	64	58	15	9	54
19 Years	82	60	2.21	1,115	652	1,283	998	315	286	1,173

Postseason

Year	W	L	ERA	G	SV	IP	H	ER	BB	SO
1995	1	0	0.00	3	0	5	3	0	1	8
1996	1	0	0.63	8	0	14	10	1	5	10
1997	0	0	4.50	2	1	2	2	1	0	1
1998	0	0	0.00	10	6	13	6	0	2	11
1999	2	0	0.00	8	6	12	9	0	1	9
2000	0	0	1.72	10	6	15	10	3	1	10
2001	2	1	1.13	11	5	16	12	2	2	14
2002	0	0	0.00	1	1	1	1	0	0	0
2003	1	0	0.56	8	5	16	7	1	0	14
2004	1	0	0.71	9	2	12	8	1	2	8
2005	0	0	3.00	2	2	3	1	1	1	2
2006	0	0	0.00	1	0	1	1	0	0	0
2007	0	0	0.00	3	0	4	2	0	1	6
2009	0	0	0.56	12	5	16	10	1	5	14
2010	0	0	0.00	6	3	6	4	0	0	2
2011	0	0	0.00	2	0	1	0	0	0	1
Total	8	1	0.70	96	42	141	86	11	21	110

Saves by Opponent

vs. Baltimore Orioles	79
vs. Tampa Bay Rays	64
vs. Boston Red Sox	58
vs. Toronto Blue Jays	54
vs. Chicago White Sox	43
vs. Texas Rangers	40
vs. Kansas City Royals	37
vs. Seattle Mariners	37
vs. Minnesota Twins	36
vs. Oakland Athletics	35
vs. Cleveland Indians	31
vs. Detroit Tigers	30
vs. Los Angeles Angels of Anaheim	28
vs. New York Mets	20
vs. Atlanta Braves	8
vs. Florida Marlins	6
vs. Colorado Rockies	5
vs. Houston Astros	5
vs. Philadelphia Phillies	5
vs. Arizona Diamondbacks	4
vs. Chicago Cubs	4
vs. Milwaukee Brewers	4
vs. San Diego Padres	4
vs. Washington Nationals	4
vs. Cincinnati Reds	3
vs. Los Angeles Dodgers	3
vs. St. Louis Cardinals	3
vs. San Francisco Giants	2
vs. Pittsburgh Pirates	0

ACKNOWLEDGEMENTS

I RECOGNIZE THAT A project of this scope could not be completed without the cooperation of a number of people. To the media relations and publicity professionals working for each of the thirty major league baseball teams, I am extremely appreciative for your help in providing me with access to your team's players and for putting me in contact with retired players. To all the player agents and their assistants, I cannot thank you enough for helping to connect me with your clients. I know their time is valuable during the season as they prepare themselves for the most difficult challenge in all of sport—to hit a round ball with a round bat squarely.

Any insecurities I held about this project's viability were quickly batted away when the player agents and team public relations coordinators told me that this book was a great idea and one that they'd look forward to reading. Since these were the very people that I was depending on to present the interview request to the players for their consideration, I was comforted to know that they were my allies in the process. I owe a debt of gratitude to all of these people who work so hard behind the scenes to make the media machine run so smoothly.

Even with all the revealing interviews to transcribe and edit, there still was much information to compile and fact-check. Several wonderful Internet destinations served as my invaluable lifeline for data, box scores, statistics, and play-by-play accounts, including baseball-reference.com, newyork.yankees.mlb.com, thebaseballcube.com, and baseball-almanac.com, all of which are terrific research tools for journalists and fun Web surfing for hard-core baseball fans.

Niels Aaboe of Skyhorse Publishing not only got this project off the ground, he steered it, and me, in the right direction. I'm deeply grateful for his guidance and wise counsel along the way. I can think of few greater gifts someone can bestow than encouraging another person's labor of love. And over the past six months, this author has received lots of encouragement. Thanks also to Sara Kitchen for shepherding the project through production.

Throughout the long period of nurturing this book, I was blessed with the perfect work environment. As a freelance author working from home, this means a loving family that understands my crazy lifestyle and supports my passion for projects like this one. A huge hug to my daughter, Rachel, who telephones me from college to receive the latest updates on my progress, and to my son, Jack, who has the softest hands of any high school infielder I've ever seen, for keeping alive my enthusiasm for baseball—the greatest game ever invented. My wife, Carolyn, is always an inspiration and her unconditional love is what keeps me going in work and in life. Over our two-decades-plus marriage she has become a pretty savvy baseball fan who can first-guess with the best of baseball's television analysts.

I am, of course, very appreciative of each of the current and former major leaguers who agreed to speak with me, whether they were successful facing Rivera or not. I was surprised by how self-deprecating many of the players were when assessing themselves in their match-ups with Rivera. Professional athletes, by nature, are a self-confident bunch, not accustomed to admitting or accepting failure, even when they are competing against the very best of opponents. But when speaking of their futile and feeble attempts to hit Rivera's cut fastball, the majority of players are able to laugh at themselves, and I found this refreshing. Even the few hitters who possess a high batting average against Rivera claim they were more lucky than good, or at the very least, upon reflection, they readily confess that their base hits were not solidly struck but rather were bloopers and bleeders, to use their parlance. Thanks to all for your participation; because of you, this book is a home run!

Finally, this book would not have been possible without the supreme domination of Mariano Rivera, the greatest closer who ever lived. Thanks for nineteen seasons of pure, unmitigated joy.

David Fischer
New Jersey, October 2013

PHOTO CREDIT

Photo of Mariano Rivera: AP Photo/Elaine Thompson